Theory of Economic Systems:
Capitalism, Socialism and Corporatism

William P. Snavely
University of Connecticut

With contributions by

Morris Singer
University of Connecticut

Dominick Armentano
University of Hartford

Charles E. Merrill Publishing Company
A Bell & Howell Company
Columbus, Ohio

Merrill's Economic Systems Series
William P. Snavely, Editor

Library of Congress Catalog Card Number: 71-76753

Standard Book Number:
675-09495-X   (hardbound edition)
675-09494-1   (paperbound edition)

Printed in the United States of America

1 2 3 4 5 6 7 8 9 10 11 12 13 14 15-76 75 74 73 72 71 70 69

To Alice, Nell, Bill and Betsy

Editor's Foreword

The Merrill Economic Systems Series has been developed to meet three clearly recognized needs. First, it is designed to provide greater flexibility and broader coverage in formal economic systems courses. To do so, the series contains a core volume and ten books covering individual countries. The core volume presents an analytical discussion, placed in historical perspective, of the major types of systems. The individual country-study volumes, written by outstanding scholars and specialists on the country, provide illustrations of the nature and operation of various systems in practice. The ten countries included in the initial series illustrate a wide range of economic systems. Those who are involved with the systems field will find it possible to choose from this extensive selection those particular country-study volumes which fit most effectively their own individual courses. As the series is expanded to include additional countries the flexibility of choice will become even greater.

The second important need which this series is designed to meet is that for collateral reading in various social science courses. Those who teach principles of economics, introductory political science, comparative government, or general social studies courses, will find excellent possibilities for assigning individual volumes for greater in-depth study of particular areas. Each book has been prepared as an entity in itself and can therefore profitably be studied either individually or as part of a more comprehensive program.

Finally, this series will provide a stimulating introduction to different economic systems for the interested reader who is concerned about this subject of major contemporary importance.

William P. Snavely

Preface

The twentieth century has been characterized by rapid, indeed revolutionary, changes in many areas of human thought and endeavor. Economic systems are no exception, for changes both in the types of systems operating in practice and in formal thought concerning them have been dramatic.

In the period between the two world wars, new economic systems in the form of communism and fascism emerged to confront established capitalistic economies. Neoclassical theorists tended to belittle the prospects for communism and other forms of socialism on the grounds that none would be able to achieve as high a degree of economic efficiency as capitalism. The shock of the 1930's depression gave rise to searching reappraisals of traditional views. As a result of this, established capitalistic systems tended to shift from relatively extensive *laissez-faire* policies to policies of increased governmental intervention designed to counteract the serious dislocations stemming from the depression. The traditional capitalistic economies thus evolved into new forms popularly referred to as mixed-capitalistic systems. The reappraisal of neoclassical views also resulted in the development of strong arguments by Lange and others to support the position that socialist systems could, theoretically, operate with a high degree of efficiency.

The clash between the dominant mixed-capitalistic nations, in alliance with Russia, and the major fascist nations in World War II resulted in the defeat of the latter. This led to a reduction in the important alternative forms of economic systems from three to two—mixed capitalism and socialism. There are, of course, many variations of these two most prominent remaining systems. In the post-World War II period, competition between these systems has been keen on both philosophical and operational levels.

The geographical extent of competition between capitalism and socialism has been greatly expanded since the war as a result of the breakdown of traditional imperialism and the emergence of a large number of new and for the most part underdeveloped nations. The attainment of more rapid rates of growth and development has become a major preoccupation of these nations, and it is only natural that the people of each of them should be seriously concerned with the question of what type of economic system seems to be most appropriate for the realization of their economic aspirations. There appears to be no universally applicable answer to this question and each country must reach its own decision concerning the extent to which the market approach or the command approach should be emphasized. The developed countries, also, must cope with the problem of the emphasis to be accorded the market and the command approaches in dealing with the economic problems which confront them.

In view of the marked increase in the number of new nations, each with its own particular variation of the market or the command approach, it has become increasingly difficult to cover adequately the field of economic systems within the framework of the traditional textbook. It is for this reason that the more flexible and more comprehensive approach represented by this series has been undertaken.

The present volume concentrates on the theoretical aspects of the basic systems—capitalism, socialism and corporatism. To provide deeper insights into these systems, an historical introduction of each is included. This is followed by an analysis of the system itself. Consideration is also given to the more important arguments in support of and in opposition to each system. The two final chapters deal with various aspects of the relationship between economic systems and growth.

Since there is considerable variation in the level at which courses in comparative economics are offered, this core theory volume has been designed for effective use at different levels. For the less formal or less advanced courses, teachers will find it a simple matter to omit the technical discussions without the loss of basic continuity. In more rigorous or more senior courses, these discussions will add analytical interest.

The country-study volumes consider the operation of various systems in practice in both developed and developing countries. Those teaching in the field of comparative economics can combine with this basic theory book those particular country-study volumes in the series which best suit the design of their individual courses. Since the country-study series is open-ended, it will in time become even more flexible and adaptable as additional countries are included.

The author owes a deep debt of gratitude to the many people who have contributed in one way or another to the development of this book. Particular thanks are due to Professor Dominick Armentano and Professor Morris Singer for the excellent chapters which they contributed and to Professor Paul Weiner for his many helpful comments and suggestions.

The author also wishes to express his appreciation to Mrs. Joanne Mitchell, Mrs. Muriel Scotta and Mrs. Barbara Sedlock who helped in the preparation of earlier drafts of the manuscript, to Mrs. Kathy Saxton who prepared an excellent index, and to the University Research Foundation which made available the outstanding services of Mrs. Charlotte Ritchie for the typing of the final draft.

Sincere thanks are also extended to Paul Becher for his continuing helpfulness and to Miss Kathy Doyle for her excellent copyediting.

Though many people have contributed to the development of this book, the author, alone, is responsible for the shortcomings which remain.

William P. Snavely
Storrs, Connecticut
1969

Contents

ix

Introduction

The Concept of Economic Systems

Man's interest in economic systems can be traced far into the past. Expressions of it are found in a number of early works, including those which are devoted to the stimulating thoughts of Plato, Aristotle and other Greek philosophers. This interest in economic systems has continued through the centuries and has reached a peak of intensity in contemporary times with the keen economic and political rivalry which has developed between those nations adhering to the principles of modern capitalism and those following in the path of communism.

The term *economic system* refers to the manner in which the answers to basic economic questions are determined in a particular society. These familiar questions, simply stated, include:

1. What products shall be produced, and how much of each?
2. What techniques of production shall be used?
3. Who shall do what work?
4. How shall the total output be distributed?
5. How shall the rates of saving and investment be determined?

This list is not intended to be exhaustive; it is presented merely to indicate the types of economic questions which must be answered effectively

1

in any society, no matter how primitive or how advanced, if that society is to have an economy which functions in orderly fashion.

The manner in which the answers to these basic questions are supplied and the pattern of ownership of productive capital and land determine, together, the nature of the economic system of a society. Since there are different ways in which answers to these questions can be determined as well as different patterns for the ownership of productive capital and land, it follows that various types of economic systems are possible. This conclusion is readily confirmed by a glance at the world today in which one sees a number of different economic systems represented among contemporary nations. This diversity is less confusing than it might at first appear, for most of the systems which have been developed among the nations of the world or at the level of abstract thought can be placed within the broad, threefold classification of capitalism, socialism and corporatism.

For the purposes of this volume, capitalism will be understood to include both the abstract *laissez-faire*-competitive model and the mixed capitalistic systems found in the contemporary world. Since terminology in the area of comparative systems unfortunately has not yet become standardized, the term *capitalism* will also be understood to include the concepts of liberal capitalism, democratic capitalism, pure capitalism and the free-enterprise system.

Socialism is used here to include both liberal socialism, which assumes free markets for consumer goods and labor but government ownership of productive capital, and authoritarian socialism or communism, in which productive capital is also government owned but decisions concerning employment and the production of consumer goods are centrally made. Liberal socialism has also been referred to as limited socialism, market socialism, democratic socialism and democratic partial socialism. The command-type economies represented by authoritarian socialism have also been called full socialism, and sometimes simply socialism.

Corporatism includes the romantic political thought of men such as Johann Fichte and Friedrich Schlegel, the philosophy of social Catholicism and social Protestantism, as well as the pragmatic, fascist forms of corporatism which developed first in Italy after World War I, then in Germany, and later in Spain, Portugal and, to some extent, a few other countries. The fascist form of corporatism has also been referred to as authoritarian capitalism.

To give the reader a better idea of the nature of the subject matter to be covered in this study of economic systems, a brief summary is presented below of the topics to be treated in detail in later chapters. It should be noted that the three broad systems discussed—capitalism, socialism and corporatism—are considered in historical perspective.

Capitalism

Capitalism in the Greek and Roman Periods

Elements of the capitalistic system had developed well before the Greek and Roman periods. In some of the ancient Greek city-states, though not continuously in all, some aspects of capitalism prevailed, but no fully developed capitalistic system emerged in the Greek period. Ancient Rome was characterized by a similar stage of rudimentary capitalistic development.

With the fall of the Roman Empire, capitalistic elements as they had previously existed largely disappeared from Western Europe and were replaced by the feudal-manorial system which continued during the several centuries of the Middle Ages. The end of the Middle Ages was marked by the gradual rise of towns and a return to production for the market. This represented the emergence of capitalism in a restricted form characterized by extensive guild regulation and control of economic activity.

The Period of Early Capitalism

Werner Sombart refers to the span from the thirteenth century to the middle of the eighteenth century as the period of early capitalism. The first part of this period, the thirteenth to sixteenth centuries, represented the period of the guild system; the second part, the sixteenth to mid-eighteenth centuries, was the period of mercantilism, or statism as it is sometimes called.

Under mercantilism, nations attempted to become as economically self-sufficient as possible in order to maximize their power positions in the course of seeking to gain their international political objectives. Though encouragement was given to the development of private industry and commerce under mercantilism, the framework of regulations and restrictions within which these activities had to operate made for a rather limited form of capitalism.

During the long span from the thirteenth to the middle of the eighteenth century, there was, as Sombart emphasizes, a prevailing feudal or pre-capitalistic approach to economic relationships. The profit motive and the incentive for wealth accumulation were weak in this period, and the relationship between the owners of productive enterprises and both their workers and their customers tended to be a highly personal one. Employers had concern for their workers in sickness and also in the infirmities of their old age. These feudal, paternalistic attitudes represented a form of social security.

Modern Capitalism

The rise of the philosophy of individualism and the rapid development of science and technology after the middle of the eighteenth century made possible the industrial revolution and the development of modern capitalism. In this period the feudal relationships which had previously afforded workers a measure of economic security were largely removed as workers were thrown on the impersonal agricultural and industrial labor markets which had developed. For a time these changes in the economic structure generated rather bad conditions for the working class. In fact, they helped to stimulate Karl Marx's strong criticisms of the capitalistic system.

After 1850, technological developments encouraged the adoption of larger-scale industrial operations, and by the last quarter of the nineteenth century, this tendency as accentuated by merger and trust movements had become quite pronounced in the leading industrial countries. This development had significant implications for the extent of competition in some industries and led Congress in the United States to pass antitrust legislation.

The Mixed-Capitalistic System

Government interventions in the United States economy through various regulations and controls, coupled with conditions of imperfect competition in most lines of production, make it appropriate to characterize the economy of this country as a mixed-capitalistic system in contrast to the *laissez-faire*-competitive model of capitalism. The decline of *laissez-faire* in the United States has been particularly pronounced in the period since World War I.

The Prospects for Capitalism

Following the brief historical survey of the institutional development of capitalism, three chapters are devoted to the prospects for this system as viewed by various economists. The discussion covers a wide range of thought on the subject, including that of classical economists, Marx and Engels, neo-classical economists, Keynes and his followers, Schumpeter and Galbraith. The discussion of Marx's conclusions on capitalism is preceded by a brief biographical sketch of this harsh critic of the capitalistic system.

The analyses of most of these economists have led them to rather pessimistic conclusions about the long-run prospects for capitalism. Their theoretical conclusions are contrasted with the high degree of adaptability and durability so far displayed by capitalistic systems in practice.

The convergence thesis, which holds that capitalistic and socialistic systems will continue to go through a process of adaptation and modification which will steadily reduce the differences between them, is also considered briefly in the context of the prospects for capitalism.

Socialism

Socialism in the Greek and Judeo-Christian Traditions

Like capitalism, socialism in theory and in practice is also considered in historical perspective to provide a better appreciation of contemporary thought concerning this system. In the Greek period, the views of Plato and Aristotle on communism, as well as the practice of a form of communism in Sparta, Lipara and Crete, are considered. This is followed by a glance at socialism in relation to the Judeo-Christian tradition. Here the teachings of Moses, Christ and the early Christian leaders are reviewed, and the differences between the communism of the Essene settlements and the early Christian groups are considered briefly.

Utopian Socialism

The next stage in the development of socialist thought began with the publication of Sir Thomas More's *Utopia* in 1516. More's famous work was divided into two parts. The first part contained a brilliant description of the unfortunate economic and social conditions then prevailing in England and other countries. The second part described the society of Utopia, which practiced an idealized form of communism. The success of the country of Utopia was based upon the assumption of a highly virtuous behavior pattern on the part of its citizens. More failed to give the secret for moving from the present imperfect state of society to the "perfect" one which he described. In doing so, he set the pattern for the long line of utopian socialist writers who followed him.

Other utopian socialists included for brief discussion are Jean Jacques Rousseau, Charles Hall, William Godwin, Count Henri-Claude de Rouvroy de Saint-Simon and Robert Owen. All of these writers were keen critics of prevailing economic and social conditions, but their thinking tended to leap from the level of criticism of existing institutions to the construction of abstract mental images of the ideal state. Robert Owen, who was notably successful in reforming and greatly improving living conditions in the mill town of New Lanark, Scotland, actually tried to establish several ideal communistic communities, including one at New Harmony, Indiana. These experiments all failed, for Owen had found no way to bridge the gap between human nature as it is and as it would have to be for man to live in the state of harmony which he sought for his communistic communities.

Karl Marx and Scientific Socialism

Karl Marx regarded the utopian socialists with contempt, for he considered them to be visionary and highly impractical. Marx ushered in the age of scientific socialism, for he was not only a sharp critic of contemporary conditions and a firm believer in the advantages to be gained from a system of communism, but, in addition, he attempted to discover the basic historical processes that would make a progression from capitalism to socialism inevitable. Marx and Engels, who was his close collaborator for many years, adopted the term *communism* rather than *socialism* to emphasize what they considered to be the important differences between their thinking and that of their utopian-socialist predecessors.

A discussion of Marx's scientific socialist thought must consider the impression made upon him by the Hegelian dialectic and his adaptation of this dialectic for use in the development of his own materialistic interpretation of history. Marx emphasized the role of the mode of production and his concept of the class struggle in formulating his thesis of the inevitability of the breakdown of capitalism and the replacement of this system by communism. Having developed his supposedly scientific explanation of the course of historical evolution by means of his theory of dialectical materialism, Marx did not go further to develop an analysis of the functioning of a communistic economy. He made the progression from capitalism to communism seem so automatic that his followers found no reason to consider whether or not such a system in practice might involve highly complex and difficult operational problems.

Though he was more scientific in his approach than the utopian socialists who preceded him, Marx's vision of a classless society in which the doctrine of "from each according to his ability and to each according to his need" is gladly accepted by all seems to call for the perfection of man's nature to a degree which appears highly utopian itself.

Edward Bernstein and Revisionism

The latter half of the nineteenth century brought marked improvements in the economic position of the working class in the more advanced capitalistic countries. As a result, the prospects for the overthrow of capitalism by a growing army of disenchanted unemployed seemed to be receding instead of drawing closer. This led Edward Bernstein and his followers at the close of the nineteenth century to repudiate the Marxian concept of the increasing misery of the proletariat under capitalism. Instead, they accepted the thesis that desired reforms should be worked for through the democratic process within the framework of capitalism. They thought that socialism, by adopting this procedure, would eventually emerge as the result of a peaceful evolutionary process rather than through a sudden revolution.

Bernstein's views had the effect of splitting the Marxists into two groups—the revisionists, who followed Bernstein, and the orthodox Marxists, who continued to accept literally the theory of the approaching proletarian revolution.

Socialism and the Resource Allocation Problem

The Bolshevik regime which was successful in gaining power in Russia in 1917 had an orthodox Marxist orientation. As a result, it is not surprising that the new regime found itself in power without having any well-developed guidelines for socialist economic planning. In fact, the question of the efficiency with which resources could be allocated in a socialist economy had been largely neglected by both classical and Marxian economists before World War I. Soon after the war, however, Professor Ludwig von Mises developed arguments to show that an efficient allocation of resources could not be achieved under socialism and that as a result this could not be an economically practical system. During the 1930's such economists as Lionel Robbins, George Halm and Frederick von Hayek developed other arguments to support the thesis that a socialist economy would be incapable of operating in a rational and efficient manner. The arguments of Mises, Hayek, Robbins and others are discussed by Professor Armentano in Chapter 8.

The pessimistic views of Mises and others were challenged first by Professor Fred M. Taylor in a professional address delivered in 1928, and then much more fully by Professor Oscar Lange in a pair of articles published in 1936 and 1937. Professor Lange developed in considerable detail the case for the realization of efficiency in the allocation of resources in a liberal socialist economy through using trial-and-error pricing. In his system, accounting or shadow prices serve as parameters indicating the terms on which alternatives are offered. With appropriate behavior patterns prescribed for the managers of public enterprises and for the central planners, Lange shows that a trial-and-error system could operate efficiently. He also argues that the same approach could be used successfully in an authoritarian socialist system in which consumer preferences are not permitted to guide the allocation of resources for the production of consumer goods and in which there is not freedom of occupational choice.

The theoretical case for socialism developed by Professor Lange was strong and succeeded in shifting the discussion of the relative merits of capitalism and socialism to quite a different plane. In the period since the appearance of his articles, the arguments concerning these two systems have tended to be more pragmatic and have been concerned with such questions as Which would tend to produce better economic and social results in practice? and Which would provide greater personal freedom? A number of arguments relating to these questions are reviewed briefly in the latter part of Chapter 9.

Corporatism and Fascism

The Concept of Corporatism

The discussion of liberal and authoritarian socialism is followed by a review of corporatism and fascism—the last of the three broad categories of economic systems considered in this work. The term *corporatism* refers to those economic, social and political systems which emphasize organization on the basis of occupation. The principle of private ownership of productive capital is an inherent aspect of corporatism, but this system is distinguished from traditional capitalism by the stress placed upon cooperation and mutuality of interests between employers and employees. At one time or another, corporatism has been associated with the efforts of religious groups, with capitalistic attempts to stem the tide of socialism, and with highly nationalistic movements.

Early Corporatist Thought

An early expression of the philosophy of corporatism is found in the works of some of the Romantic political thinkers in Western Europe in the first part of the nineteenth century. Writers such as Johann Fichte and Friedrich Schlegel rejected the doctrine of individualism on the grounds that it promoted disruptive influences in society, for instance greed and personal ambition. They believed that a system of corporatism sponsored by strong national states would best achieve the social harmony which they sought.

Catholic and Protestant Corporatist Efforts

These Romantic political thinkers had little practical influence, and the spirit of corporatism was next manifested in efforts to provide better economic and social conditions for workers within the framework of the capitalistic system. Both Catholic and Protestant religious groups played an important part in these efforts to improve the position of workers. The corporatism advocated by these groups was an economic doctrine which occupied a position between the extremes of Marxism and classical capitalism.

The Fascist Form of Corporatism

Corporatism in its most flagrantly fascist form developed after World War I, first in Italy and then in Germany. Since German fascism is treated in Professor Knauerhase's volume in this series, *National Socialism in Germany*, only Italian fascism is considered in some detail in Chapter 10.

Corporatism in the Postwar Period

The defeat of the fascist regimes in Germany and Italy in World War II did not bring to an end corporatism in its religious and fascist manifestations. Elements of a religiously motivated corporatism reappeared in some countries in the postwar period. In Germany and Italy, for example, Christian Democratic parties became the major political force. So far, relatively little progress toward corporatist developments has been achieved by these parties when in power or when sharing power in coalition governments, but their philosophical orientation reflects an element of corporatism. It can also be argued that in a mature capitalistic country like the United States a secular corporatist trend has developed as a result of the checks and balances which have emerged within the framework of large business units, powerful labor unions and a national government which has accepted an important measure of responsibility for the manner in which the economy functions.

The fascist form of corporatism has prevailed in Portugal and Spain since the war, and elements of fascism have been present at one time or another in Argentina and some other countries as well during this period.

The Problem of Evaluating Economic Systems

Sooner or later, students of comparative economic systems almost invariably raise the question, What is the "best" system? They seem to think that economists should be able to provide a definitive answer which could serve, among other things, as a guide for the leaders of the less developed countries and show them the path along which they should strive to guide their countries during the process of development. The frequent coupling of the word "comparative" with the phrase "economic systems" tends itself to suggest the idea of a qualitative ordering.

Actually, the problem of ranking economic systems is one which economists cannot solve on a purely objective basis, for a ranking process necessitates the introduction of subjective judgments. Professor Bela Balassa has developed an excellent analysis of the evaluation problem, and a brief review of the success criteria which he discusses will help to illustrate the difficulties involved in attempting to compare economic systems.[1]

Professor Balassa's Success Indicators

The five success indicators which Professor Balassa has selected for evaluation purposes are static efficiency in the allocation of resources,

---

[1]For his full discussion, see Bela A. Balassa, *The Hungarian Experience in Economic Planning* (New Haven, Conn.: Yale University Press, 1959), pp. 5-24.

dynamic efficiency, the growth rate of national income, consumer satisfaction, and the pattern of income distribution. The nature of each of these indicators will be considered briefly.

Static Efficiency

Static efficiency refers to the efficiency with which the resources of an economy are allocated in conformance with the preferences of individuals in capitalistic and liberal socialist systems, or with the preferences of the planning authority in the case of an authoritarian socialist system. The consideration here is the efficiency with which resources are allocated in the economy at a given point in time.

Professor Balassa observes that both a free-enterprise capitalistic system and a liberal socialist one would seem to be capable of achieving a high degree of static efficiency. The cost of accumulating information needed for making production and investment decisions would tend to be higher where productive capital is state owned and decisions are more centralized. On the other hand, a free-enterprise capitalistic system will tend to operate within the framework of greater uncertainty, and this will result in some unemployment of labor and other resources at times.

Both free-enterprise and liberal socialist systems would score better on the matter of static efficiency than an authoritarian socialist system which used a physical allocation of resources rather than an allocation based upon a price system. Here it would not be easy to see whether with a different allocation of resources it might be possible to increase the production of some goods without reducing the production of others—that is, it would not be easy to determine whether static efficiency had been achieved in a system in which the price mechanism is not permitted to operate within a market structure.

Dynamic Efficiency

The second success indicator, dynamic efficiency, refers to the theoretical growth rate in national income of which different systems are capable if they have the same initial resources and rates of savings. Several points have been noted by various writers in comparing the dynamic efficiency of capitalism and socialism. For example, some proponents of capitalism have argued that the profit motive would stimulate the quest for more efficient techniques of production and for innovations. Professor Schumpeter, who was himself a supporter of capitalism, pointed out that as this system matured and became characterized by large-scale firms in many lines of production, the process of innovation would tend to lose its individual character and become a more organized and routine procedure.[2] As this trend occurred, the nature of the process of innova-

---

[2]For a more detailed discussion of Schumpeter's analysis, see Chapter 5.

tion and technological development under capitalism would tend to become more like the process under socialism.

It has also been pointed out that in developing countries long-term growth rates can be raised by increasing the rate of social infrastructural investment in such things as highways and other forms of transportation, technical and other schools, and public health programs. Proponents of socialism claim that greater attention would tend to be given to investments of this type under this system than under a free-enterprise one.

Professor Balassa also mentions that some writers have claimed that the uncertainties stemming from the decentralization of economic decision making which are present in a capitalistic system can result in errors and waste which could be avoided under the centralized investment planning of socialism. The counter argument is that this centralization may make for a more stable growth rate under socialism, but free enterprise may be characterized by a greater dynamism than a system of government-owned enterprises. The result may be a higher theoretical average growth rate under capitalism.

Given the assumptions of the dynamic-efficiency criterion which include the same initial resources and the same rates of savings for the different economic systems, Balassa concludes that it is probably impossible for economists to draw meaningful conclusions concerning the comparative theoretical growth rates of capitalism and socialism.

The Actual Growth Rate

The third success indicator discussed by Balassa is the *actual* growth rate, in contrast to the *theoretical* growth rate considered under the dynamic-efficiency criterion. The factors affecting the actual growth rate include not only the kinds of things which are relevant to dynamic efficiency, but also the important matter of the rate of saving in various systems as well. In the case of saving, that is sacrificing present consumption in order to increase the rate of investment, it would seem that a socialist system in which the rates of saving and investment are centrally determined could impose greater consumption sacrifices on the public than the public may be willing to impose upon itself in a free-enterprise economy. To the extent that this situation does prevail, unless there are other offsetting factors, one would expect to find somewhat higher growth rates in socialist-type economies than in capitalistic free-enterprise ones. Though theoretically it would be possible for the government in a capitalistic country to levy tax rates which would impose burdens of forced saving upon the public as heavy as those likely to be imposed under a more centralized socialist system, in practice, as Balassa observes, it seems doubtful that this would be done. Since the matter of comparative growth rates has become a subject of considerable current economic and political interest, the final two chapters, contributed by Professor Morris

Singer, deal in some detail with the relation between systems and growth rates in the case of the less developed countries. Professor Singer also develops a theoretical analysis of the impact of the price system on the rate of growth, again within the context of developing countries.

Consumer Satisfaction

The fourth success indicator chosen by Professor Balassa is consumer satisfaction. He lists three factors as significant here. These are 1) the extent to which production targets reflect consumer preferences; 2) the extent to which the actual rate of saving reflects individual preferences; and 3) the extent to which individual preferences in regard to working time and leisure time are met. Capitalistic systems which provide wide scope for consumer sovereignty and choice of work will tend to conform more fully to this success criterion than systems in which decisions are more centrally made and in which less weight is given to the matter of individual preferences.

The Distribution of Income

The final success indicator which Professor Balassa considers is the distribution of income. As he points out, the pattern of income distribution affects the performance of an economic system with respect to the other success indicators, and at the same time it, too, can serve as one of the indicators of success. In this latter capacity, some standard for evaluating income distribution patterns would have to be established if different systems are to be compared on this basis, and Balassa correctly observes that any standard selected would involve value judgments. There is little more that the economist can say about the matter.

Success Criteria and Value Judgments

Now that Professor Balassa's success criteria have been reviewed briefly, it should be emphasized that the mere process of selecting a particular set of criteria for judging the relative performances of different economic systems involves to some extent the making of value judgments. In short, why use this set of success indicators rather than some other which might include some of the same indicators, but others as well?

Once a particular set of success indicators has been adopted, still further value judgments arise when efforts are made to apply it in evaluating systems. For example, even if each individual indicator selected should permit an objective grading of various systems to be made, there would still remain the problem of determining the aggregate scores of the systems under review. A simple adding would mean giving an equal weighting to all of the indicators used, which in itself would mean exercising a value judgment on weighting. A similar value judgment would be involved if any other weighting system were selected.

The purpose of this discussion of success indicators has been to underscore the point that the economist has no objective basis for ranking various economic systems. It is hoped that the reader will discover useful insights concerning these systems which will enable him to consider them with greater understanding and even to reach more intelligent value judgments of his own concerning their relative merits.

Capitalism in Historical Perspective

2

Definitions of Capitalism

The Tautological Definition of Capitalism

To avoid unnecessary confusion concerning the concept of capitalism and the capitalistic system, it should be understood that all economic systems which are characterized by the use of capital equipment in the process of production are, in this sense, capitalistic. In fact, as soon as primitive man first took the time to construct a crude tool or weapon to assist him in the attainment of things which he could consume, it could be said that a capitalistic system had developed. The definition of a system as capitalistic because it employs capital equipment in the process of producing consumer goods is tautological, however, and does not represent the meaning which is more usefully attached to this term.

The Traditional Concept of Capitalism

Traditionally the capitalistic model assumes that capital goods and land are privately owned, consumer demand gives direction to production, the profit motive provides the incentive for entrepreneurial activity, competition throughout the economy insures an income distribution pattern which reflects the productive contribution made by each member of the system, and the role of government is limited to such functions as providing internal law and order, protecting the country from external attack, and maintaining a stable monetary system. Some of these characteristics are also found in other systems. For example, fascism maintains private ownership of capital goods and land, and also makes use of the profit motive as the incentive for entrepreneurial activity. On the other hand, the fascist system partially replaces consumer demand with the decisions of an authoritarian governmental planning body in determining the pattern of production.

The model of limited socialism, though it makes use of consumer demand to give direction to production, differs markedly from capitalism. Under a system of limited socialism, public ownership replaces private ownership of capital goods and land, and the drive for cost minimization in public enterprises replaces the profit motive of capitalism.

The Greek and Roman Period

Though elements of capitalism had developed well before the Greek and Roman periods, it will suffice here to point out that in some, though not continuously in all of the ancient Greek city-states, a number of capitalistic features were present. Ancient Rome was characterized by a similar stage of development of capitalistic elements. It cannot be said, however, that a fully developed capitalistic system had emerged.

The Middle Ages

With the fall of the Roman Empire, those elements of capitalism which had previously existed largely disappeared from Western Europe. Under the feudal-manorial systems which emerged and which continued during the several centuries of the Middle Ages, economic life became reorganized along the lines of relatively self-sufficient manorial estates. Though all of the land in an estate was technically owned by the lord of the manor, custom and tradition decreed that part of it should be made available for the use of the serfs who lived on the manor under the lord's protection. In return, the serfs, who were legally bound to the estate on which they were born, were obligated to devote part of their time to the cultivation of the lord's land. Mutual rights and obligations between the serfs and lords of manorial estates were characteristic of feudalism, but it should be noted that the economic and social position of the serf tended to be extremely low. Some element of paternalism toward the serfs did exist in the sense that the lord of a manorial estate had the responsibility of protecting the serfs under him and even of feeding them from his own stores in time of famine.

Production on the manorial estates was for subsistence—not for sale in the market for profit. As a result there was little scope for the operation of the forces of competition. On the basis of these characteristics, this system could not be classified as capitalistic; rather it is usually referred to as feudalistic.

The teachings of the Christian religion, which had wide influence during this period, also reflected the non-capitalistic character of economic life. Church teachings held that individuals should accept their status in this life and not be concerned with trying to improve it through raising their incomes and accumulating wealth. The reward for bearing with patience the cares and difficulties of life on earth was the promise of a happier state in the hereafter. This doctrine obviously conflicts with the profit motive as an incentive to the entrepreneurial activity which characterizes capitalism.

The system of feudalism during the Middle Ages was relatively static. The class structure was rigid and individuals were frozen into the social class in which they were born. Economic innovation was largely absent, as were the growth and development which are characteristic of a dynamic economy. In fact, the Middle Ages represents a long static interlude between the Roman period and the Renaissance, which was characterized by the return of more dynamic economic and social conditions.

The Guild System

Werner Sombart, one of the outstanding writers on capitalism and its historical development, treats the period from the thirteenth to the middle of the eighteenth century as the period of early capitalism, but it is often more useful to break it down into two periods.[1] The restricted form of capitalism which prevailed during the rise of towns and before the development of strong national states—that is, the span from the thirteenth to the sixteenth century—is referred to as the guild system.

The drawing to an end of the Middle Ages in Western Europe was marked by the gradual rise of towns in which small-scale handicraft production of goods for sale on the market became increasingly important. To some extent this represented a revival of elements of capitalism, but it was a severely restricted capitalism. Each line of production tended to be organized in a guild. The guild, in turn, established rules concerning the number of workers—apprentices and journeymen—which each master craftsman could hire, the number of hours per day that the shop could operate, the standards of quality which the product must

---

[1]Werner Sombart, "Capitalism," *The Encyclopaedia of the Social Sciences* (1930), Vol. 3, p. 206.

meet, and the price which could be charged. Such regulations were rigidly enforced and obviously represented serious infringements upon freedom of competition and the drive for profits. The ability of traders to seek profits through commercial activities was also subject to legal restraint. Attempts to gain monopoly positions in the holdings of commodities so that higher prices could be charged were prohibited.

Mercantilism

The rise of national states during the period from the sixteenth century to the middle of the eighteenth century introduced new economic elements as well. States replaced towns as the sovereign power, and economic policies were introduced which were designed to increase the economic and political strength of the nation. Since these policies were largely concerned with helping countries gain a favorable balance of trade, the form of capitalism which prevailed in Western Europe during this period is called mercantilism or, alternatively, statism.

States following mercantilist policies introduced measures which would encourage the growth of home industries. Subsidies were provided to encourage the growth of productive enterprises, and tariffs and other trade restrictions were imposed to reduce the competition of imports. Efforts were made to keep wages low both directly through legal restrictions and indirectly by encouraging the growth of population. Low wages were desired as a means of keeping costs of production down so that home industries could compete more effectively in foreign markets.

The discovery and exploitation of colonies became an integral part of the mercantilist system. The advantages were obvious: colonies would serve both as a cheap source of raw materials for the industries of the home country and as markets for the finished goods produced at home. Emphasis was placed upon an inflow of gold and silver to the home country, not, as is sometimes said, because these elements were considered the sole end of mercantilism, but rather because an inflow of these precious metals would be indicative of a favorable balance of trade, which was considered to be an integral part of the development of economic strength.

Under mercantilism, nations wanted to be as economically self-sufficient as possible in order to maximize their ability to wage war in the course of seeking to gain their international political objectives. The development of large armies, navies and merchant marines was naturally part of the system.

Though encouragement was given to the development of industry and commerce under mercantilism, the framework of regulations and restrictions within which these activities had to operate represented at least partial departures from some of the basic characteristics of our capitalistic model.

Characteristics of the Period from the Thirteenth to the Nineteenth Century

To gain an understanding of the economic evolution that was taking place from the thirteenth to the middle of the eighteenth century, it is useful to divide this time bloc into the two sub-periods described above; but there are some significant characteristics which apply to the period as a whole. For example, as Sombart points out, there was a prevailing feudal or pre-capitalist approach to economic relationships. The profit motive and the desire for wealth accumulation were weak during this period, and the concept of working as a means simply of making a living which would maintain but not elevate one's station in life was of major importance. Production, for the most part, continued to be on a small-scale basis and the relationship between the owners of productive enterprises and both their workers and their customers tended to be a personal one. Employers had concern for their workers when they were sick and also in the infirmities of their old age. The carry-over of these feudal, paternalistic attitudes represented a form of social security for the working people of the period.

Though capitalistic elements were weak and not well developed during this long span from the thirteenth to the middle of the eighteenth century, they were present with sufficient force to justify Sombart's designation of this period as one of early capitalism. Schumpeter, another outstanding writer on capitalism, used a slightly different designation. He referred to the period from the thirteenth to the middle of the sixteenth century as early capitalism and the period from the middle of the sixteenth to the beginning of the nineteenth century as the period of mercantilist capitalism. These differences are not significant; they simply point to the fact that capitalism in its more modern form followed the period of mercantilism.

Developments During the Nineteenth Century and to World War I

Several significant changes which exerted their influence in the eighteenth and nineteenth centuries altered rather dramatically the nature of capitalism in Western Europe. The changes were such that Sombart designated the span from the middle of the nineteenth century to World War I as the period of full capitalism. Schumpeter's corresponding period encompasses virtually the entire nineteenth century.

The modest differences in timing selected by these two authorities are not significant for present purposes. What is important is the nature of the changes that exerted their influence during this general period, and it is to this that we now turn.

The Philosophy of Individualism

Mercantilist policies had tended to subordinate the interests of the individual to those of the state, but by the latter part of the eighteenth century the philosophy of individualism was becoming increasingly prominent. Such thinkers and writers as Rousseau, Godwin and Proudhon emphasized the importance of the individual. Godwin, particularly, expressed his faith in the power of human reason and felt that individuals should be free of oppressive state control.[2]

The development of science and technology, which resulted in innovations appropriate to large-scale production, provided the possibility of large profits for producers and merchants if governmental restrictions were removed. These expanding profit possibilities placed producers and traders in opposition to existing restrictive and inefficient political regimes and contributed to the growing sentiment for a *laissez-faire* policy on the part of government.

Economists of the period such as Adam Smith and John Stuart Mill echoed the sentiment for a policy of *laissez-faire*, and they incorporated this doctrine in their formal writings. They accepted the *laissez-faire* concept on pragmatic, utilitarian grounds. That is, they believed that this approach would result in the greatest good for the greatest number.

The spread of Protestantism with its less doctrinaire approach and greater emphasis upon personal conscience also contributed to the rising spirit of individualism. The concepts of thrift and accumulation became easily accommodated under the Protestant ethic in contrast to the traditional attitude of condemnation of conscious efforts to accumulate wealth.

The developing reaction against restrictive governments was reflected in the American and French Revolutions in the latter part of the eighteenth century and in the numerous revolutionary movements and attempted revolutions which were particularly characteristic of the first half of the nineteenth century. The abortive 1848 revolutions in Europe, though only temporarily successful in overthrowing existing restrictive

---

[2]This interesting statement appears in the first edition (1793) of Godwin's *Enquiry Concerning Political Justice*, Vol. 2, p. 380:

Above all we should not forget, that government is an evil, an usurpation upon the private judgment and individual conscience of mankind, and that, however we may be obliged to admit it as a necessary evil for the present, it behoves us, as the friends of reason and the human species, to admit as little of it as possible, and carefully to observe whether, in consequence of the gradual illumination of the human mind, that little may not hereafter be diminished.

regimes, were followed, nonetheless, by more liberal governmental policies. In fact, the latter half of the nineteenth century in England and in parts of Western Europe was characterized by a strong spirit of economic liberalism.

The Industrial Revolution

As a result of the emergence of new attitudes and new technological developments, dramatic changes in the organization and operation of productive enterprises occurred in England during the latter quarter of the eighteenth and the first half of the nineteenth century. These changes were so rapid and marked that they are referred to as the industrial revolution. Similar revolutionary changes occurred with varying lags in other countries.

The development and use of power-driven machinery was an important feature of the industrial revolution. The reductions in cost to be achieved by using such equipment resulted in the growth of factories and the decline in small-scale handicraft production in home workshops. Large numbers of artisans were squeezed out of business by the competition of factories and were forced to seek employment as wage earners in the impersonal labor market which emerged with the growth of the factory system. This separation of workers from the ownership of the capital equipment used in production—which characterized the shift from commercial capitalism to industrial capitalism during the industrial revolution—greatly weakened the workers' economic position. The employer-employee relationship became a completely impersonal one and the previously existing sense of feudal responsibility rapidly disappeared.

At the same time that radical changes were occurring in England in the production of textiles, metals, machinery and other products, dramatic changes were also occurring in agriculture. The market for raw wool was expanding rapidly and this led to an extensive shifting from small-scale diversified peasant farming to large-scale sheep raising. This change in the pattern of production required the fencing or enclosure of large areas of land, a process which is referred to as the enclosure movement. Since sheep raising is far less labor-intensive than small-scale diversified farming, a large number of peasant tenant-farmers were uprooted from the land and forced to seek employment simply as wage earners either in agriculture or in industry. The limited availability of jobs in agriculture resulted in the migration of a great many peasant families to the industrial towns and cities. The carry-over of feudal relationships which previously had afforded them some measure of personal economic security was now completely removed as they were thrown on the impersonal agricultural and industrial labor markets which had developed.

From the perspective of the latter half of the twentieth century it is difficult to appreciate fully the economic and social impact of the first fifty years of the industrial revolution in England. The flood of workers streaming to the industrial centers resulted in supply-and-demand relationships that were highly unfavorable to the workers. As a result, wages were at quite low levels and large numbers of women and even extremely young children were attracted to jobs in the factories and mines.[3] Workers were unorganized, factory legislation had not yet been introduced, and factories themselves tended to be poorly lighted and ventilated as well as unsanitary, and conditions of work were often hazardous.

Karl Marx, in commenting upon the situation of workers during this period of rapid economic and social change, referred to the fact that the old idyllic feudal ties had been severed and replaced by callous cash payment. It had not yet become evident that the working class could also benefit from the expanding production and economic growth which could take place within the framework of industrial capitalism and that new forms of social security would in time emerge to replace the feudal ties of an earlier era.

Robert Owen—Humane Industrialist and Social Reformer

The unhappy plight of the working class in England during the industrial revolution has been so widely commented upon that it need not be treated in more detail here. One exception to the general rule is so striking, however, that it should be noted in passing. This is the miracle wrought by Robert Owen, the mill owner at New Lanark, Scotland.

Owen lived from 1771 to 1858. Thus, his lifetime spanned the period of the industrial revolution in England. His father engaged in several activities, including those of ironmonger, postmaster and saddler. The fact that young Owen stopped school at seven and was already a shop assistant by the age of nine was not in his case a result of economic necessity, but rather a reflection of the practice of this period. He migrated to London at the age of ten and in the years following held several different jobs. By the time he was nineteen he had achieved a managerial position in a cotton-mill firm in Manchester. His salary at this point had reached L300 per year, which was unusually high for one so young and was a reflection of Owen's exceptional ability and energy.

---

[3]For a somewhat more favorable interpretation of the period of the industrial revolution, see F. A. Hayek, ed., *Capitalism and the Historians* (Chicago: University of Chicago Press, 1954).

Exceptional Capitalist During the Industrial Revolution

Seven years later Owen entered a partnership which bought the mills at New Lanark in Scotland. Conditions in this mill town were extremely bad at the time; virtually all of the unfortunate aspects of the industrial revolution were present. Many of the workers had been imported as very young children from workhouses in various cities. They had grown up in the harsh conditions of the times, and drunkenness and vice were widespread. Owen was a man of concern who deplored the conditions of the workers which confronted him. He was also an activist and he began systematically to try to improve the situation. In his reform efforts he met resistance from his partners and from the workers themselves, but he was able to win out over both.

Owen was an environmentalist who thought that man was innately neither good nor bad, but rather that his behavior and moral standards were determined by his environment. At New Lanark he proceeded to test his theory by bringing about a radical improvement in the conditions of living and work. He placed great emphasis upon education and introduced schools for the very young. The inclusion of music and dancing in the curriculum mark him as a progressive educator who was far ahead of his time.

To improve the living conditions of the older children and adults, Owen introduced a clean-up campaign to brighten the appearance of the town. He also tried to solve the problem of excessive drinking, which had been the workers' escape from the harsh realities of mill life. Owen was successful in reducing substantially the extent of drinking, probably more through the severe restrictions which he imposed on the operation of the pubs than through his efforts to educate the public to appreciate the finer things of life. Be that as it may, the whole character of living in New Lanark was transformed under Owen, and crime and vice virtually disappeared.

To appreciate fully how far in advance of the thinking of the times Owen was, it should be mentioned that he advocated that children should not enter the factories until they had reached the age of twelve, and even then they should not be made to work excessively long hours. This was in striking contrast to the practice at the time to put children to work in the mills at seven or eight years of age and for as long as fourteen or more hours a day. Owen based his advocacy of a more moderate approach to the working of children on the very practical grounds of taking good care of a productive resource so that its lifetime productivity could be maximized. He chided his fellow industrialists for taking good care of their inanimate machines while abusing unconscionably their human factor of production.

Owen was also critical of the extremely low wages paid to labor. He recognized that workers, constituting the bulk of the population, represented a mass market *if* they had purchasing power. He thought wages should be kept high to provide this purchasing power, and that in this way prosperity would be assured.

Further evidence of his modern thinking is found in his advocacy of the development of a good system of labor statistics so that the government could deal properly with the problem of unemployment through a system of public works.

All in all, Owen stands out as an exceptional figure during the period of the industrial revolution when labor tended to be a neglected and abused factor of production. He demonstrated through his own efforts that the lot of the mill workers in an industrial town could be dramatically improved and that the efforts and expense involved were economically justifiable; for it should not be forgotten that Owen accumulated a tidy fortune while transforming the community of New Lanark. In effect, he provided a practical demonstration of the relationship between the conditions of employment and the level of labor productivity.

During his period of activity as a successful industrialist Owen attracted wide attention, and New Lanark was visited by many English and European factory owners who were curious to see the results of his experiments. Though most were greatly impressed by what they saw, there seems to have been no extensive effort by others to duplicate his accomplishments.

Owen the Utopian Socialist

Having made his mark and his fortune as an industrialist, Owen turned to more radical experiments in social reform, in which he was not successful. He was strongly opposed to the concept of individualism and felt it to be the source of most problems. He condemned, too, the institution of private property, as he had come to believe that private property was the source of many of the antagonisms and evils in existing societies. In place of individualism and the institution of private property, Owen endorsed the concept of cooperation and a system of communism in regard to property. He also saw that the industrial revolution had separated the worker from the land, and hence from his source of food. This placed the worker in a very weak economic position.

Owen thought that the creation of small cooperative settlements combining agriculture and manufacturing with communal ownership of land and capital would provide a favorable environment within which the carry-over of socially undesirable characteristics of the first generation of inhabitants who had lived previously under the evil conditions of existing society, would be overcome and replaced by a greatly improved pattern of life. Actual experiments with his parallelograms, as he referred to his ideal settlements, in New Harmony, Indiana, and elsewhere all proved to be failures after a period of time. Owen thus encountered the dilemma which typically confronts the utopian socialists who hope to perfect man by perfecting his social environment. The question is, How can this environment be perfected if man himself has not first been perfected? And this is again the old circular problem of the chicken and the egg.

Conclusions on Owen

In concluding this brief section on Owen, it is only fair to recognize him as a man who had great practical business sense; a deep concern for the plight of the common man during the difficult early period of the emergence of industrial capitalism; and insights into problems of education, governmental responsibility for the relief of unemployment, and the significance of the wage level for aggregate demand which were a century or more ahead of their time. Furthermore, he was not attracted to the luxuries which his accumulated wealth could put at his disposal, but instead, he quite willingly parted with most of his fortune in financing his experiments with the establishment of "ideal" communities. That he lived his later years in very modest economic circumstances and without the respect and acclaim which he had once received is perhaps more a reflection upon the world in which he lived and its judgments than upon Owen himself.

Industrial Capitalism to 1850

To turn again to the broad topic of the emergence and development of industrial capitalism, it was the new spirit of *laissez-faire*, a more liberal religious attitude toward the accumulation of wealth, and major technological innovations such as the development of a practical steam engine and various kinds of power-driven machinery that made the development of industrial capitalism possible. It took, in addition, a substantial number of people who were willing to undertake the role of entrepreneur and assume the risks involved, together with the driving force of competition to make it a reality. The basic characteristics of the capitalistic system are, in fact, usually summarized under the headings of *laissez-faire* and competition, and the term *laissez-faire-competitive system* is a standard synonym for the term *pure capitalistic system*.

The development of industrial capitalism in the period from 1775 to 1850 was characterized by the increasing use of power-driven machinery, the standardization of steps in the processes of production which made possible a high degree of division of labor and the employment of much unskilled labor, and the development of marketing and financial arrangements and institutions appropriate to the rapidly rising industrial output. It was also a period of great social change in England as the working class adjusted to new and impersonal economic conditions.

Karl Marx in his well-known work, *Das Kapital*, which was published after the lot of the working class in England had begun to improve, devotes many pages to discussions of the miserable conditions of laborers during the rise of capitalism. He does not seem to have appreciated the fact that these conditions could be characteristic of one stage of the development of capitalism in a country like England, without being an inevitable feature of the system as it matured.

Industrial Capitalism After 1850

The development of industrial capitalism in the period which lasted until the middle of the nineteenth century was characterized by relatively small-scale productive enterprises; but in the period following 1850, and particularly in the last quarter of the century, there was a marked growth in the scale of industrial operations. Contributing to this were important technological improvements in the production of iron and steel which facilitated the growth of railroads and other forms of transportation. Transportation improvements had the effect of providing access to larger and larger markets, and this, in turn, provided the incentive for marked increases in the scale of industrial production. The development of improved machines having interchangeable parts and the increasing adaptation of power machinery to the steps in productive processes made it physically feasible to expand the scale of production. At the same time, the growing use of the corporate form of industrial organization, expanding capital markets, and the growth of financial institutions made increases in the scale of production financially possible.

By the latter quarter of the nineteenth century the stage of development of technology, organizational structure, and capital and financial markets encouraged a very rapid growth in the scale of production. It was in this period that growth and consolidation resulted in the emergence of a few giant firms in the chemical, coal, oil, steel and other industries. This consolidation movement had important implications for competition.

One of the assumptions of the model of capitalism is that conditions of pure competition prevail. This simply means that it is assumed that the number of firms in each line of production is sufficiently large that no one firm is able to exert any noticeable influence on the market price through its own actions, and that it is easy for firms to enter or leave industries. It is also assumed in the model that workers are unorganized and bargain individually with employers. Under these assumptions, market prices would tend to be determined at levels which provide firms with normal but not excessive profits, and wages would reflect the value of the marginal product of labor.

Where one or a few firms do manage to gain a dominant position in an industry, however, the competitive situation becomes somewhat different. Here an individual firm may be able to influence market prices in ways which will enable it to make excessive profits. This is done by restricting the volume of output in order to keep prices higher than would have been the case had conditions of stronger competition prevailed. Workers also tend to be at a bargaining disadvantage if they are unorganized and must bargain with firms which hold monopoly or quasi-monopoly power. In such cases, wages may be kept below the levels which would have been realized under more competitive conditions.

In the United States, Congress became alarmed at the growing trend toward industrial concentration and monopoly power and in 1890 passed the Sherman Antitrust Act in an effort to prevent undesirable monopoly developments. Additional legislation has since been enacted to supplement the Sherman Act. It is interesting to note that this restraining legislation was made necessary by the fact that the most successful competitors in some cases were those firms which seemed to be able to drive out weaker competitors and thus attain dominant positions in their industries.

Financial Capitalism

The Sherman Act did not succeed in stopping the trend toward increasing concentration of economic power. Businessmen found that they could still control a number of business firms by the development of holding companies. The holding-company approach to economic concentration was not prohibited by the Sherman Act, and it was widely used in the period to 1914 and again during the decade of the 1920's.

The period of capitalism ushered in by the industrial revolution has been referred to as industrial capitalism, and in the United States until almost the end of the nineteenth century, the industrial entrepreneur was of dominant importance. The marked growth in the holding-company movement which was underway by the end of the century was made possible by the marshalling of huge financial resources by those with banking and other financial connections. Since these promoters were more financial than industrial entrepreneurs, it is useful to refer to the period from roughly 1895 to the beginning of the depression of the 1930's in the United States as the period of financial capitalism.

The Improving Position of Workers After 1850

The economic condition of the working class in the major capitalistic countries improved markedly during the second half of the nineteenth century. The development of more efficient machinery, increased labor productivity and the rapid expansion in industrial growth greatly increased the demand for labor. The previous labor market situation, which was characterized by a major over-supply of labor, was dramatically changed in labor's favor. As a result, labor was able to share through rising real wages in the industrial growth of the period following 1850. It was also possible for labor to make some headway in developing labor organizations. The labor movement found greater strength in England and Germany during this period than it did in the United States, but even in this country an important beginning was made. Though the membership in American labor unions was nearly 900,000 by the end of the century, it was not until the protective legislation of the 1930's was passed that the labor movement here gained its major strength.

The Decline of *Laissez-faire* and Competition

In the years since World War I, in what Sombart refers to as the period of late capitalism, important changes have occurred in the economies of Western Europe and the United States in regard to the practice of *laissez-faire* and the extent of competition. Though the illustrations of the decline of *laissez-faire* and competition to be mentioned here are taken from the experience of the United States, similar and even more dramatic changes were occurring abroad.

There had already been some important departures from the practice of *laissez-faire* during the nineteenth century in the form of such things as restrictions on banking and interstate commerce, as well as antitrust legislation. Beginning with the immediate pre-World War I period, however, the trend away from *laissez-faire* has been most pronounced. As a general explanation of this trend one could say that it has resulted from the efforts of various groups in society to bring about solutions to problems which were affecting them adversely, and more recently from the attitude of the government that it has the responsibility to intervene in order to correct serious economic and social difficulties as they are recognized and identified. The emergency periods of World Wars I and II and the major depression of the 1930's brought about a marked acceleration in the rate of departure of government, particularly the federal government, from a *laissez-faire* policy.

Since space will not permit a careful discussion of each of the very large number of government interventions since 1914 which run counter to the concepts of *laissez-faire*, a random and very incomplete listing must suffice. The reader will be able to add to this list on his own.

Labor Regulations

There have been many regulations dealing with labor and labor problems since 1914. Laws have been passed to prohibit child labor, to limit the number of hours of work demanded of women and men, to prescribe standards of safety and comfort in working conditions, to guarantee and protect the rights of workers to organize and bargain collectively, to limit immigration, to establish minimum wages, and to establish procedures for arbitration and mediation. The strength of organized labor has, of course, greatly increased in the present century. This situation has led business leaders and others to suggest that labor unions also be placed under the restraints of anti-monopoly legislation. Originally the unions were subject to the Sherman Act, but they were exempted from antitrust regulation by the Clayton Act.

Industrial Controls

Legislation and regulations affecting industrial firms have included such things as tariffs and quotas on imports, price controls, rationing of strategic materials, and quotas on the output of oil wells. Also included are pure food and drug and transportation regulations, extension of antitrust regulations, retail-price maintenance, profits and excess profits taxation, collection of social security and sales taxes, and the treatment of employees as mentioned above. Legislation has also been enacted concerning the nature of advertising, weights and measures, and non-discrimination on the basis of race, color or creed in employment and in the provision of service.

Regulation of Financial Institutions

Limitations and restrictions affecting financial institutions have also been important. These have included a whole host of regulations on commercial and savings banks concerning such things as reserve percentages to be maintained; types of assets to be held; maximum interest rates to be paid on savings and time deposits; and prohibitions on the issuance of bank notes, on the payment of interest on demand deposits, and on the floating of securities issued by corporations and units of government. Investment bankers and stock exchanges are restricted in the floating of new stock issues by the requirement that full and accurate information about the issuing companies be disclosed, and they are prohibited from artificially rigging the market prices of securities. Margin requirements setting a limit on the percentage of the purchase price of stocks which may be borrowed are also imposed. Among financial institutions, insurance companies, building and loan associations, and small loan companies are also subject to governmental regulations of various types.

Expansion in Governmental Activities

In addition to the proliferation of governmental restrictions and regulations of which the above listing is only a sampling, the principle of *laissez-faire* has also been intruded upon as a result of the increasing number of activities which the government conducts on its own, either directly or indirectly. At the state and local levels of government these include such things as the construction of highways and streets; the construction and operation of civic buildings including hospitals, clinics and auditoriums; and the provision and operation of primary and secondary schools as well as colleges and universities. Government also regulates the sale of water and alcoholic beverages, and the production, distribution and sale of fuel gas. The operation of bus, streetcar and subway systems as well as seaports and airports, public beaches and other recreational facilities is often under the control of state and local authorities, as is the provision of refuse disposal services and the provision and operation of low-cost housing facilities.

At the federal government level, many activities are now carried out both directly and indirectly. These include such things as the construction of dams and electric power facilities, and land reclamation, flood control and irrigation projects. The federal government operates hospitals and retail stores for military personnel. It is responsible for the operation of educational institutions and programs, as well as for the conduct of research projects and the dissemination of the results through extension programs, bulletins, and other publications. The provision of traffic control and direction-finding facilities for aircraft and boats is under the direction of the government. The government extends huge amounts of credit to the economy through the farm credit institutions, the rural electrification program, the Small Business Administration, slum clearance and urban renewal programs, the federal mortgage programs and the Federal Reserve System. An educational branch supplies substantial amounts of funds for the construction of college and university facilities, for research projects and for loans and scholarships to students. Several departments deal in fields as diverse as labor-management disputes, and food and drug research and inspection. Various federal agencies provide a large insurance and retirement program which includes insurance of bank deposits, mortgage insurance, crop insurance, unemployment and accident insurance, and retirement benefits under the Social Security, civil service and military programs. Also to be mentioned here is the responsibility that the federal government has assumed for the maintenance of full employment, price stability and a favorable rate of economic growth. Policies implemented in connection with the attainment of these objectives also represent departures from the principle of *laissez-faire.*

Though the above lists may seem long, they are by no means exhaustive. They do afford some indication of the extent of the erosion process that has taken place in regard to the *laissez-faire* policies of government over time. Also, they help to explain why systems that were classified as capitalistic in the nineteenth century have in the present century been referred to as mixed-capitalistic systems.

The Changing Structure of Competition

Marked changes in the extent and nature of competition have also occurred over time in the more capitalistic countries. There are, for example, a number of basic services of a public utility nature which are most appropriately supplied by firms holding a monopoly position in the field. It would be uneconomic to have several electric companies competing for customers in a given city with each company erecting its own set of poles and power cables, or to have more than one streetcar company running its tracks along the city streets to compete for customers. Firms having monopoly positions are also more appropriate for such services as telephones, sewage and garbage disposal, subways, commuter railroads, and gas for cooking and heating. In these public utility fields, it is the practice for government to regulate the activities of the firms granted monopoly privileges; consequently they are often referred to as regulated monopolies. Restrictions imposed upon the firms may include the setting of rates which they may charge for their services and establishing standards of service which must be maintained.

Oligopolistically Competitive Industries

Outside the field of regulated public utilities there are very few examples of firms holding essentially monopoly positions, but there are a number of areas in the economy of the United States, for example, which are characterized by oligopolistically competitive conditions. Oligopoly, it may be recalled, refers to the competitive situation in which the number of competing firms is so small that the pricing policies of any one of them will have a noticeable impact upon the sales of the others. In the United States, oligopolistically competitive conditions are found in such lines of production as automobiles, television sets, steel, aluminum, gasoline, copper, typewriters, glass, commercial passenger planes, and laundry detergents. With a little thought, the reader can expand this list substantially. Characteristically, competition among firms in an oligopolistically competitive industry usually involves factors other than price. The reason that price competition is normally avoided is that each firm in the industry realizes that if it cuts its price in an effort to increase its sales, the other firms will notice their loss of orders and may quickly reduce their prices correspondingly, or perhaps even more than the amount of the reduction instituted by the original firm. In conditions of oligopoly it is quite easy for an attempt at price competition to get completely out of hand, perhaps even develop into a cut-throat price war which may be difficult to stop. Anyone who has observed the progress of a filling-station gasoline price war will appreciate the problem.

To avoid the undesirable effects of a price war, firms in oligopolistically competitive industries usually confine their competition to advertising, product differentiation in the case of non-standardized products, and service. For example, each automobile firm tries through styling differences and appealing advertising to attract customers to its line of cars.[4] Where the product is highly standardized, as in the case of basic steel products, competition revolves more around service and delivery times rather than price differentials. In such industries, price leadership tended to develop as a means of effecting price changes from time to time as circumstances warranted, without at the same time starting a price war. The United States Steel Company played this role for many years in the steel industry, but its position as price leader has become less clearly defined in more recent years.

Local oligopolies are also of importance. For example, the number of banks in many towns and cities is rather limited, so that competition among them is based primarily upon service and advertising rather than upon interest rate differentials. Competition among pharmacies, clothing stores, and similar retail establishments may also be oligopolistic in nature in smaller communities.

As capitalistic systems have matured and the size of the typical firm in many basic industries has become extremely large, deviations from the concept of pure competition have also arisen as a result of the difficulties involved for new firms wishing to enter those industries. To illustrate the problem, consider how difficult it would be for a new automobile producer to become established in the United States. In addition to the tremendous investment in productive facilities, it would also be necessary

---

[4]It is interesting to note that when one of the automobile companies increased its warranty period rather substantially over that which had customarily prevailed in the industry, other firms felt compelled to follow suit within a year or so.

to establish a large number of dealerships around the country. The problems are indeed so formidable that no new company has succeeded in breaking into the field on a permanent basis in the United States in the post-World War II period, and during this same period, the number of automobile producers has actually grown smaller as some firms have withdrawn from the industry. Similar difficulties of entry prevail in the aircraft, steel, nickel, electrical appliance, prefabricated housing, and a number of other industries. These difficulties represent still another type of departure from the assumptions of the *laissez-faire*-competitive model. Given the present state of technology and the great economies of scale to be found in many industries, some economists consider that the emergence of oligopolistic conditions in them represents a rational economic development and that such departures from the model should not be condemned or viewed with uneasiness. Other economists disagree with this position and hold that industrial concentration may lead to undesirable economic and political control, and a lessening of the effectiveness of competition.[5]

Summary and Conclusions

While elements of capitalism can be traced quite far back into history, it is in the period since the beginning of the industrial revolution in England that the capitalistic system has assumed the greatest significance. The increasing profit possibilities resulting from the rapid growth of technology in the latter quarter of the eighteenth century and the spread of the philosophy of individualism contributed to the growing sentiment in favor of *laissez-faire* governmental policies. In this atmosphere, production grew rapidly in the nineteenth century and the capitalistic system seemed to function very much along the lines suggested by the *laissez-faire*-competitive model which classical economists had described.

In the latter quarter of the nineteenth century a trend toward large-scale production and concentration in a number of industries became quite pronounced. In time, this situation stimulated the passage of regulatory legislation to prevent undesirable business practices. From this point on, there have been increasing departures from a *laissez-faire* policy by the United States government and by the governments of other advanced capitalistic countries. There has also been a continuing trend away from the small-scale, many-producers-of-each-product pattern which is characteristic of conditions of pure competition.

As a result of their departures from conditions of *laissez-faire* and pure competition, the economies of mature capitalistic systems have become

---

[5]For an interesting discussion of this point, see Ben W. Lewis, "Economics by Admonition," *American Economic Review,* XLIX, No. 2 (1959), 384-398.

known as mixed-capitalistic systems to distinguish them from the purer form of capitalism described by the *laissez-faire*-competitive model. The evolution from capitalism to mixed capitalism should not be regarded as necessarily unfortunate or undesirable. Indeed, this evolution reflects one of the greatest strengths of capitalism which has been its ability to adjust to changing conditions and circumstances without losing its vigor and vitality and while maintaining its emphasis upon the institution of private property and the profit incentive. Today there is a rather wide range of variation among the mixed-capitalistic countries in regard to the role of government in the economy and the nature of the competitive structure of industry.

In the following three chapters, the prospects for capitalism will be examined from a number of points of view, starting with those of the nineteenth-century classical economists.

Capitalism: Malthus to Marx   **3**

Classical Economists

Thomas Malthus

Economists in the classical tradition, that is, economists who supported the doctrines of *laissez-faire* and competition, who were writing in England during the first half of the nineteenth century tended to develop a rather pessimistic view of the future. Thomas Malthus in his famous work, *An Essay on the Principles of Population as It Affects the Future Improvement of Society, with Remarks on the Speculations of Mr. Godwin, M. Condorcet, and Other Writers*, first published in 1798 and subsequently carried through six revised editions, the last of which was published in 1826, developed the thesis that population would tend to expand until it pressed against the means of subsistence. In his first edition, Malthus claimed that population tends, in the absence of checks, to rise in a geometric progression and that the means of subsistence increase at an arithmetic rate. Given these trends, he stated that it was the positive checks of war, famine, pestilence, misery and vice which held the actual rate of population increase down to the rate of increase in the means of subsistence. It was his belief that population would tend to press against the limit of the means of subsistence.

35

It is interesting to note that Malthus, on the basis of his theory, criticized the poor-law system in England at the time on the grounds that its system of doles and payments for large families was simply encouraging the impoverished sector of the population to increase still further. These laws were aggravating the problem of poverty rather than solving it, he thought.

In later editions of his work Malthus expanded his list of checks to the rate of population growth by including the preventive check of moral restraint. For Malthus, this meant marrying on the average at a later age and practicing sexual abstinence. He also included the idea that the accepted subsistence level of living could rise somewhat above a purely physical minimum of subsistence. In spite of the introduction of these modifications in his analysis, Malthus continued to be rather pessimistic about the future course of man's progress. He doubted that the preventive checks to population growth would prevail and thought it more likely that population would be kept in bounds through the misery and misfortune of the positive checks.

Writing as he was during the period of the industrial revolution in England when workers were living and working in particularly unfavorable circumstances, it is not surprising that Malthus reached such pessimistic conclusions about future population trends. At the time, he could not have anticipated the marked increases in productivity which scientific and technological improvements would bring to agriculture in England and in other parts of the world, nor could he have anticipated the advances in transportation which would make it possible for the more densely populated countries to import food from their less densely populated colonies and from other countries having an agricultural surplus. These factors contributed to the rising level of living of the British working class during the latter half of the nineteenth century.

Another development which Malthus did not foresee was the tendency for birth rates to decline in the economically more advanced countries. He thought that the growing population in England of his day was a result of the stimulating effect of the dole payments, scaled to family size. Actually, later statistical studies have indicated that England's birth rate was not rising during this period, and that it was rather a decline in the death rate which was responsible for the increasing population trend.

More Recent Population Developments

The dramatic changes in the birth rate and in the rate of population growth in a country like Japan in the post-World War II period tend to contradict Malthus' conclusion about the force of checks other than the unpleasant ones which he lists under the positive checks. The Japanese experience, as well as others, suggests that increases in the level of living may reach a stage beyond which they exert a retarding effect upon the birth rate. In India and some of the other countries in Asia, the problem of how to reach such a stage is extremely difficult to solve, and the rate of population growth in these countries remains a matter of major concern.

It is of course true that, for the contemporary world as a whole, the problem of population growth is one of the most serious and pressing ones, and this seems likely to continue to be the case for some time to come. Population pressures in many of the developing countries have contributed to the consideration which individual nations have given to the question of what type of economic system will be likely to provide the most favorable rate of economic growth and development. Different countries have tried different solutions, but no universally acceptable answer to this question has been found.

John Stuart Mill

The question of what type of economic system is best is by no means new, and some of the classical economists of the nineteenth century—most notably, John Stuart Mill—attempted to find an appropriate answer. Mill accepted the natural law of population growth which Malthus had developed. He also accepted the familiar Ricardian theory of rent which held that as the demand for food increased to the level at which it became necessary to cultivate land beyond the point of diminishing returns, an income share in the form of rent would appear which would accrue to the owners of the land. Interestingly, it was Malthus who first described the law of diminishing returns in agriculture which states that as additional equal amounts of labor and capital are added to a given amount of land, the marginal physical product will first increase, eventually reach a maximum, and finally decrease.

In accepting the Malthusian theory of population growth and the Ricardian theory of rent on land, Mill and other classical economists of the period found themselves forced to draw rather pessimistic conclusions concerning the long-run trend of economic development. They reasoned that with the growth of population in a given country, the cost of producing food would rise as it became necessary to push cultivation on good land beyond the point of diminishing returns and also to bring into cultivation land of inferior quality. Increases in the cost of food production would result in higher food prices, and these price increases would lead to rising rent returns on land of better quality. As rents rose, the landlord segment of the population would receive an increasing share of national income. Since the wages of workers could not fall below a minimum-of-subsistence level, Mill and other classical writers concluded that the increasing share of national income accruing to landlords as rents rose would inevitably be at the expense of a decrease in the return to non-agricultural capital. Mill concluded, pessimistically, that as population increased, the return to capital would tend to decline to a level at which no further net capital accumulation would be worthwhile. At this point economic growth would cease and a stationary state of the economy would be reached.

Expressed in more familiar terms, Mill was stating that the marginal efficiency of investment and the money rate of interest would tend, sooner or later, to arrive at a relationship which would make any further net additions to the physical stock of capital not worthwhile. When this relationship was reached, only replacement investment expenditures to maintain the stock of capital at its existing level would be made, and economic growth would no longer be realized. Having arrived at this pessimistic conclusion about the long-run trend of economic development of a capitalistic country like England, Mill and other classical economists of the time attempted to find some means by which a country could escape the eventual fate of economic stagnation. It was argued, for example, that England should reduce its tariff rates on the importation of agricultural products from the continent of Europe where the prices of these commodities were lower. This would have the effect of slowing the rate of increase in the rent of agricultural land in England and also of slowing the rate of decrease in the marginal efficiency of investment in that country.

Mill believed that a free-trade policy by England in regard to the importation of agricultural commodities would only postpone the time when rents on land would rise to such an extent that the return to capital would be pushed down to the level at which no further net capital accumulation would occur. Faced with such a pessimistic view of the economic future of England's capitalistic economy, Mill tried to find some solution that would provide more favorable long-run results.

In the course of his search for a way out of the economic stagnation dilemma, Mill became attracted to socialism. He studied the works of socialist authors carefully and for a time seems to have developed considerable sympathy for the socialist approach. Ultimately he rejected the idea that socialism was superior to the *laissez-faire*-competitive system on the grounds that the natural laws of population growth and diminishing returns in agriculture would be equally applicable and troublesome under socialism.

The Stagnation Thesis

It is interesting to note that the stagnation thesis developed by Mill disappeared from the mainstream of classical and neoclassical economic thought during the period of favorable economic growth and development which characterized the second half of the nineteenth century and the first three decades of the twentieth. During the devastating worldwide depression of the 1930's, however, the stagnation thesis in a somewhat modified form was revived, and for a time it received serious attention from economists in capitalistic countries. The return of more prosperous conditions in the 1950's and 1960's has caused this thesis to fade into relative obscurity once again. Given current predictions about the population explosion which is taking place in the world and the problems which it is bringing with it, particularly in developing countries, it would be rash to conclude that we have heard the last of the stagnation thesis.

Karl Marx

Though the pessimism of Mill and his generation of economists which caused the subject of economics to be referred to as "the dismal science" disappeared from the mainstream of neoclassical economic thought in the latter half of the nineteenth century, it was continued and intensified in the writings of Karl Marx. Since he was both the most profound critic of capitalism in his day and also an ardent proponent of communism, it is necessary to discuss Marx both here in the context of the prospects for capitalism and later in connection with the development of socialist thought. To appreciate fully his critical appraisal of capitalism, it is helpful to know something of his background, training and personal life. The following biographical sections on Marx are, therefore, by way of prelude to the discussion of his formal thought on capitalism.

Marx's Early Life

Karl Marx was born at Treves in Rhenish Prussia in the year 1818. This city, not far from Luxembourg, was influenced by the cultural traditions of both France and Prussia. Marx's paternal grandfather and great-grandfather were rabbis, and his mother was descended from a rabbinical family as well. His father was a member of the civil service.

In eighteenth-century Prussia, Jews were subject to various forms of discrimination. As a result, the capture of the city of Treves by French revolutionary troops in 1794, gave hope to the members of the Jewish community that the legal restrictions against them would be removed. Napoleon's defeat at Waterloo in 1815, however, was followed by a territorial redistribution under which Treves returned to Prussia, and in 1816, a number of the restrictions of the past were reintroduced. In an effort to escape these, Marx's father in 1824 accepted the Lutheran Church. His wife and children, including Karl, then age six, were also baptized into the newly-adopted religion. Young Karl was not strongly attracted to this religion, and some years later he was to express his attitude on religion in general by referring to it as ". . . the opium of the people."

Even as a youth Marx was studious and possessed of an inquiring mind. It was his good fortune to be befriended by his neighbor, Baron Ludwig von Westphalen, and his family. The Baron was a man of culture and of liberal views, and young Karl had free access to his library. The Baron found the boy to be a stimulating thinker and the two developed a close intellectual relationship. As a youth, Marx was exposed to liberal ideas both at home through his father and through the Baron next door.

His Year at the University of Bonn

Karl Marx was an outstanding student in secondary school, and in 1835 he was accepted by the University of Bonn for the study of law. The choice of law as his major field reflected more the urging of his father than Marx's own interest in the subject. He seems to have been a high-spirited student and something of a rebel during his first year in the university. Records show that he was charged with such offenses as drunkenness and carrying a forbidden weapon, which was said to have been a pistol. The records of the university are said to include the following entry concerning Marx: "Relating to conduct: it is noted that he, because of riotous noise and drunkenness, brought a one-day Karzer punishment upon himself." This meant that he was imprisoned for a day in the Karzer, or university jail, which was the usual way of dealing with a student who created a disturbance while drunk. The Karzer diet of bread and water no doubt added to the sobering impact of the confinement. The record carries the further statement that, "Otherwise, nothing detrimental in moral or economic aspects" had been discovered.

In 1836, during his year at Bonn, he was charged while on a visit to the nearby city of Cologne with carrying an illegal weapon, said by the Prussian authorities to have been a pistol. This incident seems to have caused some dispute between the officials of Cologne and those of the university concerning who had jurisdiction in the case. The city officials apparently claimed higher competence and told the university to keep out of the matter. The case was not brought to trial and the final entry indicates that it had been postponed indefinitely.

Marx's Period at the University of Berlin

Marx transferred from the University of Bonn to the University of Berlin after his first year. Though he had been a successful student at Bonn, he took his work more seriously at the University of Berlin. It was here that he became increasingly attracted to philosophy, particularly to the Hegelian school, which was then so much in vogue in the German universities. Hegel, who died in 1831, held that the dialectical process was the means through which progress had been achieved throughout history. The inevitable development of an antithesis to the existing thesis in ideas would create antagonism and conflict from which new and better ideas would emerge through a process of synthesis. This synthesis would represent the new thesis against which a new antithesis would in time develop, leading to a new synthesis. Hegel held that this process in the realm of abstract ideas had been going on throughout the sweep of history.

In the heady atmosphere of the interminable philosophical discussions of his fellow students, Marx began to find the realm of formal systems of logical thought more stimulating and attractive than the study of the law which seemed to him to be unsystematic and to lack any fundamental logical structure.

While studying diligently at the University of Berlin, Marx obviously was not fully occupied by the philosophical works he was reading and by the intellectual discussions and debates which he had with his fellow students, for he became engaged to Baron von Westphalen's daughter, Jenny. This was an extraordinary achievement which shows that Marx had not only made a highly favorable impression on the Baron, who gave his consent, but also on Jenny, whose heart he had won. Jenny was not just an ordinary girl next door. She was a lovely, intelligent, socially popular and prominent girl from a noble family who could have married a man from her own social and cultural background. Instead, she chose Karl Marx, who was then a university student with very uncertain prospects for the future, no family estate to inherit, and who actually was younger than she was by several years. Given these differences in background, the prospects for a happy marriage would have seemed open to serious question. That the marriage could have survived as a happy one over a lifetime of exceptional vicissitudes is a tribute to the character and understanding of this remarkable woman.

After Karl's engagement to Jenny, his father encouraged him in his study of the law, for he was concerned that Karl should be able to follow a profession in which he could support a family. When Marx finally came to the conclusion that he could not be happy with a career in law and decided to prepare instead for an academic career in the field of philosophy, his father was quite concerned. He thought the switch impractical, for he knew 'the difficulties that Karl would face in finding an academic appointment upon the completion of his doctorate in philosophy. But Karl would not be dissuaded, and in 1838 his father died.

Following his father's death, Marx was hard pressed for money to continue his studies, but he managed to scrape by for three more years at the university. In 1841, at the age of twenty-four, he completed his doctoral dissertation and received his degree. His fiancee's father died the same year.

A Lost Chance for an Academic Career

After completing his doctorate, Marx expected to follow an academic career. He had developed a close personal friendship during his years at the University of Berlin with Bruno and Edgar Bauer. The two brothers were members of the Hegelian group to which Marx belonged. Bruno Bauer expected to be appointed to a professorship at the University of Bonn, and he had promised to take Marx with him in the junior position of lecturer. Before these appointments were made, it became known that Marx and Bruno Bauer were the authors of an anonymous tract which contained some radical criticisms of Prussian Lutheranism. This was sufficient to block Bauer's professorship and to close the doors to an academic career for Marx.

Marx Turns to Political Journalism

Another friend, Moses Hess, helped Marx get a connection with a newly established, somewhat liberal paper called the *Rheinische Zeitung*. Marx started as a contributor of articles, but soon worked his way into an editorial position. He became much concerned with the shortcomings of the Prussian government of the time, and the critical articles which he published attracted a considerable amount of attention. In fact, the articles were so popular that the sales of the paper climbed rapidly. There was close government control of the press in Prussia in this period, however, and the Russian reaction to critical comments made about the Czarist regime in several issues resulted in Marx's forced resignation from the paper. Interestingly, after his departure, the paper lost its popular following and soon folded.

The Closing of Opportunities in Prussia

Marx had clearly demonstrated his skill as a political writer, but in doing so he had become known to the authorities as a dangerous radical. As a result, he had essentially exhausted the possibilities for a journalistic career in Prussia along the lines that would have been of interest to him. Having previously become known as one of the publishers of a tract that had removed him from consideration for an academic career in Prussia, Marx was now so widely known for his radical views that he could not expect employment as a civil servant either. With career opportunities at the bourgeois level largely closed to him at the age of twenty-four, Marx had only very limited alternatives. He could sink into the proletariat class and find work of a very menial character, or he could try to follow his intellectual interests in the only environment still readily open to him which was that of the radical movements of his day. He chose the latter course and followed it willingly, though it meant living with his family in extremely impoverished circumstances and in exile for many years.

His Marriage to Jenny von Westphalen

After his forced resignation from the editorial staff of the *Rheinische Zeitung*, Marx returned to Treves, and a month later, without a job and with only limited prospects, he married his fiancee, Jenny von Westphalen. A few months later, Arnold Ruge offered Marx the coeditorship of a new liberal publication to be called the *Deutsch-Französiche Jahrbücher*, which was to be published in Paris and sold to the Germans living in France. Ruge hoped to circulate it within Prussia also by smuggling copies across the border.

The Move to Paris

Marx and his bride moved to Paris where he undertook this new publishing venture. Only one issue of the periodical was published before it folded, but it contained two interesting articles by Marx. One of these suggested that Jewish emancipation from the discrimination of the period could only be realized by replacing commercialism with socialism. In his other article, Marx expressed the view that in Germany true political reform could only be achieved through a proletarian overthrow of the existing order and the introduction of socialism. It should be noted that Marx was already beginning to emphasize class political conflict as the means through which true social reform must be achieved. This contrasted sharply with the more doctrinaire approach followed by most socialists at the time.

With the loss of his new job, Marx was once more financially hard pressed, so his wife and new baby returned to Treves to live with his mother-in-law until he could find a new source of income. Marx himself became well acquainted with a number of the radical intellectuals who were living in Paris at the time. It was in this period that he met the poet Heinrich Heine. Heine was greatly impressed by Marx and it was through him that Marx was able to meet a number of the prominent socialists and leaders of workers' organizations who were carrying on their activities in Paris at the time.

Marx's Growing Acquaintance with Friedrich Engels

During the interlude in Paris, Marx became better acquainted with Friedrich Engels, who became both his collaborator and benefactor, and his only long-term close friend. Engels was a member of a German family that had gained success in the textile industry. The business included a branch in the British manufacturing center of Manchester, and Engels had spent time there. He was a sensitive man and the difficult conditions faced by working-class families in Manchester in the 1840's had made a deep impression upon him, Engels came to see Marx first in 1842, but at that time Marx was unimpressed by the young student who was two years his junior, and no rapport developed between them.

Engels contributed two articles to the first and only issue of the *Deutsch-Französische Jahrbücher*, and one of these developed a strong criticism of contemporary political economic thought. He expressed the view that classical economists were simply justifying the *status quo*, and were not developing theories which would indicate how the serious social and economic problems of the period could be solved. Marx was quite impressed by this article; it not only induced him to read the economic literature which he had not previously done, but also to write to Engels. From this point on, the two men drew closer together and developed an enduring friendship. As a follow-up to this initial correspondence, Engels visited Marx in Paris where the two men found through several days of intensive discussions that they shared a number of similar points of view, and that there was a mutual interest in developing a closer working relationship.

The Marx-Engels collaboration was a most interesting one. Engels was a successful businessman who got along easily with men of affairs. At the same time, he differed from most of his associates in the sensitive insights that he had concerning the difficult circumstances of the working class which lay behind the prosperity of the industrialists. The sharp contrasts between the economic position of the owners of industrial enterprises and the masses of the workers who kept the machines rolling suggested to Engels that there was something wrong with the system. In terms of personality, Engels was unassuming, with no compulsion to hold a dominant position in his human relationships. Though extremely bright and quick to grasp ideas, he was not so widely read or so profound a scholar as Marx.

Marx, on the other hand, lacked the ability to associate easily with others. He was an intellectual who studied exhaustively the subjects that attracted him, and he was impatient with views that were not in accord with his own. Alexander Gray has suggested that the personal economic difficulties which Marx faced in supporting his family and his heavy dependence upon Engels for financial assistance over many years had the effect of eroding Marx's self-confidence and of developing in him a strong inferiority complex. As Gray puts it:

He was suspicious of everyone; he quarrelled sooner or later with everyone—Engels alone excepted; he was arrogant and self-assertive; for all who did not acknowledge his superiority, he had the supremest of contempt. In his heart there was envy and bitterness and hatred; for the world at large he had neither tolerance nor love.[1]

Though this is not the place to attempt a posthumous psychoanalysis of Marx, and while Gray's assessment of his nature may have been overly harsh, for Marx appears to have had a strong humanitarian concern, it should be noted that some writers have suggested that Marx's personal problems and frustrations may have had some impact upon his attitude toward the economic and political systems prevailing at the time. Suggestions of this nature are matters of conjecture, however, and should be recognized as such.

His Expulsion from France

While living from hand to mouth in Paris in 1844, Marx made some contributions to *Vorwärts*, which was a radical periodical. This outlet for his journalistic talents was also soon closed, for the Prussian government brought pressure on France to halt the activities of those who were publishing articles highly critical of the Prussian regime. France acceded to this request in January 1845, and most of those associated with *Vorwärts* were ordered to leave France. This new expulsion meant that at the youthful age of twenty-seven, Marx was already *persona non grata* in both of the two countries in which he had hoped to make a home for himself and his family.

On being expelled from France, Marx sought refuge in Belgium. His reputation had preceded him, however, and the government would permit him to settle in Brussels with his family only on the condition that he would not engage in literary activities of a critical nature concerning Belgium. Marx was essentially without funds at the time, and it was only through a timely gift of money from Engels that Marx was able to rent accommodations and bring his wife and two daughters to join him again. Soon Engels also came to Brussels so that he and Marx could collaborate more effectively.

The Collaboration with Engels

Over the next few years the two men worked diligently to further working-class movements in various countries, and Marx went to great lengths to try to establish himself as the intellectual leader of the labor

---

[1]Alexander Gray, *The Socialist Tradition: Moses to Lenin* (London: Longmans, Green and Co., 1947), p. 298.

movements then in existence or under way. Engels and he had first collaborated on a book which sharply attacked the radical thought of Bruno Bauer and his followers. Having disposed of Bauer and his group, Marx then turned against Proudhon. He had become acquainted with Proudhon, who was an outstanding French socialist, during his stay in Paris. Proudhon was widely known for his famous comment "Property is theft," which appeared in his popular book, *Qu'est-ce que la Propriété.* In spite of the book's highly critical tone, Proudhon was not opposed to the concept of private property, but rather to the characteristic of private property that made it possible for the owner to exploit his workers. All that was needed to cleanse private property of its undesirable aspect was to replace its exploitative potential with the concept of justice, he believed. He would thus preserve the use of private property and the institution of inheritance.

Marx became disenchanted with Proudhon when he found that the latter merely wished to reform the established economic system and not to overthrow it. His rejection of Proudhon was consistent with his rejection of utopian socialists in general. Their faith in the efficacy of social reform, which was based upon the assumption that man is fundamentally good, was in conflict with his own view of individual and class behavior. Marx used Proudhon's book, *The Philosophy of Poverty or Economic Contradictions*, as a basis for discrediting him, and he wrote a stinging rebuttal satirically titled, *The Poverty of Philosophy.* In this work he attempted to show that Proudhon had contributed nothing new to socialist thought and that what he had believed to be original ideas had actually been expressed earlier by English socialist writers.

Having attacked the thought of Bruno Bauer and his post-Hegelian followers in his first book and that of Proudhon in his second, Marx, with Engels, also attacked in various essays the thought of Ludwig Feuerbach and of those who accepted his approach. Feuerbach and his followers constructed their systems of thought on the basis of their assumptions about man's nature. Though Marx recognized that Feuerbach's philosophy, which was based upon man, was an advance over Hegel's philosophy, which was centered upon the realm of the abstract idea, he strongly criticized Feuerback for his failure to go farther by taking into account the significance of class distinctions.

The Materialistic Interpretation of History

In their various writings during these early years of their collaboration, Marx and Engels were developing arguments against the "idealist" conception of history which holds that man is shaped by the influence of his religion, laws, literature, art and other institutions. They reversed the order of the functional relationship and argued that it is men who make their religion and other institutions—not the other way around. In their interpretation of history, they constructed a substitute theory which related existing institutions to underlying economic causes. This "materialistic" conception of history made economic relationships the dynamic factor which influenced the institutional superstructure of religion, law, literature and art.

The League of the Just

During their three-year collaboration in Brussels, Marx and Engels were quite active in promoting socialist ideas and organizations. They took over a weekly periodical called the *Brüseller Deutsche Zeitung*, which had a local German circulation, and they also helped to organize a local society of German workers. Of greater importance, however, they became members of the League of the Just. This was a German workers' secret socialist organization which had local branches in Brussels, Paris, some Swiss and Italian cities, and London. Wilhelm Weitling, in exile from Germany like Marx, was the leading figure in this movement. Weitling had built this organization at the cost of great personal difficulties and sacrifices, which included serving time in a Swiss prison.

Marx regarded Weitling as a rival in his quest for leadership of the German workers' socialist movement, and he was quite ruthless in his efforts to wrest control from him. The climax occurred at a Brussels meeting in 1846 when Marx demanded to know Weitling's objectives for the League of the Just. In his reply, Weitling mentioned only some rather bland generalities, and Marx reacted violently to discredit him. The ultimate result was that Marx and Engels were able to gain control of the League, which they renamed the League of the Communists to distinguish it from the utopian socialist movements of the time. At the stormy London meeting of the League held in November 1847, Marx and Engels managed to get themselves assigned the task of defining the objectives of the League. These were stated in their famous brief work, *The Communist Manifesto*, which was first published in the German edition in London in February 1848.

The Communist Manifesto

The Communist Manifesto is a remarkable document that includes a brief survey of the development of the working-class movement, criticisms of contemporary socialist thought, and a succinct statement of the objectives of the League. The *Manifesto* begins with the challenging statement "A spectre is haunting Europe—the spectre of communism." This was followed a few lines later by the exaggerated point that "Communism is already acknowledged by all European powers to be itself a power."[2] Actually, it was not socialist revolutions by the working class—Marx's proletariat—that were considered a serious threat by the autocratic rulers at the time; rather, the bourgeois liberal revolutionary potential seemed to represent the real danger to the established order.

The Spirit of Nationalism

The spirit of nationalism was quite strong at the time Marx and Engels were working on the *Manifesto*, and it was fully shared by the working class in various countries. In spite of this, Marx and Engels wrote as though the spirit of nationalism was disappearing, for they stated that "National differences and antagonisms between peoples are daily more and more vanishing. . . ." Just the opposite was the case, and the nationalistic feelings of the working class became, if anything, stronger during the remainder of Marx's lifetime. It was this nationalistic attitude which helped to thwart Marx's efforts to organize a strong international revolutionary workers' movement. Indeed, the possibilities of proletarian revolutions rather obviously receded over the years, as Marx, himself, seems to have recognized in private discussions.

The Class Struggle

In the first chapter of the *Manifesto*, the authors state that "the history of all hitherto existing society is the history of class struggle." Here Marx and Engels were emphasizing their materialistic interpretation of history. In presenting their sweeping view of historical development, they gave full credit to the bourgeois class for its great accomplishments in bringing about modern techniques of mass production and exchange. But they pointed out in vivid language that in doing so, "What the bourgeosie therefore produces, above all, is its own grave-diggers. Its fall and the victory of the proletariat are equally inevitable." Their point was that the bourgeoisie, in building up its own power, had brought into being an antagonistic class which would eventually overthrow the existing order.

The language used in Chapter I is highly colorful, as a few additional random quotations will illustrate:

> The bourgeoisie, wherever it has got the upper hand, has put an end to all feudal, patriarchal, idyllic relations. It has pitilessly torn asunder the motley feudal ties that bound man to his "natural superiors" and has left remaining no other nexus between man and man than naked self-interest, than callous "cash payment".

• • • • • •

---

[2]This and the other quotations from the *Manifesto* which follow are based upon the English translation by Samuel Moore, published in 1888.

The bourgeoisie has torn away from the family its sentimental veil, and has reduced the family relation to a mere money relation.

• • • • • •

The bourgeoisie cannot exist without constantly revolutionizing the instruments of production, and thereby the relations of production, and with them the whole relations of society.

• • • • • •

The need of a constantly expanding market for its products chases the bourgeoisie over the whole surface of the globe.

• • • • • •

The weapons with which the bourgeoisie felled feudalism to the ground are now turned against the bourgeoisie itself.

But not only has the bourgeoisie forged the weapons that bring death to itself; it has also called into existence the men who are to wield those weapons—the modern working class—the proletarians.

In Chapter II of the *Manifesto*, Marx and Engels were in effect arguing with the bourgeoisie about the nature of communism. Here their tone was taunting and in places even vengeful. They discussed the abolition of private property under communism and defended their program against the charge that it would bring an end to individual freedom and that it would abolish the family. Almost at the end of the chapter they listed a ten-point program which represented their thinking concerning an appropriate platform for the Communist League which had charged them with the responsibility of drawing up a formal program. Some selected quotations from Chapter II will help to indicate the nature of the discussion here.

The immediate aim of the Communists is the same as that of all the other proletarian parties: formation of the proletariat into a class, overthrow of the bourgeois supremacy, conquest of political power by the proletariat.

• • • • • •

The distinguishing feature of Communism is not the abolition of property generally, but the abolition of bourgeois property.

• • • • • •

The average price of wage labor is the minimum wage, i.e., that quantum of the means of subsistence which is absolutely requisite to keep the laborer in bare existence as a laborer.

• • • • • •

You are horrified at our intending to do away with private property. But in your existing society, private property is already done away with for nine-tenths of the population; its existence for the few is solely due to its non-existence in the hands of those nine-tenths.

• • • • • • •

In one word, you reproach us with intending to do away with your property. Precisely so; that is just what we intend.

• • • • • •

Abolition of the family! Even the most radical flare up at this infamous proposal of the Communists.

On what foundation is the present family, the bourgeois family, based? On capital, on private gain. In its completely developed form this family exists only among the bourgeoisie. But this state of things finds its complement in the practical absence of the family among the proletarians. . . .

• • • • • •

The bourgeois clap-trap about the family and education, about the hallowed co-relation of parent and child, becomes all the more disgusting, the more, by the action of modern industry, all family ties among the proletarians are torn asunder, and their children transformed into simple articles of commerce and instruments of labor.

But you Communists would introduce community of women, screams the whole bourgeoisie in chorus.

The bourgeois sees in his wife a mere instrument of production. He hears that the instruments of production are to be exploited in common, and, naturally, can come to no other conclusion than that the lot of being common to all will likewise fall to the women.

He has not even a suspicion that the real point aimed at is to do away with the status of women as mere instruments of production.

• • • • • •

The Communists are further reproached with desiring to abolish countries and nationality.

The workingmen have no country. We cannot take from them what they have not got.

• • • • • •

What else does the history of ideas prove, than that intellectual production changes in character in proportion as material production is changed? The ruling ideas of each age have ever been the ideas of its ruling class.

Specific Proposals

Then, near the end of Chapter II, Marx and Engels listed the measures that they regarded as appropriate in the most advanced countries. These are as follows:

1. Abolition of property in land and application of all rents of land to public purposes.
2. A heavy progressive or graduated income tax.

3. Abolition of all right of inheritance.
4. Confiscation of the property of all emigrants and rebels.
5. Centralization of credit in the hands of the State, by means of a national bank with State capital and an exclusive monopoly.
6. Centralization of the means of communication and transport in the hands of the State.
7. Extension of factories and instruments of production owned by the State; the bringing into cultivation of wastelands, and the improvement of the soil generally in accordance with a common plan.
8. Equal liability of all to labor. Establishment of industrial armies, especially for agriculture.
9. Combination of agriculture with manufacturing industries; gradual abolition of the distinction between town and country, by a more equable distribution of the population over the country.
10. Free education for all children in public schools. Abolition of children's factory labor in its present form. Combination of education with industrial production, ...

Criticisms of Traditional Socialist Thought

In Chapter III, Marx and Engels developed a critical review of feudal socialism, petty-bourgeois socialism, German or "true" socialism, conservative or bourgeois socialism, and the utopian socialist and communist systems of such reformers as St. Simon, Fourier and Robert Owen.

The concluding chapter of the *Manifesto* is quite brief. It begins with a statement of the support by the Communist League of various radical movements then under way in France, Switzerland, Poland and Germany. But the final two paragraphs of this chapter are the most important and best known. Marx and Engels concluded with the ringing statement:

> The Communists disdain to conceal their views and aims. They openly declare that their ends can be attained only by the forcible overthrow of all existing social conditions. Let the ruling classes tremble at a Communistic revolution. The proletarians have nothing to lose but their chains. They have a world to win.
> WORKING MEN OF ALL COUNTRIES UNITE!

The Revolutions of 1848

There were strong political tensions in France, Prussia, and other parts of Europe at the time that Marx and Engels were writing the *Manifesto*. For the most part, they stemmed from the desire of the bourgeois class to attain effective constitutional governments and to limit the power of ruling monarchs. As soon as the *Manifesto* was published, Marx was expelled by the Belgian government. He left Brussels and headed for

Paris where, it is interesting to note, the French revolution of February 23, 1848, began just one day before his arrival. This was a rather fitting welcome for one who had just published a volume inciting the working-men of the world to unite and throw off their chains. But this revolution and the rebellions which also soon broke out in Berlin, Budapest, Milan, Naples, Prague, Rome, Vienna and elsewhere were not the proletarian revolutions which Marx and Engels were attempting to encourage. Rather they were revolutions brought about through the efforts of bourgeois liberals.

Marx was well aware of the nature of these revolutions and rebellions. The only exception to their bourgeois liberal character occurred briefly in Paris in June 1848, when there was a limited workingmen's uprising which succeeded in holding out for a brief period but was soon put down by military force. Marx recognized this as a truly proletarian revolutionary effort, but it was so limited and so brief that it was of no immediate practical consequence. Even the larger liberal bourgeois revolutions and rebellions were all -suppressed in the period from 1848 to 1850, and the former ruling houses regained their positions of power.

From Paris to Cologne

Marx and Engels left Paris for Cologne in May 1848. They saw that German industrial workers were not in a position to stage a successful revolution at that time. The army had remained loyal, as had the peasants. Given this situation, Marx, with the help of others, established a new radical daily paper called the *Neue Rheinische Zeitung*. The paper was used as a forum to attack the bourgeois democratic parties. The government was so preoccupied with the revolt in Berlin that Marx and his colleagues were able to publish their radical paper for a short time without interference. In November 1848, the Prussian king dissolved the National Assembly, and at this point, Marx took a stand against the payment of taxes by the public and urged the use of force in resisting the government. Marx was charged by the government with treason, and publication of his paper was suspended. Surprisingly, Marx was acquitted by the jury which was of bourgeois composition.

A Second Expulsion from Prussia

Marx resumed publication of the *Neue Rheinische Zeitung*, but he had financial difficulty in keeping it going. In May 1849, he was again expelled from Prussia by the government, and this brought an end to his paper. He liquidated his household assets to raise the money needed to move his family from Cologne to Paris. In France, also, he found that he was not favorably regarded by the government. He was told that if he should wish to remain in that country, he could not settle in Paris but would have to live in a small provincial town. Marx decided not to accept the option offered him in France, and he moved on to, London where he settled for the remainder of his life. He had not expected to remain long in London, for at first he was still confident that workers' revolts would soon develop in a number of different places on the Continent and result in the overthrow of entrenched regimes. After two or three years of waiting in vain, Marx realized that the workers were not sufficiently well organized to revolt.

Marx tried to reorganize the Communist League, but after sharp internal differences of opinion developed, he terminated the organization. His attempt to establish a new periodical, again with the title *Neue Rheinische Zeitung*, was also a failure, and it went out of existence after only a few issues.

Marx's Exile in London

In addition to these discouraging failures, Marx's early years of exile in London brought extreme impoverishment. The family settled in a slum section of London in very meager quarters. The Marxes' younger son died in the fall of 1850, and an infant daughter born the following year died in the spring of 1852. These were years when the family, sometimes for several days at a time, had only bread and potatoes to eat—and not enough of these. At times, too, there was no money with which to obtain medical services when members of the family were ill. Marx had no regular employment and the family assets were exhausted. Engels, who was working in the Manchester branch of the family mills, was the primary source of income for Marx. Without his support, Marx and his wife and children would probably not have survived these early years in London. Tragedy again struck the family in 1856 when Marx lost his only remaining son.

That Marx was able to do any work at all under such miserable conditions is surprising. Actually, he continued to pour out a steady stream of writing, most of which brought him no income. The exceptions were the articles which he wrote for the *The New York Tribune*. He was invited in 1851 to serve as one of the paper's European correspondents, and to contribute two articles weekly. Marx also began at this time to work on his full-scale analysis of capitalism which was ultimately to become his magnum opus, *Das Kapital*. Volume I was published in 1867, and the remaining two volumes were still incomplete at the time of his death in 1883. Engels completed them from Marx's notes.

In addition to his writing, Marx continued to work actively in the international socialist movement during his years in London. His efforts to impose his own thinking on the movement resulted in sharp conflicts with other socialist leaders of the time. One of the leaders of whom Marx was highly critical was Ferdinand Lassalle, who organized the General Union of German Workers. Lassalle was a highly colorful personality, a man of great energy, and an extremely successful labor leader. He supported Marx and he conveyed to members of the working class popularized versions of Marxian thought that they could understand and appreciate. Lassalle's thinking differed from that of Marx in some respects, however. For one thing, he accorded a much greater role to the state. He thought that the workers should establish their own political party, strive for the institution of universal suffrage, and, when they gained control of the state, use state power as a permanent means of achieving an improved society. This was in sharp contrast with Marx's view that the functions of the state should be kept to a minimum and that it should eventually largely wither away.

The striking phrase, "the iron law of wages," is generally attributed to Lassalle. The "law" described what he considered to be the tendency of the wages of workers to fall toward a minimum of subsistence level. He based this tendency upon a kind of Malthusian concept of population growth. Lassalle held that if wages should rise above a minimum of subsistence, the number of children of workers would rapidly increase and in time the increased labor supply would push wages down again. Marx would not accept a theory of the impoverishment of the working class based upon the Malthusian "natural law" of population.

Even though Lassalle supported Marx and largely accepted his doctrine, Marx was highly critical of him. This attitude stemmed partly from Marx's inflexibility and unwillingness to accept any departures from his system of thought and partly from the fact that Lassalle's popularity with the working class made him a dangerous rival for leadership of the socialist movement. In addition, Lassalle's flamboyant personality was offensive to Marx. The competition which Marx felt from Lassalle was terminated by the latter's premature death in 1864 as the result of a duel.

The International Working Men's Association

In September of the same year, steps were taken to establish an international organization of workers, which was named the International Working Men's Association. Marx participated in the formation of this new labor movement and he quickly began to play a leading role in the organization's general council. The other members of the general council deferred to Marx's scholarship and force of personality to such an extent that he wrote the various resolutions and proclamations issued in the name of the International, and all correspondence was referred to him. The International represented a loose affiliation of a number of different labor movements centered in various countries. The primary allegiance of these movements was to local leaders and national organizations, and only to a very limited extent to the International which attempted to bring together these many divergent elements, involving perhaps nearly five million workers. Given the weak structure of the International, Marx attempted to lead the organization as rapidly as he could in what he considered to be appropriate directions. His writings for the International covered such topics as cooperation, education, and the working day.

The Antagonism Between Marx and Bakunin

During the first few years of its existence, the First International, as it is now popularly called, showed an encouraging growth and development. Beginning in 1868, however, previously suppressed differences and antagonisms began to break into the open. It was in this year that Michael Bakunin came into the International through his affiliation with a Swiss workingmen's association. A strong antagonism developed between Marx and Bakunin which contributed to the ultimate breakdown of the First International.

Bakunin, like Lassalle whom Marx had also found personally objectionable, was a striking and unusual personality. Though he was a member of the Russian aristocracy by birth, Bakunin became an ardent anarchist and a professional revolutionary. His radical activities in Russia led to terms in prison and to his being sentenced to exile in Siberia. He finally escaped from exile and made his way to Western Europe, where he became active in the revolutionary labor movement. Like Lassalle, Bakunin was more an activist than a thinker. He was, in fact, naive and impractical, and his thinking and writing reflected his strong belief in anarchism and federalism. He was highly conspiratorial and made up secret codes to be used in the conduct of his revolutionary activities. Marx thought all of this both silly and childish.

In spite of the impractical side of his nature, Bakunin was a strong personality and possessed the qualities of leadership. Those in the International who had been chafing at Marx's assumption of the primary responsibility for running the organization and who resented his giving it his philosophical direction began to align themselves with Bakunin's faction. At the annual meeting of 1869, Bakunin and Marx clashed sharply, and as an aftermath, Bakunin's faction formed a new organization known as the Democratic Alliance which was only loosely connected with the International.

The End of the First International

Various political events such as the Franco-Prussian War of 1870 and the establishment of the ill-fated Paris Commune after the war, plus continuing internal feuding and differences, led to a deterioration in the strength of the First International. Marx was finding it impossible to continue to exercise effective personal control over the organization in the face of increasing factionalism. Though the annual congress held in 1872 voted to expel Bakunin from the International, Marx and Engels decided to try to bring the organization to an end. They did this by forcing through a motion that called for the transfer of the general council from London to New York. A few meetings were held in New York, but they amounted to little, and after the 1876 meeting in Philadelphia, the First International went out of existence altogether. As in the case of the earlier Communist League, Marx also brought the First International to an end when he could no longer control it effectively and when he became convinced that it could not achieve the objectives which he had in mind. He did not live to see the establishment of the Second International which was formed in 1889.

The Easing of Financial Pressures

It should be noted that though the movements and causes with which Marx associated himself continued to prove failures, there was at least some improvement in his financial position in 1864. He inherited some money from a friend and also in this same year Engels became financially more affluent and was able to contribute greater support to Marx and his family. Later, when Engels sold his share of the mills, he established a pension for the family. From 1864 on, Marx was relieved of the acute financial pressure which had plagued him previously, and his family could live somewhat more comfortably.

Marx's Success

This is as far as it is possible here to explore the life of Karl Marx, a remarkable scholar who at the very beginning of his career found conventional bourgeois employment opportunities largely closed to him, and who thereafter devoted his life to the cause of the industrial proletariat, the class which he thought was destined ultimately to overthrow established capitalistic systems by force. Though his life was marked by a succession of failures, Marx did succeed in writing an impressive critical analysis of capitalism, *Das Kapital*. It is this ponderous three-volume work which has led some economists to classify Marx as the last classical economist and the first scientific socialist. It is also *Das Kapital* which has earned Marx such an important place among those who have given inspiration to contemporary communist and socialist movements. The reputation and mark in the world which he failed to make during his own lifetime have been realized in the years since his death to an extent which Marx, even with his deep conviction in the correctness of his views on the future of capitalism, would scarcely have anticipated.

From this brief survey of Marx's life, we turn now to his formal analysis of capitalism as developed in *Das Kapital*.

Capitalism: Marx's Analysis

4

Capital

Marx and Engels had clearly outlined their philosophical view of capitalism and the inevitability of its breakdown in *The Communist Manifesto*. In *Das Kapital*, which will be referred to here by its English title, *Capital*, Marx set himself the task, among other things, of developing rigorously the propositions which had been merely stated in the earlier work.

Having described in the *Manifesto* his narrow view of social classes which divided society into only two groups—the capitalists who own capital goods and the proletariat or workers who do not—Marx attempted to prove in *Capital* that the exploitation of the workers by the capitalists would lead to the ultimate breakdown of capitalism. To support his exploitation thesis, Marx made the labor theory of value the foundation of his argument. This led him into logical difficulties which only served to weaken his case.

The Labor Theory of Value

David Ricardo

In adopting the labor theory of value, Marx was following David Ricardo with whose work he was thoroughly familiar. Ricardo had argued that goods which are scarce and have utility tend to have exchange values which reflect the relative amounts of labor used in producing them. Ricardo showed that rent did not play a part in the determination of value since the price of agricultural commodities was determined by the cost of production on marginal land which did not yield a surplus in the form of rent. He also eliminated capital as a factor in the determination of relative exchange values by assuming that capital and labor are used in the same proportion in various lines of production. Thus capital could be disregarded and differences in labor time used in the production process would be sufficient to establish relative values in the market. Under this analysis, the general price level could be a function of the quantity of money in circulation, but relative prices would remain a function of the relative quantities of labor used in production.

It is obvious, of course, that capital and labor are not used in the same proportions in all lines of production. Some industries are more labor intensive and others are more capital intensive. Where such variations occur, it would not be meaningful to base relative values solely upon the amount of labor used in the production process. It should be remembered, however, that in Ricardo's day production was still mostly on a rather small-scale basis, and variations in the quantity of capital used in different lines would not have appeared to be so great.

It was necessary for Ricardo to take account of the fact that labor was not a standardized factor, for there are marked differences in the skills possessed by different workers and also in the skills required in different lines of production. He glossed over this problem by suggesting that appropriate valuations for the various degrees of labor skill would easily and quickly be established in the labor market. But this answer involves some circularity of reasoning. To illustrate, assume that it takes fifteen minutes of unskilled labor to shine a pair of shoes and thirty minutes of skilled labor to weave a basket. For simplification, also assume that the cost of materials in each case is zero. From this information alone it is not possible to determine the relative values of skilled and unskilled labor. But if it is known that the market price of a shoe shine is 25 cents and the market price of the basket is $2.00, then it can be deduced that one unit of skilled labor is worth four units of unskilled labor. In this case, however, it has been necessary to know market values first before labor values could be determined; while under the labor theory of value, it is the labor content of various goods that is supposed to establish their relative market values.

This kind of circularity-of-reasoning difficulty plus the unrealistic assumption that labor and capital are used in uniform proportions in different lines of production made Ricardo's labor theory of value rather unsatisfactory, and it had been generally abandoned by economists by the time that Marx wrote *Capital*. Marx found the labor theory of value so useful for developing his concept of exploitation under capitalism that he chose this earlier and by then less satisfactory theory of value as the foundation on which to base his argument.

Marx's Exploitation Thesis

To gain a better understanding of Marx's exploitation thesis, it will be helpful to follow the discussion as he developed it. In doing so, it will be necessary to introduce some of the terms and special concepts which he used.

Constant Capital

Marx used the term *constant capital* to include what is now referred to as fixed capital and raw materials. He was not always careful to indicate clearly when he was referring to the stock of constant capital and when he was referring to the flow of constant capital as represented by the depreciation of fixed capital plus the using up of raw materials in the course of production.

1. c = the depreciation of a firm's fixed plant and equipment (c_1) plus the value of raw materials used (c_2) during the period of production.

Stocks and Flows of Constant Capital

The total stock of constant capital $(C = C_1 + C_2)$ is linked to the flow of constant capital (c) by the rates of turnover of c_1 and c_2. For purposes of illustration, it will be assumed that the period of production used for accounting purposes is one year. Thus c_1 would represent the dollar amount of depreciation of the firm's plant and equipment during the given year and c_2 would represent the total value of raw materials used. If the expected useful life of the fixed plant and equipment of firm A is ten years, then this would be the turnover period (t_1) for c_1, and

2. $C_1 = t_1 c_1 = 10c_1$.

The turnover period for raw materials (t_2) would be much shorter. If firm A carries an average inventory of raw materials equal to two months' production requirements, then its turnover period (t_2) for c_2 would be one-sixth of a year, and

3. $C_2 = t_2 c_2 = 1/6 \, c_2$.

The Cost of Labor

The third component of the firm's cost of production in Marx's model is the cost of labor represented by the annual flow of wage payments (v). If wages are paid weekly by firm A, then the turnover period of its working capital used for wage payments (t_3) would be 1/52 of a year, and its stock of working capital required for wages (V) would be:

4. $V = t_3 \, v = 1/52 \, v.$

The Firm's Annual Cost of Production

The annual cost of production for an individual firm, as Marx viewed it, would thus be:

5.   Annual cost of production of the firm $= c_1 + c_2 + v = c + v.$

It will be useful from this point to use the combined expression, $c + v.$

The Firm's Total Stock of Capital

Also, the total stock of capital invested by the firm could be expressed in the form:

6.   Total capital stock of the firm $=$
     $t_1 \, c_1 + t_2 \, c_2 + t_3 v = C_1 + C_2 + V = C + V.$

The Contribution of Constant Capital to Value

It should be noted that Marx considered that constant capital added an amount of value to production that was just equal to the loss of value incurred in the form of physical depreciation in the case of fixed plant and equipment and in the form of the reduction of the physical inventory of raw materials as that component of constant capital was incorporated in the product being produced. Since he also held the view that the value of fixed plant and equipment as well as of inventories of raw materials was exactly equal to the value of the labor time embodied in their production, he was saying in effect that constant capital components could add no more to the value of the goods they helped to produce than the value of the labor time congealed in them, by which Marx meant the value of the labor time used in their own production. As Marx stated it:

> The maximum loss of value that they [the means of production] can suffer in the process, is plainly limited by the amount of the original value with which they came into the process, or in other words, by the labour-time necessary for their production.[1]

In attributing the value of the components of what he calls constant capital solely to the value of the labor time embodied in their production, Marx is saying in effect that the value of capital goods does not reflect

---

[1] *Capital*, Moore and Aveling translation of the third German edition (Moscow: Foreign Languages Publishing House, 1961), I, 205.

in part their relative scarcity as measured by the rate of interest and by a possible rent component if their supply is restricted by patent protection or other barriers. It is interesting to note that the Communist regime in Russia followed Marx's thinking in rejecting the concept of an interest component in the determination of relative values. As a result, it has been difficult for Russian planners to determine the relative efficiency of alternative methods of production. For example, should a new electric power plant be designed as a hydroelectric plant which would require a large capital expenditure for a dam but would have lower operating costs, or should it be designed as a fossil fuel plant which would require a smaller initial capital outlay but would have higher operating costs? Without some measure of the relative scarcity of capital such as an interest rate, proper cost estimates of the electricity generated by the two alternative methods could not be determined. Russian planners met this problem for a time by using a substitute for the rate of interest called the coefficient of relative effectiveness, which in practice served the same function.[2] More recently, Russia has begun to use an interest charge on loans to industry in order to achieve greater efficiency in the use of capital.

The Total Value of a Firm's Output

If $c + v$ represents a firm's total cost of production during a given time period in Marx's model, what does he have to say about the total value of the firm's output during the same period? This he states as follows:

7. Total value of a firm's output during a given period $= c + v + s$.

Surplus Value

The s term in the expression above stands for surplus value in Marx's terminology. Surplus value is a very important concept in the Marxian system for it is a reflection of the exploitation of labor under capitalism.

For Marx, surplus value would arise under capitalism from the nature of the bargaining process between employers and laborers. He held that wages would be established in the market at a rate which represented the value of the labor time required to produce the means of subsistence for labor. He referred to this rate as the value of the worker's labor power. In working for the capitalist, the laborer may contribute to the value of the product being produced an amount equal to the value of his labor

---

[2]For an interesting discussion of the coefficient of relative effectiveness, see the discussion in Harry Schwartz, *An Introduction to the Soviet Economy* (Columbus, Ohio: Charles E. Merrill Publishing Company, 1968), pp. 99-100.

power—that is, his daily wage rate—during only six hours of working time. The greater bargaining strength of the capitalist enables him to require the worker to continue for a longer period, for example twelve hours, which Marx used to represent the length of the working day. If the worker contributed the value of his labor power—his daily wage—in only six hours, the value which he contributed to the firm's product during the remainder of his working day would accrue to his employer as surplus value. Marx regarded this as exploitation of the laborer by the capitalist, for it represented in his model an appropriation of value contributed by the laborer which was made possible by the superior bargaining position of the owners of capital.

GNP and NNP

The total annual value of the product produced by an individual firm, in Marxian terms, can be represented, as indicated in equation 7, by the expression $c + v + s$, and by subtracting its costs of production, $c + v$, we get the remainder, s, which for Marx would represent the firm's total surplus value for the year.

The expression $c + v + s$ is equal to the gross value of the annual output of an individual firm. By aggregating this expression, with some modifications, for all the firms in the economy, the equivalent of GNP viewed from the standpoint of income shares can be derived. To get GNP, it is necessary to subtract from c the value of raw materials (c_2) used by each firm in the process of production. This deduction is necessary to avoid double counting in the process of aggregation, for the raw materials used by a firm are counted in the value contributed by the firm which produced them. In aggregating the values produced by individual firms, then, only the depreciation (c_1) component of c should be included.

It is also necessary to include the value of personal services contributed by doctors, nurses, teachers, lawyers, entertainers, etc., to arrive at the equivalent of GNP, for Marx does not include this component in his discussion of value produced. With these adjustments, GNP can be expressed as:

8.   GNP $= \Sigma\ (c_1 + v + s + \text{personal services})$.

Also, if depreciation (c_1) is subtracted, the remainder is equivalent to Net National Product as shown in equation 9.[3]

9.   NNP $= \Sigma\ (v + s + \text{personal services})$.

It is interesting to note that the Communist regime in Russia followed

---

[3]An interesting discussion of this extension of Marx's expression for the gross value contributed by the firm to the aggregate output of the economy is developed in Paul M. Sweezy, *The Theory of Capitalist Development* (New York: Monthly Review Press, 1956), p. 63.

Marx in omitting services from the measure of the productive contribution of the economy. Only rather recently has Russia begun to give some consideration to the inclusion of services in its aggregate measure of productive activity.

The Rate of Surplus Value

To turn from aggregates back to the individual firm, Marx discussed three ratios which are of significance in his model. The first is the rate of surplus value, which he also called the rate of exploitation.[4]

10.   The rate of surplus value $= \dfrac{s}{v}$.

To use the figures which Marx assumed in his numerical illustration, if in a particular productive situation $c = \$410$, $v = \$90$, and $s = \$90$, then the rate of surplus value $s/v = \$90/\$90 = 100$ per cent.

What did Marx mean to describe by his rate of surplus value? Essentially, he was attempting to show the extent to which the capitalist by virtue of his bargaining strength was able to force his workers to contribute value to the firm's output in excess of the amount paid to the workers in the form of wages. This represented for Marx an appropriation of value by the capitalist which was simply an exploitation of labor.

Marx regarded the wage system of capitalism to be little different from a system using slave labor. In the latter, the slave owner provides directly a mere physical subsistence for his slaves and extracts an optimum amount of labor time from them; while in the former the capitalist pays a wage that provides a bare subsistence for the worker and his family, and extracts as much labor as is practicable from the worker. As will be noted in more detail later, Marx did think that wages could at times rise above a subsistence minimum under capitalism, but he thought there would usually be a reserve army of unemployed which would result in such competition by workers for jobs that wages would tend to remain close to the subsistence level most of the time.

It should be noted that the numerical value of the rate of surplus value, s/v, depends upon the length of the working day and the portion of this day that it takes the worker to contribute an amount of value to the firm's product that is equal to the value of the daily goods consumed by the worker and his family. The part of the day which it takes the laborer to contribute to the product an amount of value equal to the value of the wage he receives, Marx referred to as necessary labor time. During the remainder of the day, the worker would contribute surplus labor time to the firm. Again, if the length of the working day is assumed

[4]See *Capital*, I, 215-219.

to be twelve hours and it takes only six hours for the worker to contribute the value of his daily wage—the value of his labor power—the rate of surplus value (rate of exploitation) would be 6/6 or 100 per cent. This rate would be increased if improvements in agricultural techniques reduced the amount of time required to produce the food consumed by the worker and his family. For example, if the amount of necessary labor time declined from six hours to four hours, the rate of surplus value would be 8/4 or 200 per cent.

Marx also recognized that wages could be pushed above the subsistence level at times of rapid capital accumulation by an increase in the demand for labor large enough to absorb the reserve army of unemployed temporarily into active employment. In this case, necessary labor time might rise to say eight hours, and the rate of surplus value would then fall to 4/8 or 50 per cent.

The rate of surplus value would also be affected by changes in the length of the working day. Marx discussed the problems that are involved in attempting to increase the rate of surplus value by imposing longer hours on the workers. If the worker is forced to work too many hours his health and efficiency would be impaired. The determination of what has come to be accepted as a normal working day is the result of a struggle between the capitalist class and the working class, in Marx's view. In his discussion of the working day, Marx cited a number of illustrations of pathetic abuses of labor through the excessively long hours imposed upon workers before a more reasonable normal working day had been established in practice and verified by labor legislation. This section of *Capital* makes interesting though depressing reading.[5] In spite of his many illustrations of the abuse of labor through long hours, Marx when discussing his concept of the long-run declining rate of profit under capitalism does not believe that capitalists will be able to effect any significant modifications in this trend through attempts to increase the rate of exploitation by lengthening the working day. This is a reasonable position for him to take within the framework of his analysis, for there are limits to the extent to which such a trend could be retarded by this means. These limits stem from the absolute limit of twenty-four hours in the day and the need of workers for sleep.

Marx assumed that the rate of exploitation, s/v, is uniform in all industries. In his model, this assumption is a link in the logic by which he attempted to demonstrate a tendency for the average rate of profit to decline under capitalism.

The Rate of Profit

The second ratio that Marx described is the rate of profit, which can be expressed as in equation 11.

---

[5] *Ibid.*, I, 231-302.

11. Rate of profit $= \dfrac{s}{c + v}$. [6]

This ratio can also be stated in terms of the capital stock by multiplying the terms in the denominator by the appropriate turnover periods.

12. Rate of profit $= \dfrac{s}{t_1 c_1 + t_2 c_2 + t_3 v} = \dfrac{s}{C_1 + C_2 + V} = \dfrac{s}{C + V}$.

Using the same figures assumed in his illustration of the rate of exploitation ($c = \$410$, $v = \$90$, and $s = \$90$), Marx calculated the rate of profit as:

13. Rate of profit $= \dfrac{s}{c + v} = \dfrac{\$90}{\$410 + \$90} = 18$ per cent.

Marx wished to emphasize the difference between his ratio of surplus value—100 per cent using the figures above—which for him indicated the extent of exploitation of labor by the capitalist, and the less revealing figure of profit—18 per cent in this case—more customarily used by classical economists. It should be noted that in both his rate of surplus value and his rate of profit ratios, Marx was relating surplus value, s, to capital used in the process of production. In the rate of surplus value, s is related to variable capital only, while in the rate of profit it is related to total capital, $c + v$, used in the course of production.

Marx assumed that in a competitive capitalistic economy the rate of profit would tend to be pushed toward equality both among the individual firms in a given industry and among firms in different industries. Mobility of labor and capital were assumed to account for this equalization tendency.[7]

The Organic Composition of Capital

The remaining ratio, which completes the set of basic relationships which Marx used, is the organic composition of capital.[8] Marx expressed this as:

14. The organic composition of capital $= \dfrac{c}{c + v}$

To assume that the rate of exploitation, s/v, and the rate of profit, $s/(c+v)$, tend to be equal for all industries, it would also have been necessary for Marx to assume that the organic composition of capital, $c/(c+v)$, is the same in all lines of production. Obviously, however, there are significant differences among industries in regard to the amount of capital used per worker. Some are more labor intensive than others, as Marx himself was well aware.

[6]*Ibid.*, III, 42.
[7]See *Ibid.*, III, Chap. X; and Sweezy, *op cit.*, pp. 68-71.
[8]*Capital*, I, 612.

If the organic composition of capital, $c/(c+v)$, differs among industries, while the rate of profit is assumed to be the same everywhere, this implies that the market values of various goods do not correspond solely to the value of the labor time required to produce them. Marx found himself confronted with this dilemma, and instead of taking the logical step of dropping his labor theory of value in favor of a more generalized cost of production theory, he attempted in Vol. III to salvage the theory which he had developed in Vol. I. Marx's clinging to a theory of value which gave rise to certain logical difficulties was a reflection of his strong desire to prove in formal fashion that labor is exploited under capitalism.

Marx's Transformation Analysis

In attempting to reconcile the fact that labor values of commodities differ from their market prices without dropping his labor theory of value, Marx developed in Vol. III a transformation analysis which was supposed to illustrate the transformation of labor values into market prices.[9] He constructed a table showing the transformation process for five different industries, each having a different organic composition of capital, but all having the same rate of exploitation (s/v = 100 per cent in each of the five industries). Marx's own table is reproduced in Table 4-1, with slight modification.

In column 1, Marx listed the total amount of constant capital and variable capital for each of the five industries. In every case, $C + V$ = 100, but the mix of C and V differs from industry to industry. Marx assumed a turnover period of 1 for variable capital, so $V = v$ in all industries. The turnover rate of constant capital is less than 1 throughout as is evident from the difference between the figures which Marx assumed for C in column 1, and those which he assumed for c in column 2.

Since Marx was here assuming a rate of exploitation (s/v) of 100 per cent, the figures for s in column 3 are identical to the figures for V (since $V = v$) in column 1. In column 4, the cost-price ($c + v$) of the commodities of each industry are listed. Then, by adding the surplus value (s) figures of column 3 to the cost-price figures ($c + v$) of column 4, he got the value-of-commodities ($c + v + s$) figures of column 5. If the goods of these five industries exchanged for each other according to their true labor contents, the value-of-commodities figures of column 5 would also correspond to the actual market prices of these commodities. But Marx pointed out that it is the practice under capitalism to add a "general rate of profit" to the cost-price of commodities in order to get the prices of production at which products are sold in the market.[10]

---

[9]See *Ibid.*, III, Chap. IX.
[10]See *Ibid.*, III, 155.

TABLE 4-1. The Marxian Transformation Process

1 Capitals	2 Depreciation and raw materials c	3 Surplus value s	4 Cost-price of commodities c + v	5 Value of commodities c + v + s	6 Average rate of profit	7 Amount of profit	8 Price of commodities	9 Deviation of price of commodities from the value of commodities
I. 80C + 20V	50	20	70	90	22%	22	92	+ 2
II. 70C + 30V	51	30	81	111	22%	22	103	− 8
III. 60C + 40V	51	40	91	131	22%	22	113	−18
IV. 85C + 15V	40	15	55	70	22%	22	77	+ 7
V. 95C + 5V	10	5	15	20	22%	22	37	+17
TOTAL 390C + 110V	202	110	312	422		110	422	0

As shown in column 6, Marx calculated the general or average rate of profit to be 22 per cent. He used the formula $\Sigma s / \Sigma (C + V)$ to derive the average rate of profit here. Substituting figures in the formula, he got $110/(390 + 110) = 110/500 = 22$ per cent. By applying the average rate of profit of 22 per cent to the total capital $(C + V = 100)$ for each industry, a profit mark-up of 22, as shown in column 7, must be added to the cost-price figures of column 4 to get the price of commodities figures listed in column 8. As the final column in his table, Marx listed the difference between the price of the commodity and the value of the commodity for each industry. Though for no industry does the value of its commodity equal the price of its commodity, the sum of the differences turns out to be zero. By this demonstration, however, Marx has not proved that on the average the relative values of commodities as reflected in their labor content is just equal to their relative prices. Instead of proving it, he has forced this result in his model by assuming total profit to be just equal to total surplus value.

As Sweezy points out, Marx himself apparently was not entirely satisfied with his process of transforming values into prices of production. But his dissatisfaction with his transformation process did not alter his conviction that prices of production were derivable from the values of commodities as reflected in their labor content.[11]

Marx's Breakdown of Capitalism Thesis

Marx could have accepted a more generalized cost-of-production theory of value and still have been able to argue that laborers were in a sense exploited because their relative bargaining position was considerably weaker than that of the capitalists who employed them. This would not have satisfied him, however, for it would have implied that if workers could somehow strengthen their bargaining position, the exploitation of labor could be reduced or perhaps eliminated within the framework of the capitalistic system. This he was not willing to accept, for he was attempting to prove the inevitability of the breakdown of capitalism, and he needed to be able to show a permanent and increasing trend of class antagonism to make his point. The labor theory of value was an extremely useful, though invalid, link in his argument. Other important points which he developed in support of his breakdown thesis are described briefly below.

The Investment of Surplus Value in Constant Capital

Marx assumed that most of the surplus value which capitalists appropriate would be invested in constant capital. He mentioned two factors

---

[11]For an interesting comment on this point, see Sweezy, *op. cit.*, pp. 115-116.

that account for this tendency. First, he seemed to imply that it is part of the mentality of capitalists to increase their investment in constant capital. As he put it,

> Therefore, save, save, *i.e.*, reconvert the greatest possible portion of surplus-value, or surplus-product into capital! Accumulation for accumulation's sake, production for production's sake: by this formula classical economy expressed the historical mission of the bourgeoise . . . .[12]
>
> If to classical economy, the proletarian is but a machine for the production of surplus-value; on the other hand, the capitalist is in its eyes only a machine for the conversion of this surplus-value into additional capital.[13]

In addition to the capitalist mentality which leads to the investment of surplus value in constant capital, Marx mentioned a second factor. This is the pressure of competition under capitalism which forces capitalists to expand their investment in constant capital in order to incorporate modern technology in their productive enterprises. This latter point was of particular importance in Marx's analysis, for he considered that surplus value is only realized in those enterprises which are producing with the most efficient equipment. In his terminology, the amount of socially necessary labor time involved in its production determines the value of any commodity, and by socially necessary, he means labor time devoted to production under up-to-date technological conditions.[14]

The Reserve Army of Labor

Marx thought that the accumulation of constant capital would tend over the long run to contribute to unemployment. He introduced the concept of the reserve army of labor by which he meant the pool of unemployment that he believed would be a permanent feature of capitalism. Marx thought that this pool of unemployment would keep workers at a bargaining disadvantage and thus cause their wages to remain low. He recognized that at times the accumulation of capital might be sufficiently rapid to draw down the reserve army of labor and cause wages to increase as a result of the improved bargaining position of the workers, but he saw this as only a temporary phenomenon since the decline in surplus value resulting from rising wages would in time cause the rate of capital accumulation to lag behind the rate of growth in the labor force. Unemployment would again increase and the real wages of workers decline.

Marx also thought that during periods when real wages were relatively high as a result of a lumping of capital investment which would tempor-

---

[12]*Capital*, I, 595.
[13]*Ibid.*, I, 595.
[14]*Ibid.*, I, 39.

arily increase the demand for labor, the pressure to develop new and more efficient labor-saving capital equipment would increase. As more efficient capital equipment was developed and introduced, labor would be displaced. Thus Marx implied that technological unemployment is also a factor in the long-run growth of the reserve army of labor which he considered to be characteristic of capitalism.

The Falling Trend in the Rate of Profit

In addition to contributing to the growth of the reserve army of labor, the accumulation of capital would, according to Marx, also cause a downward trend in the rate of profit.[15] The growth of constant capital would cause the organic composition of capital, $c/(c + v)$, to rise. This, in turn, would cause the rate of profit, $s/(c + v)$, to fall. To have a declining rate of profit accompanying an upward trend in the organic composition of capital, it is necessary to introduce a special assumption about the behavior of the rate of surplus value, s/v, and in this discussion Marx assumed that it remains constant. This assumption leads to a contradiction in his analysis of which he does not seem to have been fully aware.

It does follow quite obviously that if s/v remains constant while $c/(c + v)$ is increasing, $s/(c + v)$ must decline. Since Marx considered that a rise in the organic composition of capital would mean an increase in the amount of capital used per worker, labor productivity and total output would rise over time as the organic composition of capital, itself, increased. With a constant rate of exploitation, workers would get a constant fraction of total output, and if total output were growing as a result of a rising trend in the organic composition of capital, the real wages of workers would have to increase. Thus the argument that Marx used to support his theory of the falling rate of profit tendency under capitalism seems to contradict his view that the real wages of workers would tend, except for temporary increases, to remain at a subsistence level.[16]

Reason for Logical Weaknesses in Capital

In concluding this brief discussion of some of the logical weaknesses in Marx's analysis, it may be well to ask how one so versed in philosophy and the rigor of logical reasoning could have developed a formal system which contained serious internal weaknesses in several of the underlying arguments. Basically, Marx's logical difficulties seem to arise from the fact that he knew in advance what he wanted to prove—the inevitability of the exploitation of labor under capitalism and the ultimate breakdown

---

[15]See *Ibid.*, Vol. III, Chaps. XIII-XV.

[16]For an interesting and more complete discussion of this point, see Joan Robinson, *An Essay on Marxian Economics* (London: Macmillan and Co. Ltd., 1957), Chap. V.

of the system itself. This, in turn, forced him to develop arguments to support his conclusions.

Marx's Rejection of the "Natural Laws"

Marx worked under a further self-imposed constraint, for he was unwilling to accept any of the "natural laws" such as the Malthusian "law" of population growth. The Malthusian doctrine, coupled with the law of diminishing returns, would have provided him with a stronger argument in support of his thesis that wages would tend to fall to a minimum of subsistence level. He would not accept this "natural" tendency, for it would be applicable regardless of the type of economic system that was present. Marx wanted to demonstrate that an extremely poor condition for workers was a special characteristic of capitalism and that it would not prevail under communism, in which the instruments of production were governmentally owned.

The Social Concern of *Capital*

Class Conflict Doctrine

Given the weaknesses inherent in some of the basic arguments that Marx used to support his conclusions, how can one explain the wide attraction of *Capital* over a long span of time? In contrast to classical economic analysis, which paid little attention to prevailing social problems, the Marxian theory was very much concerned with the extremely low level of living of the working class and the conflict of interest that prevailed between workers and capitalists. Instead of the concept of harmony of interest, which was assumed by classical economists, Marx held that in a capitalistic system class antagonism would become increasingly severe and lead ultimately to the overthrow of this system by the working class and to the establishment of communism in which class distinctions based upon the ownership of the means of production would be eliminated. His doctrine of the exploitation of laborers under capitalism naturally appealed to many among the working class who felt themselves in an insecure position and at a major disadvantage in bargaining individually with employers. Marx, of course, did not anticipate the extent to which the growth and development of labor unions under capitalism would in time help to overcome the bargaining disadvantage of the working class.

The Problem of Economic Crises

Marx's analysis of economic crises under capitalism, though only very sketchily developed before his death, also reflects his concern with concrete social and economic problems. As Schumpeter points out, economists had tended to look only at major crises in isolation, and it is to Marx's credit that he recognized that there are cyclical movements of which the crisis phase is merely a part.[17] The fact that he did not develop fully and clearly his theory of cycles before his death should not detract from the contribution which he made in recognizing the significance of cyclical movements under capitalism. Marx held that the recurring crises would become increasingly severe and that during the crisis phase of the cycle weaker capitalists would be forced into bankruptcy. This process would result in growing monopoly tendencies as capital became increasingly concentrated in the hands of the more powerful capitalists.

In recognizing and discussing cyclical fluctuations, however incompletely and inadequately, Marx again was dealing with prevailing social and economic problems in a more realistic way than they were then treated in classical economic analysis. It was not until the period of the 1930's that traditional economists really began to pay adequate attention to the cycle problem. Marx, of course, could not have anticipated the extent to which techniques for dampening cyclical swings would be developed within the framework of capitalism.

The Trend Toward Monopoly

Marx's recognition of a growing monopoly tendency under capitalism was also evidence of his concern for actual economic and social problems. The monopoly trend under capitalism which he predicted became so serious in the United States during the late nineteenth century that Congress found it necessary to pass the Sherman Antitrust Act, and legislation in this area has been considerably expanded since that time. Again, Marx did not anticipate the extent to which such a problem could be managed effectively without the destruction of the capitalistic system.

The Breadth of Marx's Approach

Also contributing to the wide appeal which *Capital* has had is the fact that in it Marx was attempting to develop a general theory to explain the historical process of economic and social development. Though he did not successfully accomplish his objective, his grand design was so sweeping that it was rather natural that his work should attract wide attention over the course of time.

---

[17]See Joseph A Schumpeter, *Capitalism, Socialism, and Democracy* (2nd ed,; New York: Harper & Row, Publishers, 1947), pp. 40-41.

Marx's Appeal to the Disadvantaged

Finally, it seems reasonable to conclude that part of the attraction which Marx has exerted in the past and which his memory and works continue to evoke at the present time stems from the fact that he was addressing a particular appeal to the "have nots" of the world. He was telling this large, disadvantaged majority of the world's population that its harsh lot in life stems from the existence of an improper pattern of ownership of productive capital, and that all that is needed to correct the situation is to abolish capitalism and replace it with communism. This is a beguilingly simple solution to the harsh problem of widespread poverty, and it is hardly surprising that in many places the pressures to try the way of socialism have been strong. The idea that socialism provides a universal formula for effective economic development and the overcoming of the problem of poverty is still widely held throughout the world. And so Marxian thought continues to be very much alive a century after the publication of *Capital*.

Capitalism: Neoclassical to Galbraithian Thought

5

The Problem of Cyclical Fluctuations

It has been stated in an earlier chapter.that the pessimism of John Stuart Mill and other classical economists concerning the course of economic development under capitalism or any other form of economic system, and the pessimistic predictions made by Karl Marx concerning the future of capitalism, were overshadowed by the rapid rate of economic growth and development experienced by the capitalistic economies of Western Europe and the United States during the latter half of the nineteenth century and the first two decades of the twentieth. But this period of growth was not without its problems. As mentioned earlier, the threat of excessive monopoly developments in the United States stimulated the passage of restrictive legislation by Congress. With the monopoly problem kept in some restraint in the United States by the Sherman Act and other legislation, the capitalistic economy of this country, as well as the countries of Western Europe, continued to be plagued by another source of difficulty which Marx had described, namely, cyclical disturbances.

Cyclical Fluctuations in the United States

To confine the discussion of the cycle problem to the United States for the sake of brevity, it is interesting to note that this country experienced a succession of economic disturbances in the period from the Civil War to the major depression of the 1930's. As outlined by Professors Thorp and Mitchell, the state of the economy over the period from 1865 through 1925 can be summarized as follows:[1] From 1865 to 1867 the economy moved from a wartime boom to a depression. By 1869, prosperity had returned, to be followed by a recession in 1870 and then two years of prosperity in 1871-72. This was followed by a long period of depression extending from 1873 to 1878, after which conditions were prosperous from 1879 to 1882. Recession and depression returned from 1883 to 1886, while prosperity continued for the most part from 1887 to 1890. In 1891 there was a short depression, from which prosperity had returned in 1892, only to be followed by a long period of depression extending from 1893 through 1897. Reasonably prosperous conditions then returned and lasted with some mild and brief interruptions from 1898 through 1906. From 1907 through 1908 the United States experienced a severe panic and depression which was followed in the period from 1909 through 1915 by, for the most part, mild prosperity interrupted by brief periods of recession or mild depression. The years 1916-17 were years of war-induced prosperity, and were followed by a recession in 1918. A sharp boom developed in 1919 and extended into 1920, to be followed by the severe but short depression of 1920-21. Conditions from 1922 through 1926 were for the most part mildly prosperous, while the remainder of the decade of the 1920's was characterized by the development of an excessive speculative development in the stock market. The stock market crash beginning in September 1929 ushered in the catastrophic depression of the 1930's, from which the country had not fully recovered when it became an active participant in World War II in December 1941.

The Optimism of Neoclassical Economic Thought

In spite of this record of instability which had characterized the economy of the United States as well as the economies of the other major capitalistic countries of the world in the latter part of the nineteenth century and the first two decades of the twentieth, the general tone of neoclassical economic thought, which had by then evolved, was optimistic. It was widely believed that an economy operating under conditions of *laissez-faire* and competition would tend toward long-run equilibrium conditions characterized by full employment and a pattern of distribution which would reflect the value of the contribution of each factor of

---

[1]For an excellent summary of the historical trend of economic activity to 1926 in the United States, England, France, Germany, Austria, Russia, Sweden, The Netherlands, Italy, Argentina, Brazil, Canada, South Africa, Australia, India, Japan, and China, see Willard Long Thorp and Wesley C. Mitchell, *Business Annals* (New York: National Bureau of Economic Research, Inc., 1926).

production employed. One can easily understand that a system which tended automatically to move in the direction of full employment and which also promised distributive justice in an economic sense would have wide appeal.

It was recognized, of course, that the capitalistic economies of the United States, England and other countries did not go smoothly and continuously toward a state of full-employment equilibrium, and that there were cyclical fluctuations around this basic long-run trend. These temporary aberrations were not regarded by most neoclassical economists as being of sufficient concern to warrant a significant change in the capitalistic system. The aberrations were not considered, as Marx viewed them, destined to become increasingly severe until they ultimately led to the overthrow of the system by a growing army of disenchanted unemployed. The measures suggested for dampening the cyclical fluctuations were for the most part monetary in nature. They concerned such things as regulating the structure of interest rates or the money supply in order to reduce tendencies toward over-spending and over-investment in some periods which would more or less inevitably be followed by periods of economic contraction.

In view of the very favorable trend of economic growth and development in Western Europe and the United States during the latter quarter of the nineteenth century and the first decade of the twentieth, it is not surprising that neoclassical economists did not share the pessimism either of Mill and other classical economists or of Marx in regard to the longer-run prospects of capitalism. The laboring class had shared in the benefits of this favorable period of growth as reflected in an upward movement in real wages. In addition, workers were making some progress in overcoming their bargaining disadvantage with employers by organizing themselves into labor unions.

The Discrepancy Between Neoclassical Optimism and Economic Reality

Though the general trend of the development of capitalism had become favorable, the recurring periods of recession and depression were accompanied by the problem of unemployment and failures among banks and non-financial businesses. In regard to bank failures, in the United States nearly 3,000 banking institutions were forced into bankruptcy in the period from 1864 to 1920; over 5,000 failed in the brief span from 1921 through 1929; and almost 9,000 banks failed in this country from 1930 through 1933.

The human misery resulting from the sharp increases in unemployment during recession and depression periods was looked upon as an unfortunate but largely unavoidable aspect of the economic system, and it was hoped that it could be reduced as the operation of the financial system improved. Until the major depression of the 1930's, the idea that the central government should play an active and direct part in attempting to mitigate the effects of a cyclical downswing in the economy was alien to the thinking of traditional economists. The *laissez-faire* concept was so widely prevalent that it was generally held that prudent governmental fiscal policy called for balanced budgets even during depression years.

Laissez-faire, Pure Competition, and Say's Law

Until the 1930's, there was no theoretical framework to indicate how and why a program of governmental intervention beyond monetary policy measures could be helpful in reducing the extent of cyclical swings. Neoclassical economists accepted by and large, at least implicitly, the concept of Say's law which is popularly, though crudely, summarized in elementary economics texts as "Supply creates its own demand." By this was meant that in the process of production, income is generated in the amount of the value of the goods produced, and so there would be sufficient purchasing power available to purchase the total output of the economy at prices yielding a normal investment return. Thus, neoclassical economic thought included the notion that general over-production, or correspondingly, a deficiency in aggregate demand, would not occur in an economic system characterized by conditions of *laissez-faire* and pure competition. It was also implicit in neoclassical thinking that for any level of income, the portion of aggregate income not spent for consumption would all be channeled into investment expenditures.

Keynes' Interpretation of Neoclassical Doctrine

In neoclassical economics, as interpeted by the late Lord Keynes, it was fluctuations in the interest rate which were supposed to maintain a relationship of equality between savings and investment. Thus, whatever the level of income might be, there would be no problem in maintaining it, for the part of income not spent on consumer goods would be used for investment expenditures as a result of appropriate movements in the interest rate. This concept of the rate of interest as the variable which would maintain a relationship of equality between savings and investment, when coupled with Say's law, suggested that since "supply creates its own demand," there would be no obstacle to the attainment of a full-employment level of income. Also, once achieved, this could easily be maintained since the interest rate would adjust as needed to channel savings at that income level fully into investment expenditures. This was indeed an optimistic line of thought which held that with conditions of *laissez-faire* and pure competition there would be no bar to the attainment of a full-employment level of income and no problem in continuing at this level over time. It is not surprising that neoclassical economists held so long to such favorable conclusions concerning the behavior of capitalistic economic systems in spite of the fact that their formal theory did not coincide closely with the competitive structure and actual behavior patterns of contemporary capitalistic economies.

During the period when neoclassical economic thought was dominant in England and the United States, Marx's concept of the inevitability of recurring cyclical fluctuations under capitalism would have seemed more realistic to those who were being adversely affected by recession and depression developments. Yet Marx seems to have made remarkably little impression upon neoclassical economists themselves.

The Depression of the 1930's and the Reappraisal of Neoclassical Economics

The advent of the catastrophic depression of the 1930's which had a world-wide impact caused an extensive reappraisal of neoclassical thought and the prospects for capitalism. With some fifteen million or more men unemployed in the United States during the depths of the depression, there is little wonder that a number of intellectuals as well as others began to ask seriously whether Marx might not have been right after all in his prediction of the growing reserve army of labor and the eventual breakdown of capitalism. During this period it was relatively easy for a sensitive person with a strong social conscience to become a Marxist; indeed, a number of people at the time did embrace covertly or overtly the principles of communism. Traditional neoclassical economics had nothing to offer in this period of dire emergency but a prescription of *laissez-faire*—reducing governmental expenditures to keep the budget in balance and patiently waiting for this depression, like others before it, to run its course. By the third year of the depression this had ceased to be either a comforting or a satisfactory doctrine.

Old ideas die slowly, however, and it is interesting to recall that even Franklin D. Roosevelt ran on the platform of a balanced budget during his campaign against the Republican incumbent, Herbert Hoover, in 1932. In his campaign speeches Roosevelt was highly critical of Hoover for having let the federal budget run into a sizeable deficit. Once in office, Roosevelt was soon convinced by his liberal advisers that conditions were so critical that strong policies by the federal government were needed to alleviate them, even at the expense of major deficits. At the same time, economists were forced to re-examine their thinking in the light of their dissatisfaction with neoclassical prescriptions in a time of such serious and long-continued depression conditions.

The Keynesian Revolution

The late Lord Keynes, drawing upon a number of separate strands of economic thought then current, produced a brilliant synthesis in his famous book, *The General Theory of Employment, Interest, and Money*, published in 1936.[2] Having been trained in the neoclassical tradition, Keynes had come to the realization that neoclassical economic thought was inadequate as a guide to policy in contemporary capitalistic systems. With the publication of this path-breaking book, Keynes gave new direction to economic thinking and set in motion what has been called the Keynesian revolution. Though Keynes' thinking as expressed in *The General Theory* has been subject to various criticisms and modifications over the years since the book was published, contemporary economic thought clearly reflects Keynes' influence.

In *The General Theory*, Keynes took issue with the implicit neoclassical notion that the interest rate was the variable which would keep savings and investment equal at any level of income. Instead of viewing savings as primarily a function of the interest rate as in neoclassical thought, Keynes held that savings are primarily a function of the level of income. Thus for an economy to achieve a full-employment level of income, it was necessary for it to generate a rate of investment expenditures equal to the rate of savings at that income level. Keynes pointed out that there was no automatic tendency in contemporary capitalistic systems for the rate of investment needed for full employment to occur. In his model, the rate of investment was determined by the marginal efficiency of investment schedule and the rate of interest. He pointed out that the marginal efficiency of investment is a highly volatile function which reflects the current state of business expectations. These expectations are affected by a whole host of factors, and the investment function is therefore subject to wide fluctuations.

As Keynes viewed it, at times when the marginal efficiency of investment schedule has declined sharply as a result of a pessimistic outlook on the part of businessmen, it would not be possible in contemporary capitalistic systems for the interest rate to fall sufficiently low to call forth the rate of investment needed to provide a full-employment level of income. Institutional factors such as the need to insure against risk of loss from loans and the administrative costs of lending activities help to set a limit below which the interest rate cannot fall. Efforts on the

---

[2]See John Maynard Keynes, *The General Theory of Employment, Interest, and Money* (New York: Harcourt, Brace & World, Inc., 1936).

part of central banks to reduce the interest rate below its traditional lower limit by pumping liquidity into the banking system would not be successful, Keynes said, for they would simply result in increased holdings of idle cash balances. This is the familiar concept of the liquidity trap which maintains that as the interest rate falls toward its traditional lower limit, the demand for holding liquid (money) balances becomes increasingly elastic. Also contributing to this increasing elasticity, Keynes suggested, is the rising probability that the interest rate will move upward in the near future. This probability makes it unattractive to lenders of funds to invest at low interest rates since the capital values of such investments will decline when the interest rate rises.

The Stagnation Thesis of the 1930's

Since Keynes was writing in the context of the 1930's depression, it is not surprising that he suggested that in mature capitalistic economies the marginal efficiency of investment would tend to be low more or less continuously and would tend to cause chronic involuntary unemployment. This tendency toward economic stagnation would require active steps by the government to relieve the pressures of unemployment, he thought. He suggested that programs of deficit-financed public works would be an appropriate way of attacking the problem.

The doctrine of secular stagnation received important support among economists during the 1930's depression period and during World War II. It gave rise to considerable uncertainty concerning the long-range prospects for mature capitalistic systems and, in a sense, restored to economic thinking a measure of the pessimism characteristic of John Stuart Mill. Keynes, like Mill, was a defender of capitalism, and it was Keynes' intention to indicate how mature capitalistic systems could be preserved in the face of tendencies toward secular stagnation. His prescriptions were extensively criticized at the time by businessmen and others who were fearful that such intervention by the government in the operation of the economy would quickly lead to socialism.

The Decline of the Stagnation Thesis Since World War II

The remarkable strength demonstrated by the U. S. economy in the post-World War II period has resulted in the virtual disappearance of the stagnation thesis in the more blatant form in which it appeared in the 1930's. Though there have been several recessions in the United States since the war, these have been fairly mild and relatively short-lived. The problem of combating a major depression has been replaced by concern about maintaining a favorable growth rate without excessive inflation. The decade of the 1960's has demonstrated that the contemporary mixed-capitalistic system of the United States still has great vitality and a capacity for impressive economic growth.

It is a tribute to Keynes that his concept of governmental concern and responsibility for the level of operation of the economy under capitalism has received wide acceptance. It is generally held today that appropriate governmental fiscal measures should be used in conjunction with monetary policy to maximize the attainment of the combined goals of full employment, a favorable growth rate, and reasonable price stability. Secular stagnation is no longer regarded as a spectre which is likely to lead to the early breakdown of mature capitalistic systems.

The Schumpeterian Thesis on the Breakdown of Capitalism

At this point it is appropriate to ask whether there is anything inherent in the capitalistic system which is likely to threaten its survival. The late Professor Joseph Schumpeter, one of the most brilliant economists of his generation, stated his position on this question quite succinctly when he said: "Can capitalism survive? No. I do not think it can."[3] He summarized his thinking on this point in stating:

> The thesis I shall endeavor to establish is that the actual and prospective performance of the capitalistic system is such as to negative the idea of its breaking down under the weight of economic failure, but that its very success undermines the social institutions which protect it, and "inevitably" creates conditions in which it will not be able to live and which strongly point to socialism as the heir apparent.[4]

What makes this thesis so startling is the fact that it was not presented by an avowed socialist, but rather by an eminent economist who had a strong sentimental attachment to the capitalistic system. As a social scientist, however, Professor Schumpeter did not let his subjective preferences interfere with his exercise of objective judgment when he attempted to analyze the future prospects for this particular economic system. The question to be considered briefly here is, What reasoning did Professor Schumpeter use to support his thesis?

Innovation and the Vitality of Capitalism

Schumpeter points out that in evaluating capitalism one must not look into the details of the system at a moment in time. To do so might lead one to draw erroneous conclusions from the monopolistic and oligopolistic conditions present in various industries. Instead, since capitalism

---

[3]Joseph A. Schumpeter, *Capitalism, Socialism, and Democracy* (2nd ed.; New York: Harper & Row, Publishers, 1947), p. 61.
[4]*Ibid.*

is a system of economic change, one must look at the system over a period of time to discern its true nature. In doing so, it becomes evident that capitalism is characterized by continuing change stemming from the introduction of new commodities, new techniques of production and transportation, the development of new markets, and the introduction of new types of industrial organization. It is this process of change, which Schumpeter summarizes under the term *innovation*, that makes for a dynamically competitive situation over time under capitalism. Thus today's monopolies are not free from competition but rather face the threat of new innovations which will destroy their advantageous position in the course of time. As Schumpeter puts it, "This process of Creative Destruction is the essential fact about capitalism. It is what capitalism consists in and what every capitalist concern has got to live in."[5] In short, he regards the process of innovation as the factor which gives capitalism its vitality.

Entrepreneurial Activity and the Development of Capitalism

The innovators or entrepreneurs have played a basic role in the development of capitalism. These were the businessmen with the ability to uncover innovational possibilities and the drive to bring them to fruition. As Schumpeter said:

> To undertake such new things is difficult and constitutes a distinct economic function, first, because they lie outside the routine tasks which everybody understands and secondly, because the environment resists in many ways that vary, according to social conditions, from simple refusal either to finance or to buy a new thing, to physical attack on the man who tries to produce it. To act with confidence beyond the range of familiar beacons and to overcome that resistance requires aptitudes that are present in only a small fraction of the population and that define the entrepreneurial type as well as the entrepreneurial function. This function does not essentially consist in either inventing anything or otherwise creating the conditions which the enterprise exploits. It consists in getting things done.[6]

The Declining Role of the Entrepreneur in Mature Capitalistic Systems

As a capitalistic system matures, Schumpeter points out, the role of the individual entrepreneur declines in importance. The process of innovation ceases to be primarily carried on by bold and imaginative individuals and becomes increasingly the routine function of teams of corporate

---

[5]*Ibid.*, p. 83.
[6]*Ibid.*, p. 132.

officials. This tendency for innovational activity to become impersonal and routinized within the modern corporate structure has important implications for the future of capitalism, according to Schumpeter.

He considers the individual entrepreneurs to be the foundation of the bourgeois class. Thus, as entrepreneurial activity becomes primarily a function of corporate administrators, the profit income of entrepreneurs will be replaced by the wages (salaries) of administrators who collectively carry on the process of innovation within the structure of corporations. The success of capitalism in bringing about an automatization of progress at the same time tends to lead to its own breakdown. Though Schumpeter, like Marx, considers that in a mature capitalistic system there will be a tendency for larger, well-organized firms to drive out and absorb smaller and less efficient firms and to bring about the decline of the bourgeois class, his theory of the breakdown of capitalism does not rest upon a growing and increasingly restive reserve army of unemployed labor.

As a capitalistic system matures and the role of the individual entrepreneur with his proprietary interest in his business declines sharply in importance, three groups become primarily involved in the development of corporate enterprises. Schumpeter lists these as the salaried top officials together with the salaried managers and lower managerial personnel, the large stockholders, and the small stockholders. Schumpeter claims that the officials and managers of non-family-owned corporations tend to assume the outlook and attitude of employees and do not identify themselves closely with the interests of the shareholders.[7] Though the large stockholders of corporations may be quite concerned about the success of the firms in which they hold investments, Schumpeter emphasizes that they are not in a position to exercise the kinds of functions which would be their responsibility if they held an individual or family proprietorship position. And finally, he thinks that small stockholders are so far removed from the managerial and operational functions of corporations that they tend to develop a hostile attitude toward the firms in which they have invested and toward big business and the capitalistic system in general.

Developing Indifference Toward the Institutions of Capitalism

Schumpeter considers that the evolution of these attitudes of indifference and hostility will prove fatal to capitalism in the long run. He states the point in colorful language as follows:

> The capitalist process, by substituting a mere parcel of shares for the walls of and the machines in a factory, takes the life out of the idea of property. It loosens the grip that once was so strong—the grip in

---

[7]The increasing tendency toward incentive stock bonuses for top officials of corporations and for profit-sharing and stock-purchase plans for other employees in the period since the publication of Schumpeter's book suggests that he may have overstated this point somewhat. See *Ibid.*, p. 141.

the sense of the legal right and the actual ability to do as one pleases with one's own; the grip also in the sense that the holder of the title loses the will to fight, economically, physically, politically, for "his" factory and his control over it, to die if necessary on its steps. And this evaporation of what we may term the material substance of property— its visible and touchable reality—affects not only the attitude of holders but also that of the workmen and of the public in general. Demater- ialized, defunctionalized and absentee ownership does not impress and call forth moral allegiance as the vital form of property did. Eventually there will be *nobody* left who really cares to stand for it—nobody within and nobody without the precincts of the big concerns.[8]

The Hostility of the Intellectuals

To develop a sufficient degree of hostility against the capitalistic system to cause its breakdown, Schumpeter points out that there must be some groups present in whose interest it is to encourage and organize resent- ment and hostility against the system. In short, there must be leaders of the opposition. And it is just here that he thinks a unique characteristic of capitalism takes on great significance. This is the characteristic, not present under any other economic system, of sponsoring and encouraging an influential group that has a vested interest in social unrest. What group is this? It is not members of the communist, socialist and other radical parties overtly dedicated to the overthrow of the capitalistic system. Rather it is the group which Schumpeter refers to as the intel- lectuals.

Admitting that it is not easy to define the characteristics of the mem- bers of this group, he mentions several factors which help to identify them.

> Intellectuals are in fact people who wield the power of the spoken and the written word, and one of the touches that distinguish them from other people who do the same is the absence of direct responsi- bility for practical affairs. This touch in general accounts for another— the absence of that first-hand knowledge of them which only actual experience can give.[9]

Schumpeter considers it impossible for a capitalistic system to suppress what he refers to as the intellectuals. He makes the point that bourgeois business interests will defend the freedom of the intellectuals, because if that is lost, so too will be the freedom of action enjoyed by private busi- ness under capitalism. In Schumpeter's view, only a non-capitalistic sys- tem such as socialism or fascism which is non-bourgeois oriented will be able to restrain effectively the intellectual group.

---

[8]Ibid., p. 142.
[9]*Ibid.*, p. 147.

What is it that makes the intellectuals such a threat to capitalism? It is their inevitable tendency to be critical, and stingingly critical at that. Thus their criticisms of capitalistic classes and institutions will eventually help to undermine the system, according to Schumpeter. The marked growth in mass media—books, newspapers, radio and television—increases the effectiveness of intellectual criticism and greatly enlarges the audiences of demagogues. Also the marked expansion in higher education as capitalism matures produces more "white collar" workers than can be absorbed into positions consistent with their expectations. There is thus generated a growing group of frustrated and discontented intellectuals who are critical of the system.

Schumpeter says that it is natural that intellectuals should invade labor-union politics in mature capitalistic systems. Because of the gulf between them and the rank and file members, the intellectuals find it necessary to cater to left-wing segments and other militant minorities in order to maintain positions of influence in the movement. The intellectuals thus tend to change significantly the character of capitalistic labor movements.

The sum and substance of the activities of the intellectuals is that

> . . . public policy grows more and more hostile to capitalist interests, eventually so much so as to refuse on principle to take account of the requirements of the capitalist engine and to become a serious impediment to its functioning. The intellectual group's activities have however a relation to anti-capitalist policies that is more direct than what is implied in their share in verbalizing them. Intellectuals rarely enter professional politics and still more rarely conquer responsible office. But they staff political bureaus, write party pamphlets and speeches, act as secretaries and advisers, make the individual politician's newspaper reputation which, though it is not everything, few men can afford to neglect. In doing these things they to some extent impress their mentality on almost everything that is being done.[10]

Growing Antagonism Toward Capitalism

So, for Schumpeter, it is in these somewhat subtle but important ways that the intellectuals, over the course of time, will subvert the capitalistic system. Given the increasingly antagonistic administrative and legalistic climate in which they must operate, Schumpeter believed that

> . . . entrepreneurs and capitalists—in fact the whole stratum that accepts the bourgeois scheme of life—will eventually cease to function. Their standard aims are rapidly becoming unattainable, their efforts futile. The most glamorous of these bourgeois aims, the foundation of an industrial dynasty, has in most countries become unattainable already,

---

[10]*Ibid.*, p. 154.

and even more modest ones are so difficult to attain that they may cease to be thought worth the struggle as the permanence of these conditions is being increasingly realized.[11]

The Changing Character of the Bourgeois Family

In addition to the changes brought about by the growth of large capitalistic corporations which tend to reduce greatly the scope for true entrepreneurial activity and to bring about a routinization of bourgeois thought processes, Schumpeter referred to a sociological change which tends to occur as capitalistic systems mature. This is the tendency for the character of the bourgeois family to change markedly and in a direction antithetical to the preservation of capitalism.

In developing this latter point he described the large bourgeois family characteristic of the earlier stages of capitalism. In the nineteenth century the large town house, and in many cases the country retreat as well, were part of the pattern of bourgeois life. The basic family objective was that of founding a dynasty in the economic rather than in the political sense. The time horizon of the family was thus long run rather than short run. Saving, investment and the building up of the family business for the benefit of future generations was the natural order of family economic life. It is in this phase of the development of capitalism that the interests of the bourgeoisie are consistent with the system's institutions and that this social class is a staunch defender of the system.

As capitalism matures, important changes in the bourgeois family occur, Schumpeter pointed out, and these run counter to the preservation of the system. The possibilities for founding family economic dynasties become greatly reduced as business increasingly becomes organized along the lines of large, impersonal corporations. With this change, parents begin to take a different outlook on children and their role in family life. The tendency toward rationalization of family as well as economic behavior leads to a weighing of the costs and advantages of parenthood. Whereas the balance was automatically considered to rest on the side of large families during the earlier stages of capitalism, in the mature phase the prevailing bourgeois attitude tends to shift markedly in favor of having only a small number of children. With the decline in importance of the family, the romantic and heroic role of the entrepreneur in struggling to build for the long-run future of his progeny becomes increasingly less significant. This further erodes the bourgeois capitalistic mentality as the system matures.

Schumpeter pictured the bourgeoisie as becoming increasingly meek and willing to compromise in the later stages of capitalism. He saw this

---

[11]*Ibid.*, p. 156.

as symptomatic of the growing loss of faith of the bourgeoisie in the system. As he put it:

> Thus the same economic process that undermines the position of the bourgeoisie by decreasing the importance of the functions of entrepreneurs and capitalists, by breaking up protective strata and institutions, by creating an atmosphere of hostility, also decomposes the motor forces of capitalism from within.[12]

Schumpeter's Conclusions on the Transformation of Capitalism

It was Schumpeter's objective to outline the reasons which led to his conclusion that there is inherent in capitalism a tendency toward self-destruction. Or, as he suggested, perhaps *transformation* is a more appropriate term here than *self-destruction*, since in destroying its particular institutional framework, capitalism is at the same time bringing about the conditions for socialism—the system which he thinks will next emerge.

Schumpeter thus reached the same conclusion as Marx in regard to the inevitability of the change from capitalism to socialism, but by quite a different process of reasoning. It is appropriate at this point to consider whether or not Schumpeter's arguments are likely to prove valid with the passage of time. Since he was basing his argument on the long-run tendency of capitalism, and since in this connection he regards a century as being in the short run, only rather general and tentative comments are possible.

Has There Been a Significant Decline in the Vigor of Capitalistic Systems?

It does seem perfectly obvious that capitalism has gone through a significant evolutionary development over the past century. During this period the process of innovation has tended to become primarily the result of organized, group action within the framework of modern corporations rather than of the activities of bold and imaginative individuals. It is also evident that during this period significant changes in the average size and organization of the bourgeois family have occurred. With fewer children, greater reliance on home appliances and less on the employment of outside domestic help, the size of houses has tended to decline; in urban areas, apartment living has greatly increased. But do these changes at the same time represent a serious decline in the vigor of the capitalistic system?

In regard to the decline in relative importance of the individual entrepreneur in the process of innovation, it should be noted that the higher officials of large corporations in which innovational activities have become bureaucratic and routinized through team research and group decision

---

[12]Ibid., p. 162.

making have been found in studies that have been made to work extremely hard and with great dedication to further the economic interests of their firms. Though the payment of bonuses related to profits is quite common for higher echelon personnel in modern corporations, studies suggest that there are other motivations than mere financial rewards which induce top corporate managerial officials to work so diligently in their jobs. Other important inducements include pride of accomplishment and the desire to be associated with a flourishing and successful enterprise.

Though it is true that average bourgeois family size has declined and that it is now more difficult to found a family economic dynasty, this does not appear to have had a seriously inhibiting effect upon the drive of bourgeois businessmen. The desires to improve family conditions through increased consumption, to educate one's children as well as possible, to provide for one's old age, and to leave an estate to be passed on to one's progeny appear still quite strong enough to induce vigorous work efforts in business activity. There would seem to be no reason to think that they will not continue to do so for a long time to come. The "hippie" drop-out and "radical left" protests against the "establishment" of the 1960's have represented such small minority movements that they do not seem to provide grounds for a contrary conclusion.

The reader may take issue with these comments by saying that while they may apply reasonably well to such countries as the United States and West Germany, they do not seem to be applicable to Great Britain in the period since World War II. Britain, under two Labor governments in this period, has socialized several industries, central banking, and the health services. This is perfectly true, but the circumstances there have been somewhat unusual. The impact of the war plus loss of income from the breaking up of the empire made the problem of financing the modernization of some British industries a serious one to solve through private investment alone. Since one of the country-study volumes in this series is devoted to the postwar British economy, it will be left to the reader to draw his own conclusions after reading it concerning the significance of the economic developments in that country for Schumpeter's predictions about the course of capitalism. It should be added here, however, that in spite of the limited socialization that has been carried out in Britain, there is not a great difference between the contemporary British and U. S. economic systems.

Are the Criticisms of the Intellectuals Constructive or Destructive?

Before closing the discussion of Schumpeter's analysis, passing comment should be made concerning his conclusions about the destructive role of what he refers to as the intellectuals. He is correct in pointing out that it is the nature of intellectuals to be critical. The basic question though would seem to be whether their criticisms tend to be directed in a constructive manner primarily at the weaknesses and shortcomings of the system. If they are, the activities of the intellectuals could, over time, tend to strengthen capitalism by stimulating desirable reforms in it. Perhaps much of the intellectual criticism directed to the need for social improvements during the desperate unemployment years of the 1930's and again in the post-World War II period in connection with problems of discrimination, health care and urban blight, when studied in retrospect, will appear to have stimulated economic solutions which helped to strengthen and prolong the life of capitalism.

The Durability of Capitalism

Capitalism in historical perspective has proved to be a durable system in the more highly developed countries in which it has developed. Its durability has stemmed in part from its adaptability to changing problems and circumstances. Though capitalism today in a country such as the United States differs markedly from the *laissez-faire*, pure competition system described by classical economists, which developed with relative purity in England during the period of the industrial revolution, the basic concepts of private property and relative freedom of individual economic initiative remain strongly entrenched. If these institutions can be effectively preserved while modifications in the capitalistic system continue to occur in meeting new problems over the course of time, capitalism in its mixed form may have a long lifetime. On the other hand, if new problems cannot be solved satisfactorily within the institutional framework of private property and individual freedom of economic initiative, then the predictions of Marx and Schumpeter about the ultimate replacement of capitalism by some form of socialism may well come to pass—though not necessarily as a result of the chain of causation which either of them suggested.

The Galbraithian Thesis on the Breakdown of Capitalism

Professor Galbraith, while partly building on points developed by Schumpeter, also has some additional observations of his own about the evolving nature of capitalism.[13] Like Schumpeter, Professor Galbraith believes that the success of the individual entrepreneur has brought about the rise of the large, modern corporations in which entrepreneurial activity has become routinized and bureaucratic. Galbraith, too, believes that the diffusion of stock ownership prevents corporate shareholders

---

[13]For a complete statement of his views, see John Kenneth Galbraith, *The New Industrial State* (Boston: Houghton Mifflin Company, 1967).

from exercising significant decision-making power. Also, bankers and financiers do not have effective control because increasing use by larger corporations of internally generated funds has decreased their dependence upon the credit facilities of the financial sector of the economy. In addition, Professor Galbraith observes that the size and complexity of modern corporations make the top executives little more than figureheads who lend approval to the proposals which have evolved through the work of the various layers of committees. Thus it is the middle-income specialists who man the committees—what Galbraith calls the "technostructure"—that currently perform a major share of the entrepreneurial function in a mature, capitalistic economy such as that of the United States.

The "Technostructure," Planning, and the Breakdown of the Free Market

In these observations, Galbraith is essentially re-emphasizing points previously made by Schumpeter. Galbraith draws an additional conclusion from the shift in the entrepreneurial decision-making function from the individual to the technostructure. He sees in this trend the breaking down of the free market, which is one of the basic institutions of capitalism. This stems in part from the increasing use of planning by modern corporations. The technostructure plans advertising programs to insure its market; it plans production schedules to meet the projected demand; and these plans are made relevant by the ability of firms to control their prices by protecting themselves from price competition. From the Schumpeterian viewpoint, this emphasis upon planning in and of itself does not necessarily mean that it is leading to the breakdown of vigorous competition as Galbraith claims. On the other hand, there are numerous economists who believe that the changing structure of industry in the United States has had serious market implications.

Schumpeter on the Introduction of Innovations

Schumpeter in an earlier classic work pointed out that in a capitalistic economy most successful innovations introduced by entrepreneurs do not come about as a result of spontaneous expressions of demand by consumers but rather as a result of the successful education of consumers by entrepreneurs to want the particular new products or services being introduced on the market.[14] Thus the use of advertising to develop new consumer tastes and to attract consumers to particular products would,

---

[14]For an excellent discussion of the nature of entrepreneurial activity and economic development, see Joseph A. Schumpeter, *The Theory of Economic Development* (Cambridge, Mass.: Harvard University Press, 1949).

in Schumpeter's view, be entirely consistent with entrepreneurial activity appropriate to a free-market economy.

Schumpeter on Innovation and Shifting Monopolistic Positions

Again, Schumpeter considered the fact that numerous firms are able to establish pricing policies in the contemporary capitalistic system of the United States, thus indicating the enjoyment of some degree of monopolistic power, does not necessarily imply that the demise of the competitive market system is at hand or has already occurred. He argued that the attainment of a competitive advantage in the nature of a monopolistic market position is the essence of successful entrepreneurial innovation.[15] In his opinion, in a strong capitalistic system in which there is vigorous entrepreneurial activity producing a steady stream of innovations, monopolistic positions gained would usually not be long lasting, for they would likely soon be encroached upon by still newer innovations which were competitive with them. To illustrate his point, when one cigarette company brings out a new and supposedly improved filter, it may be able to capitalize on it through intensive advertising for a time. The success which it may realize in the form of increased sales is an open invitation to competing firms to develop and introduce different and perhaps even more effective filters. Through intensive advertising, these firms in turn will attempt to increase their sales, and if possible entice customers away from the first firm's brand. And so the process of innovation goes on, Schumpeter thought, resulting in an ever shifting pattern of monopolistic positions brought about by competitive entrepreneurial activity. This dynamic view of monopolistic tendencies does not satisfy economists who are concerned about their impact upon market structures and behavior.

The Significance of Rising Federal Defense and Space Expenditures

Professor Galbraith introduces an interesting and significant point when he brings out the fact that rising defense and space expenditures by the federal government have made a significant number of firms almost entirely dependent upon government orders. Frequently in the case of these firms the government also directly finances their research and developmental expenditures. In spite of the heavy dependence of these firms upon a single buyer, one still finds rather strong competition among the major defense contractors. In short, selling competition is still keen in spite of the oligopolistic nature of their market structure. As yet there does not seem to be any serious likelihood that the government will move

---

[15]For a discussion of this point also, see *Ibid.*

in the direction of undertaking actual manufacturing in order to become its own supplier of major items used in the defense and space programs. Similarly, the fact that total governmental expenditures currently give rise to between one-fifth and one-quarter of all economic activity in the United States does not necessarily imply a drift away from capitalism toward socialism. It could be said to suggest some drift in the direction of fascism, however.[16]

The Adaptability of Capitalism

In concluding the discussion of this chapter it should be emphasized again that capitalism in practice has so far proved to be a very durable system. Perhaps its primary source of strength is its adaptability. Though contemporary capitalistic systems differ markedly in a number of respects from the classical ideal—the *laissez-faire*-competitive system—the differences have developed from the efforts to find solutions to specific problems which would still preserve as much of the *laissez-faire*-competitive spirit of capitalism as possible. That such problems as monopoly tendencies, cyclical instability, and weak labor bargaining positions have been dealt with reasonably effectively in capitalistic systems such as that of the United States is evidence of the flexibility and adaptability of this form of economic system and of the fact that Marx's predictions about the causes for the collapse of capitalism were unduly pessimistic. Though the changes and modifications introduced in the course of solving these problems make it appropriate to refer to the contemporary economy of this country as a mixed-capitalistic system, the fact should be emphasized that the mixed-capitalistic system still embodies only limited governmental intrusions into the operation of the economy and that the driving force of competition is still quite strong.

The Pessimism of Marx, Schumpeter and Galbraith

Though Professor Schumpeter, like Marx, expressed a pessimistic outlook concerning the eventual prospects for capitalism, he did not expect this system to evolve into some form of socialism for many years to come. He did feel that the transformation was inevitable in the long run, however. His argument concerning the destructive impact of the declining importance of the individual entrepreneur and of the increasingly critical attitude of the intellectuals toward this system may yet prove to be valid. On the other hand, if capitalistic systems over the course of time do demonstrate an inevitable tendency to evolve into some form of socialism,

---

[16]For an interesting discussion of the relationship between the government and the industrial system in the United States, see Galbraith, *op. cit.*, pp. 296-342.

it may be for reasons other than those which he suggested, or those more recently discussed by Professor Galbraith.

Another Thesis on the Possible Breakdown of Capitalism

Is it not possible, for example, that some combination of sociological and psychological factors other than those mentioned by Marx, Schumpeter and Galbraith may prove in the long run to pose a greater danger for capitalism? For example, is it not conceivable that as the population of a country grows denser over the course of time, the increasing psychic tensions which result will call forth ever greater governmental control and regulation of human activity, including economic activity, until at some point the economic system passes over the threshold from capitalism to socialism? Should there be any real validity to this thesis, it suggests that the preservation of individual freedom, including economic freedom, may depend upon man's ability to achieve a population balance which will maintain tension levels within reasonable limits.

The Convergence Thesis

In closing this section dealing with the prospects for capitalism, it should be mentioned that just as there are theories which suggest an inevitable tendency for capitalism to evolve into socialism, so there are also theories which suggest that authoritarian socialism will inevitably evolve toward a more liberal system. A synthesis of these theories has led to the convergence thesis, which has received increasing attention in recent years. This thesis holds that both capitalism and authoritarian socialism, as they now exist in various countries, will continue to go through a process of change which will result in a tendency for the two systems to converge or take on increasing similarities characteristic of some intermediate type of economic system.

Socialist Thought: Early History Through the Utopians

6

Introduction

Elements of socialist thought and examples of communism in relatively advanced societies developed both in ancient Greece and in small Jewish communities which existed for a time along the north shore of the Dead Sea and which were destroyed by the Romans shortly after their destruction of Jerusalem in the first century. The communist societies which developed in these early periods emerged either in response to the drive for the attainment of maximum military efficiency, as in the case of the Greek examples, or in response to the spirit of asceticism, as in the case of the Jewish communities of the Essenes.

During the early Christian period, examples of relatively small groups living under rather ascetic conditions are found, but the resulting semi-communal way of life seems to have stemmed more from the reactions of those inspired by their faith in a new creed to their personal and economic persecution by traditional society than by a philosophy of communism. Indeed, as Christianity passed beyond the stage of persecution to wide acceptance in Western Europe, the philosophy of living expressed by religious authorities and teachers was not communistic.[1]

---

[1]The monastic life of monks and nuns has represented over many centuries a type of ascetic communism, but this is in the nature of a minor exception to the general pattern of social organization.

Socialist thought as it developed in the period from roughly the sixteenth century to the time of Marx is best described as utopian in nature. By this is meant that the socialist writers of this period tended for the most part to consider the existing social problems and difficult lot of the masses of the people to be the result of the shortcomings of existing imperfect societies. The individual was thought to be inherently good or at least neutral—neither good nor bad—as he entered the world, and it was believed that the harmful effects of exposure to the existing evils of society resulted in his moral deterioration. To abolish greed, exploitation, crime and other undesirable aspects of the existing way of life, the utopians thought that it was only necessary to reform society by reforming political, social and economic institutions.

The utopian socialists tended to face a more or less common logical dilemma. That is, how can man living in the existing evil conditions of society and already corrupted by it, bring about the reforms needed to establish the perfect society with its harmony of life which they envisaged and to which they aspired? Some of the utopians assumed away the dilemma simply by starting their discussion with a description of their conception of a perfect society and the happy way of life which it would provide for its citizens. Others wrestled with the problem and proposed various political, social and economic reforms which were idealistic but highly improbable of attainment given the firmly entrenched position of existing vested interests. Their approach was moralistic in contrast to that of later scientific socialists who attempted to develop a logical historical basis for their thesis that socialism is the inevitable successor of capitalism.

Socialist Thought and Practice in the Period of Ancient Greece

Though aspects of socialism can be traced to considerably earlier epochs, the Greek period is a convenient one from which to begin a discussion of the historical development of this type of economic system. This stems from the fact that in ancient Greece both well-developed philosophical discussions of communism as well as actual examples of the practice of communism are found.

The Socialist Thought of Plato

On the philosophical side, Plato was the leading Greek proponent of communism. In his famous works, *The Republic* and *The Laws*, he was concerned with the broad question of how to improve the state, which he considered to be in poor condition. He objected to the democratic concept which gave all citizens an equal vote in elections and thought that the democratic process would not place the most capable experts in power but would result in political disorganization and inefficiency. To overcome these problems, Plato advocated placing the responsibilities of government in the hands of experts, known as guardians of the state. This elite group would consist of two sub-groups, the administrators who were to conduct the affairs of the state and the soldiers who were to provide physical protection for the state and its citizens. Plato regarded the responsibilities of the guardians as being of such importance that the members should not only be carefully selected but also should, in effect, be a separate class having no personal possessions or materialistic entanglements. The guardians, as Plato spoke of them, should live under communal conditions, being supported in regard to food and the simple basic necessities of life by the rest of society. By removing the guardians from activities associated with earning a living and the accumulation of personal wealth, Plato considered that they could give their full attention and concern to the special functions entrusted to them by the rest of society.

Though Plato was certainly at least sentimentally attached to the idea of a communal society in which women, children, goods and property would be held in common, scholars differ in regard to the extent to which he advocated the practice of communism. Some interpret his writings as advocating communal living only for the elite guardian group in society, while others see in his works the advocacy of the practice of communism by the society as a whole. Whatever his true intention may have been, Plato remains of interest in the history of the development of socialist thought as an early writer who described at length what he considered to be the advantages of communism. It would be appropriate to classify Plato as a utopian socialist since he tended to view the evils of society as stemming from the existing environment and institutional arrangements rather than from any inherent shortcomings in the nature of man. Further, he failed to show how it would be possible to replace the existing system with the system which he describes.

Aristotle's Criticisms of Plato's Communism

Aristotle was critical of Plato's doctrine of communism on several grounds. For one thing, he considered that Plato was expecting too great a degree of unity for the state. Given the inherent differences among individuals, Aristotle thought it unrealistic to hope for the extent of harmony and unity represented by Plato's ideal state. Aristotle also thought that property held in common would tend to be neglected and not properly maintained. In addition, instead of contributing to harmony among men, common ownership could well prove to be a source of dissension, for those who worked harder than others would tend to be dissatisfied with only an equal share of the pie.

Finally, Aristotle took issue with Plato's environmentalism. Instead of blaming the ills of society on the existing bad social environment as Plato did, Aristotle suggested that this environment might simply be a function of inherent shortcomings in man's nature.

Though a number of other Greek philosophers also had various comments to make on the subject of economic and social systems, space does not permit their inclusion here.

The Practice of Communism in Sparta

Not only is the period of ancient Greece of great interest from the standpoint of the development of philosophical thought concerning communism, but it also provides some unusual cases of communism in practice. Sparta, of course, is the best known example of the use of communism by a Greek state.[2]

Exactly how Sparta's system of communism evolved is not fully known, but major credit for it is often given to Lycurgus. In the idealized accounts, Lycurgus is said to have considered the existing, highly unequal distribution of wealth in Sparta to be grossly unfair and to have been able to convince the people of the state to accept a more equal redistribution of land. In these accounts he is also credited with having been able to change the Spartan's love of luxury to a willingness to live under the demanding conditions associated with efficient mobilization for military operations. Whether Lycurgus was able to bring about such a transformation singlehandedly is open to question, but what does seem clear is that Sparta achieved a uniquely organized way of life in which the individual became disciplined to serve the state to the full in whatever he was called upon to do.

The training and educational programs for the males of Sparta were completely directed toward making them outstanding soldiers. So vigorous was this training and so plain the manner of living of the citizens of the state that the term *Spartan way of life* is currently applied to living in simple and difficult circumstances. It seems reasonable to conclude that both the rigorous military training introduced by the Spartans and the

---

[2]The use of single labels for systems is a useful simplification, but in some cases it does have the disadvantage of obscuring more complex relationships. For example, there were also fascistic elements in the Spartan system, but in selecting a single simple label, it is more meaningful to refer to Sparta as a communistic society.

extent to which they adopted a communal way of life were inspired by the threat of war and the need to prepare for it as effectively as possible. Viewed in this light, Sparta's communism could be considered a result of military pressure rather than of conviction reached through concern for existing economic and social problems.

The communal living of the military class in Sparta was supported by the productive efforts of an exploited serf class whose members were known as helots. The helots were badly treated and intensively exploited. In effect their position was that of slaves. The virtues of the Spartan living of the military class seem less impressive when it is remembered that the economic foundation for this way of life was based upon slave labor.

Other Examples of the Practice of Communism During the Greek Period

Though Sparta represents the most significant example of the practice of communism during the ancient Greek period, some other communities probably resorted to communal living at times when they were seriously threatened with invasion by their enemies. It is known, for example, that on the island of Lipara at least a limited form of communism was used in order to achieve maximum military efficiency during the period when there was a more or less continuing threat of attack from the sea by hostile forces. Later the communistic organization of the economy was relaxed, and this fact suggests that the regimentation of life which this system made possible was acceptable as a short-run emergency expedient, but not on a permanent basis.

On the island of Crete a form of communism similar to Sparta's was followed for a time. In Crete, also, the members of the military class practiced communal living, and in doing so were supported by a large segment of the population which lived essentially in conditions of slavery.

Socialism and the Judeo-Christian Tradition

While clear-cut examples of formal thought concerning communism as well as examples of this system in practice are found in ancient Greece, the Judeo-Christian tradition, which will now be considered briefly, does not provide similarly concrete cases. Though some scholars have suggested that elements of socialist thought are found in Old Testament writings and that communal living was practiced by some of the early Christian groups, the extent of both socialist thought and the practice of communism in the Judeo-Christian tradition seems to have been very limited indeed.

The Teachings of Moses

If the teachings of Moses in the Old Testament are taken as expressions of an acceptable code of behavior for the Jewish people, there is nothing which calls upon the people to adopt some form of socialism. Inherent in the teachings of Moses seems to be an implicit acceptance of the principle of private property. His various injunctions for the proper treatment of the poor are meaningful only within the context of an economic system based upon the principle of private property. For example, his famous "Law of the Corner" calls upon those who harvest their land to leave the corners of the fields unharvested so that the poor might glean these leftover sections of the crop. Had he been an advocate of socialism this law would not have been meaningful, for the land and its crop would have belonged to the state and the grain in this case would presumably have been allocated to individual citizens through the state's distribution system. Moses' teachings in regard to the cancellation of debts after every seventh and fiftieth year also imply the acceptance of a system of private property.

The Teachings of Christ

The New Testament findings are similar to the Old with respect to property. There is nothing to suggest that Christ advocated that the system of private property be replaced by a socialistic system of state ownership. He did condemn greed and the practice of usury, and he also implied that it was difficult for the rich to be highly moral. His teachings on these matters seem to have been in the nature of exhortations to individuals to use their possessions in a moral manner rather than in the nature of a call to socialism, however.

The Teachings of the Early Christian Leaders

As Christianity became the accepted religion, replacing the pagan Roman gods, the teachings of the leaders and interpreters of the new religion did not advocate the adoption of a communal way of life, according to most interpretations of their pronouncements. Though some students of their works have given them a socialistic interpretation, it is generally accepted by scholars that the early leaders of Christianity did not condemn private property *per se*. What they did condemn was greed, a love of wealth, and excessive efforts to accumulate a fortune. Early spokesmen for Christianity such as St. Clement of Alexandria, St. Basil, St. Ambrose and St. Thomas Aquinas were harsh in their denunciation of an attitude of covetousness in regard to property and wealth. But at the same time, they did not say that to be a Christian one had to give all his possessions to the Church or to the poor and adopt a communal pattern of living. Rather it was their objective to emphasize the point that to achieve salvation one could not be overly preoccupied with materialistic matters, but must pay due attention to matters of the soul. For the man of wealth this meant having concern for those who were impoverished. The giving of alms by the rich from their surplus was advocated, but individuals of wealth were not called upon to give to the point of reducing their station in the social and economic structure. This latter point was clearly stated by St. Thomas Aquinas.

Though there appears to be nothing in the Judeo-Christian philosophy which demands the abolition of the institution of private property and the adoption of socialism, nonetheless it has been said that there are several examples of the adoption of socialistic systems in practice within the framework of this tradition. One clear case is that of the Essenes. This interesting Jewish communal society represented a unique offshoot from the mainstream of Jewish life. It is not known how or why this particular social group developed, but a number of interesting aspects of this society are matters of record.

The Settlements of the Essenes

The Essenes developed settlements along the northwestern shore of the Dead Sea, probably beginning as early as 100 B.C. They showed a high degree of ingenuity in the physical construction of their communities. They used a large common eating hall around which were various other structures including buildings for storing supplies and remarkably well-plastered underground cisterns for the storage of water. Since their settlements were in an arid area where the limited rainfall was concentrated in the period of the winter months, it was necessary for them to collect water during this season and store it for use over the long dry period of the year. Ingenious water conduits were built from their villages near the sea up the slopes of the steep hills which rose just behind them to channel to their storage cisterns the water which would rush down the gullies and draws when the rains fell. In looking at the still impressive remains of an Essene settlement at Qumran, one is impressed by the cooperative efforts which must have gone into its development.

The Essene Philosophy and Way of Life

In terms of their philosophy, the Essenes were quite apart from the mainstream of Jewish tradition. They practiced a rather extreme asceticism in an attempt to free the soul from the temptations of the flesh. They ate sparingly and excluded women from their society. This meant that their ranks had to be replaced by the recruitment of new members from the outside.

The ascetic communism of the Essenes was not practiced in monastic isolation from the rest of the world. They continued to follow their individual trades and occupations in various villages and towns in the area, and many of the Essenes lived among other people as well. They did not shut themselves off from the world but rather attempted to resist what they regarded as worldly temptations.

It has been said that the Essenes placed the wages which they earned in a common pool. Since those living in their communities had their meals and living accommodations in common, the members of the sect had very little use for money. The pool of earnings was simply used for the common needs of the community.

The religious philosophy of the Essenes was made known to many outside of their own membership and may have exerted some influence on the development of Christianity. The religious scrolls found a few years ago stored in earthen jars in the caves near what had been the site of the Essene settlement at Qumran were probably placed there for safekeeping at the time of the Roman destruction of Jerusalem in the first century A.D. At the same time, the Essene settlements along the Dead Sea were also destroyed and this seems to have ended the formal existence of this interesting early sect which practiced an ascetic form of communism.

Differences Between the Communism of the Essenes and of Early Christian Groups

While there seems little reason to question the fact that the Essenes followed a religiously motivated form of communism during the period of their existence as a distinct sect, there is good reason to doubt that the early Christian groups at Jerusalem and elsewhere lived under truly communal conditions as has sometimes been claimed. Since the teachings of Christ as revealed in the New Testament did not advocate the abolition of private property and the adoption of a communal way of life according to the interpretation of most biblical scholars, there were thus no doctrinaire pressures on the early Christians to adopt some form of communism. They were, however, admonished to develop a spirit of brotherly love and a sense of Christian concern for their fellow men. This meant that in the face of early persecutions and while they were still small minority groups living in the midst of hostility, the early Christians practiced a spirit of togetherness and mutual support which may at times have resembled communal living. Rather than representing a communistic society, however, it seems more likely that this simply reflected a strong sense of sharing the fruits of private property and private enterprise with the less fortunate members of the same religious faith.

In addition to providing some sense of historical perspective in regard to the development of both formal thought concerning socialism and the nature of the communistic types of economic systems actually adopted in much earlier periods, this discussion has a further purpose. This is to show that neither the earlier thoughts expressed about communism nor the primitive socialistic systems which developed afforded any useful guidance for the operation of socialist economies in modern industrialized societies. The same thing is true of the works of the long line of utopian socialist writers extending from Sir Thomas More in the early sixteenth century to Karl Marx and the development of scientific socialism in the middle of the nineteenth century. The utopians often were perceptive observers of existing social ills, but, as noted previously, they failed to show the practical steps needed to progress from the present state of imperfection to the idealized society which they envisaged. A very small sampling of utopian socialist writers will help to make the point.

Utopian Socialists

Sir Thomas More

One of the best known writers of the utopian genre is Sir Thomas More. He was a successful member of the British Civil Service and eventually rose to the position of Lord Chancellor. That he was a man of unusually high principles is shown by his refusal to appease King Henry VIII when to have done so would have saved his head and continued his successful career. Further evidence of his moral character is found in his famous work, *Utopia*, which was published abroad in Latin in 1516.

More's Criticisms of Economic and Social Conditions

Utopia is divided into two parts. The first describes the unfortunate social and economic conditions in England and other countries at the time. Unemployment was then a serious problem in England and led many men in desperation to resort to stealing to keep themselves and their families from starving. At the same time, the laws against crime were extremely harsh, and theft carried the penalty of death on the gallows. Not only did More object to such severity, but his social conscience was also outraged by the idle nobility who lived lavishly on the exploited labor of their tenants. In addition, he looked upon existing governments as conspiracies of the rich against the rest of society. The social criticisms in part one are not offered directly by More, but are stated as part of a travel story supposedly told to More by a Portuguese adventurer named Raphael Hythloday. In making this mythical character his spokesman, More was doubtless exercising caution in printing what would have been highly explosive thoughts had they come from his own mouth and particularly if they had been published in English rather than in Latin which could be read by so few people at the time. Even with these precautions, publishing his *Utopia* was a rather risky thing for More to do.

More's Utopian Society

In part two of *Utopia*, Raphael Hythloday describes the ideal communistic society in the country of Utopia which he visited. This mythical island had somehow managed to escape the evils of Western European societies described so vividly in part one. In Utopia the institution of private property had been abolished, and the pattern of life was simple. Work was expected of virtually everyone, including women. The size of the work force plus the favorable natural endowment of the island made it possible to limit the work day to six hours, which was still sufficient to provide a comfortable surplus of output. Agriculture was regarded as a virtuous occupation and all citizens were required to acquire skill in this type of work as well as in one other occupation.

Though the high levels of employment and productivity contributed to the surplus of goods produced, so also did the modest pattern of consumption of the Utopians. Clothes were standardized, meals were eaten in common in large public dining rooms, and conspicuous consumption was absent. Though large quantities of gold and silver flowed in as a result of the island's favorable balance of payments, these metals had a stigma of dishonor attached to them in the Utopian society. They were thus used only for such things as chains for slaves and not as ornaments for the citizens, who eschewed all jewelry and individual decorations.

It is interesting to note that slaves were used in Utopia to do the more unpleasant jobs which included such things as the slaughtering of animals; they were not used to support an idle class of citizens. Since virtually all citizens worked, the slaves were merely of marginal economic importance, though doubtless More considered them important contributors to the esthetic life of the Utopian citizens. While it may seem odd that More in attempting to describe an ideal society would include a place for slaves, his purpose probably was to demonstrate a better use for criminals and the flotsam of society than hanging, as was the practice in England at the time.

More did not overlook the population problem that might be expected to develop in such a pleasantly endowed land as Utopia. He dealt with it forthrightly by attributing to the society the practice of sending out colonies to settle on the mainland supposedly lying conveniently nearby. If necessary, these colonies would be imposed upon the indigenous population by force.

In concluding this account of More's *Utopia*, it should be emphasized again that he combined an acute awareness of and concern for the evils and shortcomings of existing society with an account of life in a supposedly ideal communist society, but with no explanation of how it would be possible to get from one to the other. In short, More failed to cope with the transition problem which was also inadequately treated by the long line of utopian socialist writers who followed him. A few additional examples of utopian socialist thought will help to illustrate the point.

Jean Jacques Rousseau's Social Philosophy

Jean Jacques Rousseau, a noted French writer on government of the eighteenth century, was highly critical of the existing economic, social and political conditions which he observed. He regarded the marked inequality in the distribution of wealth and income which provided a limited number of people with luxurious living in a state of idleness while the masses worked long hours, in poor conditions, and for very low wages, as being grossly unfair. In his famous work, *Discourse on the Origin of Inequality*, he painted a dismal picture of conditions at the time. In his opinion, a basic contributor to the prevailing maldistribution of wealth and income was the institution of private property, particularly in regard to land. He felt that land should not be appropriated for the benefit of a small number of land owners, but that it should be available for the benefit of the entire community. In his view, the fall of man from his earlier ideal life of primitive equality began in this manner:

> The first man who, having enclosed a piece of land, took it into his head to say: "This belongs to me," and found people simple enough to believe him, was the true founder of civil society. What crimes, wars, murders, what miseries and horrors would have been spared the human race by him who, snatching out the stakes or filling in the ditch, should have cried to his fellows: "Beware of listening to this imposter; you are lost if you forget that the fruits belong to all and that the earth belongs to none."[3]

Rousseau, like Marx a century later, looked upon the existing legal structure as the means by which the owners of property protected their vested interests against the masses who owned little or nothing. In practice, the legal structure represented the means for preserving the status quo—freezing the existing pattern of land and wealth distribution. Rousseau regarded using the law to ensure the continued enjoyment of the fruits of the land by those who lived in idle luxury to be immoral and unjust.

Also to be found in Rousseau's writings is an anticipation of the concept of class conflict which was developed more fully by Marx. In pointing out the sharp economic and social distinctions between the property-owning and non-property-owning classes, Rousseau was in effect describing the existing basis of class conflict.

As a critic of social evils, Rousseau was obviously a keen observer of

---

[3]Jean Jacques Rousseau, *Discourse on the Origin of Inequality*, as quoted in Alexander Gray, *The Socialist Tradition* (New York: Longmans, Green and Co., 1947), p. 81.

the institutions and mores current in mid-eighteenth century France. But what does he have to offer on the positive side?

In the first part of his *Discourse,* he paints a utopian picture of primitive man living in the forest in isolation with none of the trappings and impediments of modern society. Here man is pictured as being truly free and completely happy. In conditions of such splendid isolation, questions of right and wrong or good and evil do not arise.

As Rousseau views it, man's fall from his blissful state of perfect happiness started when he first began to establish social relationships and to live in particular habitations. The establishment of the family unit was an important step along the path leading to inequality, appropriation and exploitation. As family units began to settle in close proximity to one another, the concept of property and ownership became more clearly defined. Also the opportunity for comparisons of individual qualities and of possessions now presented itself. Here emotions of envy, greed and jealousy began to develop and these helped to stimulate the acquisitive instinct. From this point man's fall was continuous and inevitable.

Having contrasted vividly the evils of existing society with his utopian concept of primitive man living in a state of isolation, Rousseau failed, as do other utopian writers, to show how man can get from his present unhappy condition to the perfect state which he has pictured.

Rousseau has been included here among utopian socialist writers because of his views concerning society and the institution of private property. He believed that the unfortunate aspects of society stemmed from private ownership, and he felt that land and property should be held in common. This establishes him among the socialist writers, and his concept of the ideal living conditions for man provides the utopian flavor to his writings.

Charles Hall's Criticisms of Contemporary Conditions

Charles Hall, an English physician whose long life span covered the period from shortly before the middle of the eighteenth through the second decade of the nineteenth century, was a man of unusual sensitivity to the social problems of the time. He did not confine his practice to the wealthy class, but ministered extensively to the working class as well. In treating the poor, he had a unique opportunity to observe their economic difficulties in England during the earlier stages of the industrial revolution. What he saw disturbed him so much that he was inspired to write a book, which he called *The Effects of Civilization on the People in European States.*

In this book Hall makes the point that the progress of civilization, which has brought with it the development of many new commodities stemming from scientific advances, has not benefited the masses of the people, but only the small upper-class minority which has been in a position to enjoy these developments. Hall further suggests that these advances which contributed to the development of new goods and a more advanced technology have actually had the effect of worsening the condition of the majority of the population.

It is easy to see how the unfortunate situation of the working class during the earlier period of the industrial revolution in England could lead a sensitive person like Hall to this pessimistic conclusion. This was the period when the enclosure movement was flooding the labor markets of the towns and industrial cities with displaced agricultural workers. This situation kept wage rates at pitifully low levels and made it necessary for women and even very young children to take jobs and work extremely long hours—often under highly unsanitary and hazardous conditions. When ministering to working-class families, Hall was able to see the bad conditions under which they were forced to live and the effects of this on their physical well-being.

Hall saw that being forced from the land and the pursuit of agriculture had taken away such security as workers had had and placed them in the impersonal position of industrial laborers. As a result, those with wealth—in effect, the capitalists—were able to force the workers to accept the terms which they established. Hall recognized the exploitative aspects of early capitalism later discussed in great detail by Marx, and he also understood the opposition of interests between the two basic groups which Marx dramatically described under his concept of class conflict.

To correct existing inequities, Hall thought that all land should be turned over to the state to be redistributed to the public at large. To preserve equity, he also favored following a system of periodic land redistribution. In addition, he would prohibit or at least severely restrict the manufacturing of luxury commodities. Hall was thus advocating the return to a simple, healthful agricultural way of life through the mechanism of an initial socialization of all land. That his vision was utopian, he would have been forced to admit, for with all legal and political power so firmly in the hands of the owners of wealth and property as he considered them to be, how could the reforms which he advocated be implemented in practice? Whatever his shortcomings as a reformer may have been, Hall remains an unusually interesting observer and critic of the economic and social problems which were present during the early period of the industrial revolution.

The Environmentalism of William Godwin

Another English writer of interest in the history of utopian thought is William Godwin, whose famous book, *Political Justice*, was published in 1793.[4] Godwin was a staunch environmentalist who thought that man is

---

[4]*Political Justice* is the abbreviated title for this book, the complete title of which is *An Enquiry Concerning Political Justice, and Its Influence on General Virtue and Happiness.*

inherently neither good nor evil, and that his character is entirely shaped by his environment. In looking at existing social conditions he concluded that the political and legal institutions merely served to safeguard the interests of the rich at the expense of the poor who comprised the bulk of the population. Godwin considered the lot of the poor to be so bad in relation to the circumstances of the relatively small group of wealthy persons in whose favor all institutional arrangements were cast, that it was inevitable for the poor to have a highly hostile attitude toward the existing state.

In his opinion of the proper distribution of property, Godwin has a rather novel point of view. He does not call for the assumption of all property rights by the state in traditional socialist fashion, but rather considers that property belongs to those whose need for it is greatest. And just how does one redistribute property according to the test of need? Godwin considers man to be a highly rational animal who in a proper environment could reason out the knotty problem of an equitable property distribution.

To achieve his utopian state of things, Godwin recognized that the behavior pattern of contemporary man would have to be changed. To accomplish this, an improved environment would be required. He cannot show us how to achieve the favorable circumstances needed, however, and with Godwin, as with the other utopian writers, the mechanical problem of transition is left unsolved.

In his view that, ideally, reason should replace the formal constraint of law and that the role of government should be greatly reduced, Godwin also represents a link in the development of anarchist thought. His connection with socialist thought stems from his belief that the existing pattern of wealth and property distribution was highly unjust, and that instead all property should be used in a manner that would contribute to the greatest good of society as a whole. Godwin had great faith in man's intellect and reason, and he was hopeful that through the further development of these attributes of the mind, man would be able to progress toward the utopian state which he envisioned.

Saint-Simon's View of Social and Political Contradictions

Another interesting figure in the history of utopian socialism is the French nobleman, Count Henri-Claude de Rouvroy de Saint-Simon. Saint-Simon's life was both extremely active and highly colorful, and he definitely was not a typical member of the idle aristocracy of his day. As a youth he fought with the American colonists against the British in the Revolutionary War. He was most impressed by the economic and social conditions which he saw in the New World where there was no entrenched aristocracy to exploit the poor and where all men had a reasonable opportunity to realize their potential. Given his attitude concerning the uselessness of the nobility, it is not surprising that he found it easy to give up his aristocratic title at the time of the French Revolution. Though he was imprisoned for a time, he escaped the more violent end that befell so many of the titled class during that period.

In 1802, he published his *Letters from an Inhabitant of Geneva to his Contemporaries*, and this was followed throughout the remainder of his life by a succession of pamphlets and other writings expressing his ideas as they evolved over the course of time. His continuing theme was that the old feudal order based upon the foundation of agriculture had passed its usefulness and was not applicable to the new economic and social conditions which had emerged with the rise of industry. It was Saint-Simon's objective to provide guidelines appropriate to the new stage of economic development.

He felt that Church leaders had got out of touch with reality and were no longer able to provide appropriate spiritual guidance, and that the old aristocracy was quite incapable of providing effective political and economic guidance in the new industrial society which was emerging. Saint-Simon turned, therefore, from the traditional sources of leadership and tried to suggest new and more appropriate sources. He came to the conclusion that spiritual leadership should be entrusted to a group of scholars composed of representatives from such areas as art, biology, mathematics, music, physics and writing, and that political power should be entrusted to a selected group of industrial leaders. He thought that both groups of leaders should be nominated by the public.

Saint-Simon considered idleness an abomination and he believed that all men had an obligation to work so that the common welfare might be maximized. He did not take a strong and unequivocable position on the question of property ownership, and in this respect his writings do not reflect a clear-cut socialist doctrine. Though he was strongly opposed to any idle *rentier* group, he does not seem to have rejected the principle of private property so long as the owners also were hard-working. His position on private property was so mild that Saint-Simon does not fully qualify for classification as a socialist writer. That he has traditionally been so classified stems from the fact that his disciples propounded a much more positive socialist doctrine. Saint-Simon, himself, was a believer in complete equality, but for him it was equality of opportunity rather than socialization of property. While condoning the private ownership of property, he at the same time would require that property and wealth be used for the benefit of society as a whole.

In emphasizing the contradiction represented by the continued existence of a feudalistic government in an era of industrialization in France,

Saint-Simon's thoughts were anticipations of the later more fully developed Marxian dialectic. Saint-Simon was aware that as the mode of production changed, the existing institutional superstructure might come in conflict with and exert a retarding effect upon the new economic development. He recognized that France at the time was faced with the type of contradiction which Marx later formalized in his concept of the conflict between the thesis and the antithesis.

Another tenuous link between Saint-Simon's thought and Marxian doctrine can be recognized. Though Saint-Simon does not speak of a class conflict as does Marx, he does emphasize in his last work that the efforts of society should be directed toward the improvement of the conditions of the most numerous class. There is the implication here that this class, which is the working class, has been exploited in the existing society.

Robert Owen, Reformer and Social Experimenter

Another interesting figure in the utopian socialist tradition is Robert Owen. Since his beliefs and accomplishments have already been discussed in detail in Chapter 2, it will suffice to include only some brief additional observations here. It should be remembered that as long as Owen directed his efforts to the introduction of social reforms within the framework of a capitalistic mill town during the difficult period of the industrial revolution in England, he was eminently successful. This success stemmed in part from the autocratic power which he had to close down the pubs to reduce drinking and drunkenness, but more importantly from his humanitarianism which had the happy side effect of greatly increasing worker productivity in his mills. In introducing better working conditions, shorter hours and higher wages, Owen tapped a productivity reserve in his workers that more than compensated for these expenditures. His efforts to remove young children from the factories and to provide them several years of schooling and healthful development, as well as his policy of providing less arduous working conditions for women proved also to yield favorable economic results. These various reforms were not ones which called for any fundamental change in human nature. Rather they provided an opportunity for men *as they were* to realize more fully their capabilities.

When Owen turned from his reform efforts within the existing economic and social structure to his attempts to establish ideal communistic communities, he was notably less successful. His experiments at New Harmony, Indiana, and elsewhere called for a greater submersion of self-interest in favor of working for the common good than was realizable among the people who joined his socialistic settlements. These idealistic experiments all failed within a relatively short time because of the usual utopian shortcoming. That is, Owen, like the utopians who had preceded him, had found no way to bridge the gap between human nature as it is and as it would have to be for man to live in the state of harmony found in the utopian vision.

It has been possible here to mention only a few of the large number of utopian socialist writers. In spite of their common analytical shortcoming, they are an interesting group. On the positive side, their often telling criticisms of existing economic and social conditions have, over the course of time, directly or indirectly stimulated numerous helpful reforms.

Socialist Thought: Scientific Socialism 7

Marx and Scientific Socialism

In turning at this point from what has been described as utopian socialist thought to what is referred to as scientific socialism, it will be helpful to consider the basic distinction between these two streams of socialism. It was noted in the preceding chapter that the utopian writers were keen critics of prevailing economic and social conditions. Their thinking tended to leap from the level of criticism of existing institutions to the construction of abstract mental images of the ideal state. As mentioned previously, they largely, if not completely, ignored the transitional problem, which became the province of the scientific socialists.

The Nature of Scientific Socialism

Scientific socialists were not only critical observers of contemporary conditions and firm believers in the advantages to be gained from a system of socialism, but in addition, they attempted to discover basic historical processes that would make a progression from capitalism to socialism inevitable. In short, scientific socialists did concern themselves with the transition problem; indeed, they went to great lengths to develop a concept of history which would seem to support their doctrine of the inevitability of socialism. Marx, the first and most outstanding of the scientific socialists, attempted to combine economic, political and sociological factors into a theoretical structure which would make it possible to predict their historical progression. The fact that many of his predictions have not proved accurate with the passage of time merely points to the enormity and complexity of the problem of forecasting the course of social processes.

The Approach Followed by Marx and Engels

Marx and Engels rejected the utopians as being unscientific, and in order to emphasize the important differences between their thinking and that of their socialist predecessors, they adopted the term *communism* rather than *socialism*. This terminological shift is reflected in the opening sentence of *The Communist Manifesto* which rings out with the challenging assertation: "A specter is haunting Europe—the spector of Communism."[1] They considered that their approach, which involved the careful analysis of all relevant data, enabled them to discern the basic laws of historical social development. Marx's analysis resulted in the development of his doctrine of dialectical materialism, or as it is often phrased, his materialistic or economic interpretation of history. His approach was based upon an adaptation of the Hegelian dialectic.

The Hegelian Dialectic

Hegel's writing is rather involved and obtuse and one must become familiar with his special use of language to understand him. His thinking was highly abstract and his analysis was at the level of ideas. As an objective idealist he thought that ideas had a reality of their own, and his philosophical system was concerned with the logical conflicts among ideas. He argued that each idea or abstraction is confronted by its opposite, and from the conflict between the two there emerges a new abstraction which is a synthesis of the original thesis and antithesis. In Hegel's view this dialectical process was leading to the realization of the *absolute* at which point *the idea*, completely free from conflict, would have been realized. For Hegel, the state is the supreme embodiment of the materialization of *the idea*. Thus the concept of state shows an historical evolution toward that form in which there is complete freedom. When the state form which ensures absolute freedom has been realized, the Hegelian dialectical process comes to a halt.

---

[1] Karl Marx and Friedrich Engels, *The Communist Manifesto* (New York: Washington Square Press, 1964), p. 55.

The Culmination of the Hegelian Dialectical Process

Hegel considered the appropriation of property to be man's initial step toward freedom, in contrast to Rousseau who considered this to be the first step in his descent from freedom. Hegel further considered the function of the state to be that of protecting private property, but in the proper context. Thus, the use of law and the state to protect the exercise of selfish passions which resulted in the serious social problems which he observed at the time was improper. His solution to the problem of injustice called for the adoption of an authoritarian state in which an honest and capable administrative bureaucracy would provide social justice. It is interesting that he thought the contemporary Prussian state represented the ideal form in his own period. He thought that history had assigned to the Prussian state the role of spreading the concept of *the idea*, and that when this had been universally received, the antithesis would no longer be present. The dialectical process would thus be brought to a halt.

It must be emphasized that these comments on Hegel in no sense do justice to his system of thought, which is extremely complex and involved. They are merely intended to provide a very general and sketchy outline of some of the basic points which he developed in his schema.

The Impact of Hegelian Thought

Hegel's impact on philosophical and political thought was great. Included among those influenced by him were Georges Sorel, the intellectual leader of the syndicalist movement in France; Benito Mussolini, the leader of Italian fascism; and of course Marx and Engels. Actually the immediate followers of Hegel were divided into two groups. The first of these continued the conservative idealist philosophy of the master while the other developed a more radical materialistic philosophical approach. Feuerbach was the outstanding figure in the latter group, and in his philosophical system the focus was shifted from the realm of the abstract *idea* to *man*. Marx was impressed by this more materialistic approach, but he thought that Feuerbach had not developed it fully since he was dealing with man as an abstraction.

Marx and Engels' Adaptation of the Hegelian Dialectic

In their own adaptation of the Hegelian dialectic, Marx and Engels moved from the level of abstraction to a consideration of the historical process of social development. They started with the premise that production and exchange form the basis of every social system. In their view, what is produced and the mode of production, together with the manner in which the product is exchanged, determine the pattern of distribution and the class structure of the society. They concluded that social changes and political revolutions do not stem from man's growing appreciation of the abstract notion of the principle of social justice. Instead, they are a result of changes which have occurred in the realm of production and exchange, and it is in the economics of any particular period of history that the root causes of social change are to be found, not in the philosophy of the time.

Marx and Engels inverted the idealist concept of history which held that art, the legal structure, literature, and religion determine what men are; and held instead that it is man who determines the nature of the existing legal and political framework. Or expressed in more materialistic terms, it is the mode of production which determines the juridical and political superstructure. As Marx expressed it in *The Poverty of Philosophy:*

> In acquiring new productive forces, men change their mode of production; and in changing their mode of production, in changing the way of earning their living, they change all their social relations. The hand-mill gives you society with the feudal lord; the steam-mill, society with the industrial capitalist.[2]

Engels also summarized Marx's materialistic interpretation of history in the comments which he made at Marx's grave. He stated that Marx

> . . . discovered the law of evolution in human history; he discovered the simple fact, hitherto concealed by an overgrowth of ideology, that mankind must first of all eat and drink, have shelter and clothing, before it can pursue politics, science, religion, art, etc., and that therefore the production of the immediate material means of subsistence and consequently the degree of economic development attained by a given people or during a given epoch, form the foundation upon which the state institutions, the legal conceptions, the art and even the religious ideas of the people concerned have been evolved, and in the light of which these things must therefore be explained, instead of *vice versa* as had hitherto been the case.

The Role of the Mode of Production

Marx used the term *mode of production* frequently in developing his materialistic concept of history. For him the mode of production prevailing at any time was the factor which largely determined the nature of the legal, political, artistic and religious superstructure of the society. It should be understood, however, that he did not mean by the mode of production merely the level of purely physical productive technology

---

[2]Karl Marx, *The Poverty of Philosophy*, Martin Lawrence edition, p. 92.

prevailing in a country at any given time. He meant by the term something much broader, for to Marx the mode of production included not only the level of productive technology, but also the relationship between workers and those who directed them, the processes of exchange, and the pattern of income distribution.

Marx's Concept of the Class Struggle

Another important aspect of Marx's materialistic interpretation of history is his concept of the class struggle. In fact he viewed all history as a series of class struggles. He referred to the conflict which has prevailed in various past epochs between the master and his slaves, the lord and his serfs, the master craftsman and his apprentices and journeymen, and finally, in the age of capitalism, between the capitalists and their workers. The thesis and antithesis of the dialectical process are reflected in these class struggles and developing out of each of them has been a new synthesis which has in time been opposed by its own antithesis.

In the capitalistic system existing in his own age, Marx saw a strong class conflict between the bourgeoisie (capitalists) and the proletariat (workers). He considered this to be the natural result of the development of a mode of production in which the physical means of production (capital) were owned by the capitalists and the human factor of production (labor) was forced to work on terms set by the capitalists themselves. In the development from feudalism to capitalism, Marx saw that the security which workers had had while under the protection of manorial lords had been lost. Under capitalism only the impersonal relationships of the market remained and workers were in a very inferior bargaining position *vis-a-vis* the capitalists. As a result, Marx saw that the capitalists were able to exploit to a great degree the workers whom they employed.

Since Marx's exploitation thesis based upon his labor theory of value has already been discussed critically in Chapter 4, it will not be necessary to consider it in detail here. Suffice it to say that the conflict between workers and capitalists represented part of the antithesis which Marx thought would contribute to the overthrow of the existing thesis— capitalism—and result in the introduction of communism.

Consistent with his concept of dialectical materialism, Marx thought the whole legal, political and social superstructure of capitalism had become inconsistent with the existing mode of production. This superstructure had evolved through the influence and direction of the capitalist class and these institutions were designed to protect the interests of capitalists and preserve the status quo. But the current mode of production had given rise to an irreconcilable class conflict which contained the seeds of destruction of the existing system.

The Culmination of the Marxian Dialectical Process

Marx considered the capitalistic system to be economically unstable. He thought that cyclical fluctuations were inherent in the system and that competition among capitalists would cause these to become increasingly severe over time. This, he reasoned, would result in a growing army of the unemployed which ultimately would rise up, overthrow the existing system, and replace it with what he considered to be its logical successor, communism.

It is interesting to note that just as Hegel had considered the Prussian state of his time to represent the culmination of his dialectical process at the abstract level of ideas, so Marx believed that his own system of dialectical materialism would reach the ultimate stage when communism had replaced capitalism. By eliminating classes and therefore the possibility of class conflict, Marx thought that no antithesis to communism would arise.

Marxian Thought on the Stage of Full Communism

Having developed his supposedly scientific explanation of the course of historical evolution by means of his theory of dialectical materialism, Marx did not then proceed to develop a careful analysis of the functioning of a communistic economy. He merely spoke of the certainty of the coming of communism and implied that it was to be the long-run system of the future. Marx made it sound so automatic that his followers found no reason to question whether such a system in practice might involve highly complex and difficult operational problems. He did suggest cautiously, however, that it might take quite a long time to reach the stage of full communism in which the state will have withered away and his vision of from each according to his ability and to each according to his need will have been realized in practice.

The Utopian Aspects of Marxian Doctrine

While Marx has been classified as a scientific socialist because of his efforts to construct a comprehensive theory that would explain the process of social evolution, he also appears to be somewhat utopian in his conclusions about the final state of socialism. The vision of a classless society in which no antithesis is present and in which the doctrine of from each according to his ability and to each according to his need is gladly accepted by all seems to call for the perfection of man's nature in this world to a degree which, at least from the perspective of this generation, appears highly utopian indeed. In the final analysis, he may prove to have been as much of a utopian as the utopian socialists of whom he was so critical.

Some Aspects of Post-Marxian Thought

The followers of Marx for the most part also concentrated their attention on developing explanations of the inevitability of the breakdown of capitalism or, in the case of the revisionists, on explaining how socialism would replace capitalism through an evolutionary rather than a revolutionary process. Like Marx, they did not attempt to analyze in detail how a socialist system could be made to operate effectively in practice. To appreciate the development of post-Marxian socialist theory, it will be useful to comment briefly on the thinking of some of the outstanding followers of Marx.

Luxemburg's Analysis of Capital Accumulation

Rosa Luxemburg thought that Marx's analysis was incomplete since it had not dealt with the fact, as she saw it, that in a closed capitalistic system no appreciable capital accumulation could occur. Her reasoning was that in a static, circular-flow, closed economy, the surplus value produced would all be consumed by the capitalists. But in a dynamic closed system the situation would be different, she reasoned. In this case, the constant capital portion of the value of total output would go for the replacement of constant capital used up, the variable capital portion would be spent by the workers for their subsistence, but in the case of the surplus value that had been created in the process of production, a problem would arise. Part of the surplus value created would be consumed, and this caused no logical difficulty, but the remainder of surplus value which capitalists wanted to accumulate would be a different matter. To whom could the goods which would give rise to this portion of surplus value be sold? The laboring class could not buy them, for their wages would be used up in buying the variable-capital portion of total output. And if capitalists sold this part of surplus value to each other for consumption purposes, then no capital accumulation would take place.

If it were argued that this portion of surplus value might be capital goods which capitalists exchanged among themselves, this in turn would pose the problem of how the increased supply of goods resulting from the growth in capital goods could be sold when they appeared on the market. Rosa Luxemburg thought that there was no solution to this problem within the framework of a closed capitalistic system. This led her to conclude that the part of surplus value which capitalists wished to use for augmenting the stock of capital goods must be sold to consumers who were not living in a capitalistic system. This meant, in effect, that the goods representing the portion of surplus value to be used for capital accumulation in the capitalistic countries would have to be sold in more primitive markets where capitalism had not yet developed.

This line of argument supported the doctrine of imperialism which held that competition among capitalistic countries to acquire control over non-capitalistic markets would become increasingly severe and would lead to recurring imperialistic wars which would hasten the fall of capitalism.

Rosa Luxemburg's analysis was widely criticized by Marxists. It was pointed out that one serious weakness in her argument stemmed from her assumption that during the process of capital accumulation the income and consumption of the working class would not increase. This assumption was not consistent with Marx's own analysis, for he recognized that periods of capital accumulation would usually result in an increase in variable capital which would be reflected in temporary increases in wages and a rise in the level of living of workers above the subsistence norm. In this situation the workers would be able to buy, at least until wages fell again, that part of the increased output resulting from capital accumulation not bought by capitalists out of the surplus value accruing to them.

Edward Bernstein and Revisionism

Edward Bernstein, who lived from 1850 to 1932, started a trend of socialist thought which became known as revisionism. Bernstein knew Engels well and he was initially a follower of Marxian doctrine. Around the close of the nineteenth century Bernstein began to have second thoughts, however, and he repudiated the Marxian concept of the increasing misery of the proletariat under capitalism and the inevitability of the violent overthrow of the system. He was able at this point to look back on nearly half a century during which the economic position of the working man had improved markedly in the more advanced capitalistic countries. Bernstein also could observe that Marx's thesis of the increasing failure of smaller businesses during the stage of mature capitalism when a growing monopoly trend would be present was not being borne out by actual developments in the business world. Though some very large-scale firms had emerged in certain lines of production, Bernstein was impressed by the multitude of lesser firms throughout the economy which seemed to be operating quite profitably and successfully.

Having concluded that capitalism was not likely to suffer a violent collapse in the relatively near future, as Marx had predicted, Bernstein advanced the thesis that desired reforms should be worked for through the democratic process within the framework of capitalism. In this manner, socialism would eventually emerge as the result of a peaceful evolutionary process rather than through a sudden revolution. Universal education was also to be a factor in what for Bernstein was to be a sensible progression to socialism.

Bernstein in Relation to the Fabian Socialists

Bernstein's doctrine parallels closely the thinking of the Fabian socialists in England who made their concept of socialism quite respectable in that country in the latter part of the nineteenth and the early part of the twentieth century. The views of Bernstein and the Fabians differ, however, in regard to the role of the state. The Fabians wanted the state to assume an ever expanding role in the economy. They consciously sought out things that needed to be done and often initiated them as private undertakings in the expectation that as the importance of the particular function became more widely recognized, the state would finally take it over. Bernstein, on the other hand, was leery of having the state assume an excessive amount of economic and other responsibilities, and he would have it function as a partner rather than as sole owner or operator.

The Split Between the Revisionists and the Orthodox Marxists

Bernstein's revisionism seems in the perspective of time to have been an attempt to make Marxian doctrine more reasonable and realistic in the light of the impressive social and economic progress made under capitalism which Marx had neither anticipated nor taken into account. Coming as it did from one who had been a faithful follower of Marx, it caused quite a sensation among Marxists. Indeed it had the effect of splitting them into two groups, the revisionists who followed Bernstein, and the orthodox Marxists who held tenaciously to the basic Marxian precepts including his theory of the approaching proleterian revolution.

Orthodox Marxists began to attack vigorously the revisionist arguments, including Bernstein's attempt to refute what he considered to be Marx's breakdown theory of capitalism which Bernstein said held that crises would become increasingly severe until finally the capitalistic system would in effect collapse from above. At this point the strength of the proletariat would have grown to such an extent that it would easily be able to take over from the collapsing capitalistic structure and replace it with a communistic system. Actually, Marx's discussion of the breakdown of capitalism is rather vague and contained in scattered references, so that what he had in mind is a matter of conjecture.

Karl Kautsky and the Breakdown Thesis

Many orthodox Marxists tended to accept Bernstein's interpretation of Marx's breakdown thesis but tried to refute Bernstein's counter-arguments. Karl Kautsky was an exception. He held that Marx had not advanced the thesis that under capitalism recurring business crises would become increasingly severe until finally one of such severity would be reached that it would cause the collapse of capitalism and the ushering in of communism. Kautsky's position was that though Marx did consider that the long-run trend of capitalistic economies would be downward, it would not be any one short-run cyclical swing around the downward trend line that would be the ultimate factor in the collapse of capitalism. Also, the increasing strength of the proletariat, which would eventually enable it to rise up and destroy the system from below, would be a more important factor than Bernstein suggested. This is the way that capitalism would fall—not through its collapse from above.

The so-called breakdown thesis was debated from different points of view during the period from 1900 to the outbreak of World War I, and it continued to be discussed in the postwar period as well. But in the meantime an event of decisive importance had occurred. This was the coming to power in Russia in 1917 of the Bolshevik regime, which had an orthodox Marxian orientation.

The Arrival of Communism in Russia
The Problem of Planning

The foregoing discussion of scientific socialism should have made it clear that the kinds of questions on which Marx and his followers concentrated were concerned with the manner in which the transition from capitalism to communism would take place. Notably lacking were discussions of how a socialist system could be made to operate effectively once it had been brought into being. Lenin, as the leader of the new order in Russia, found the absence of detailed guidelines for socialist economic planning to be acutely embarrassing. Having little in socialist economic analysis which could provide the planning guidance needed, the new regime turned to the planning experience of Germany and the United States during World War I for planning ideas. It is said that Lenin's government even attempted to employ Bernard M. Baruch, who had been head of the War Industries Board in the United States during the war, as an adviser on economic planning.[3]

A few people did give some consideration to the problem of how a socialist economy could be made to operate effecticely in practice. One of these was Professor Karl Ballod of the University of Berlin whose book, *Der Zufunftstaat*, published in 1898, dealt with this problem.[4] Professor Ballod's analysis was oriented toward Germany, but Lenin, who was

---

[3]For an interesting discussion of this point, see Harry Schwartz, *An Introduction to the Soviet Economy* (Columbus, Ohio: Charles E. Merrill Publishing Company, 1968), p. 83.

[4]For a brief discussion of Professor Ballod's work, see *Ibid.*, pp. 83-84.

familiar with it, was so impressed by some of his proposals that he adopted them for use in Communist Russia. Given the magnitude of the planning problems faced by the new regime, Ballod's ideas were of only modest help, and most of Russia's problems had to be handled on an *ad hoc* basis for there was no comprehensive set of practical planning procedures available.

Theoretical Aspects of Socialist Planning

The central economic problem which faces a socialist system is that of determining an efficient allocation of resources. This occurs so automatically under capitalism through the mechanism of market forces in the free markets for factors of production and finished goods that the question of how allocative efficiency could be attained under socialism was essentially neglected by both neoclassical and socialist writers until the period after World War I. Two economists who did consider the theoretical aspects of the problem before the attainment of power by the Bolsheviks in Russia were Vilfredo Pareto and Enrico Barone. Pareto, first in 1897 and again in 1910, dealt with the question in his writings.[5] He outlined the nature of the mathematical problem that would be involved in determining an efficient allocation of resources under socialism. He pointed out that even if it is assumed that all of the product demand, resource availability, and production function data for the entire economy were known, which he first of all regards as "an absurd hypothesis," there would still remain the problem of putting all of these data together in a set of simultaneous equations which would have to be solved to get the answers to the resource allocation problem. The number of simultaneous equations would be so large that their solution would be impossible. Thus Pareto emphasized that though a solution to the problem was theoretically possible, it could not be solved satisfactorily in any practical sense.

Barone developed a follow-up to Pareto's approach in an article published in 1908.[6] He pointed out that a new socialist regime could start with data on the prices, salaries, interest, rent, profit, saving, etc., from the preceding capitalistic system—though the problem of gathering such information would be enormous—and try to work from there. Again, though theoretically possible, he did not believe that in practice economic efficiency could be achieved through the process of centralized decision making.

---

[5]Vilfredo Pareto, *Cours d'économie politique*, (Lausanne, Switz.: 1897), II, 364 ff., and *Manuel d'économie politique* (Paris: 1910), pp. 362-64.

[6]Enrico Barone, "Il ministerio della produzione nello stato collettivista," *Giornale degli Economisti*, 1908.

The Delay in Instituting Comprehensive Planning in Russia

As a practical matter, the new regime in Russia found it quite difficult to institute comprehensive planning. Lenin's government began rather modestly by setting long-range goals for electrical and industrial expansion. This was followed in 1921 by the establishment of the State Planning Committee. During the early years of its operations, this planning agency concentrated on developing annual control figures which would be useful in constructing forecasts of the expected development of the economy for the ensuing year. Not until 1928, when the First Five Year Plan was adopted, did the government feel in a position to undertake comprehensive planning for the economy as a whole. From this point on, there has been a succession of formal plans which have carried Russia to its current position of a major economic power.

The question of how efficiently a centrally planned socialist economy could use its resources was naturally raised by neoclassical economists. Some claimed that it would be quite impossible for a communist system like that in Russia to achieve anything approaching the efficiency of resource use found in capitalistic economies. It is interesting to study the arguments used to support this position, particularly those by Professors Ludwig von Mises, Lionel Robbins and F. A. von Hayek, who occupied leading positions among critics of socialistic planning. These will be considered in the next chapter.

Resource Allocation Problems Under Socialism 8

By Professor Dominick Armentano

Early Criticisms

The question of the efficiency with which resources could be allocated in a socialist community was a relatively neglected issue among both classical and Marxian economists before World War I. Though such economists as H. H. Gossen and E. Cannan, in works published in 1854 and 1893 respectively, hinted at the difficulty of rational economic calculation in the absence of the private ownership of the means of production, neither pursued the subject in great detail.[1] A Dutch Professor, N. G. Pierson, investigated the same problem somewhat more carefully in a neglected article first published in 1902, in which he suggested that a communist society would find it impossible to decide the

---

[1]H. H. Gossen, *Entwicklung der Gasetze des Menschlichen Verkehrs und der daraus fliessenden Regeln fur menschliches Handeln* (Braunschweig: 1854), p. 231, and E. Cannan, *A History of the Theories of Production and Distribution* (3rd ed.; London: 1917), p. 395. Both of these works are cited in Frederick A. von Hayek, "The Nature and History of the Problem," in *Collectivist Economic Planning*, ed. F. A. von Hayek (London: George Routledge & Sons, 1935), p. 26.

most economical way of employing material things since value criteria would be nonexistent in the absence of trading or exchange relationships.[2] It was not until the closely reasoned arguments of Professor Ludwig von Mises were presented in an article published in 1920, however, that the crucial issue of economic calculation was finally brought to the forefront in the controversy over the economic practicability of socialism.[3] It is with the writings of Professor von Mises that any serious study of resource allocation under socialism must necessarily begin.

The Criticisms of Professor von Mises

Mises' Theory of Value

To comprehend Mises' remarks concerning the efficiency of resource allocation in a socialist community, it is necessary to review briefly his general theories of economic value and the nature of economic calculation.[4] Economic value, for Mises, is an intensive, subjective response within the mind of man pertaining to the usefulness or utility of economic commodities or factors. More specifically, value is a personal preference that man's mind places on particular units of particular things. Value is not, therefore, something intrinsic within material objects, nor is it something that arises independently within man; it is an individual preference dependent on a subjective estimation of utility. Thus, value for Mises is always relative and always dependent on the thing valued and on the valuer.

Since Mises regards the nature of economic value as being entirely subjective, he holds that different estimations of value by men toward units of goods are to be expected. Further, since men are fundamentally interested in increasing their net utility or value, he deduces that different estimations of value are likely to lead men into exchange relationships with the goods or factors which they possess. Once involved in such exchange relationships, men tend to exchange units of goods or factors which they personally value less for units of goods or factors which they personally value more. For example, if A trades a unit of "x" which he owns to B for a unit of "y", he indicates (at the moment) that he values a unit of "y" more than a unit of "x". Likewise, B indicates that he values a unit of "x" more than a unit of "y". Because the nature of value is subjective, Mises concludes that the exchange of units

---

[2]N. G. Pierson, "The Problem of Value in the Socialist Community," reprinted in *Collectivist Economic Planning*, pp. 41-85.

[3]Ludwig von Mises, "Economic Calculation in the Socialist Commonwealth," reprinted in *Collectivist Economic Planning*, pp. 87-130.

[4]A modern restatement of Mises' theories can be found in his treatise, *Human Action* (rev. ed.; New Haven, Conn.: Yale University Press, 1963), pp. 200-211.

of goods or factors becomes mutually beneficial to each party and each gains value through the trade.

The Problem of Measuring Value

While the values of units of goods or factors can be ranked by order of personal preference, and while subjective utility can be gained or lost through trade, Mises maintains that value itself cannot be cardinally measured. Cardinal measurement always implies a precise standard or unchanging unit of calculation; no such objective standard or unit exists in Mises' subjective theory of valuation. The values that men place on goods or factors can be ranked ordinally, that is, goods or factors can be compared as having more or less value than other goods or factors. Ordinal ranking, in fact, necessarily precedes any exchange of goods or factors between men. But Mises considers objective cardinal measurement of value in terms of finite numbers or units to be impossible, given the subjective nature of economic value itself.

The Problem of Economic Calculation

Since values are not objective and not cardinally measurable for Mises, they do not lend themselves to economic calculation. At this point, economic calculation can be taken to mean the method for determining the priorities of using, combining and allocating the scarce economic factors of production in such fashion that economic efficiency and maximum satisfaction are achieved from their utilization. Economic calculation in the case of factors of production requires, by its very nature, a process of measurement in precise units of the advantages to be gained or the losses to be sustained by the use of physically non-comparable factors in the production of specified commodities. In brief, Mises indicates that it requires cardinal measurement. Since subjective valuation cannot provide a universally comparable base or common denominator, and since such a denominator is necessary before resources can be combined efficiently, Mises concludes that subjective valuation by itself is insufficient for rational economic calculation.

Rational Production in an Exchange-less Economy

Mises does admit that subjective valuation and ordinal ranking might suffice to effectuate a rational production process in a self-sufficient, exchange-less economy. Here a farmer, for instance, might not find it too difficult to "come by a distinction between the expansion of pasture farming and the development of activity in the hunting field."[5] Since the

---

[5]Mises, "Economic Calculation in the Socialist Commonwealth," in *Collectivist Economic Planning*, p. 96.

processes of production in this example are relatively limited, and since the factors of production have few alternative uses and are not exchanged, a direct comparison on an ordinal basis of the gains and losses of specific factors employed in one direction *vis-a-vis* the gains and losses of specific factors employed in the other direction might be possible.

Rational Production in an Exchange Economy

In an exchange economy where the factors of production are diverse and have a multitude of alternative uses, or when the choice lies between "the utilization of a water-course for the manufacture of electricity or the extension of a coal-mine or the drawing up of plans for the better employment of the energies of latent coal,"[6] the problem of rational economic calculation and rational decision making becomes impossible with non-comparable, non-homogeneous ordinal values. As Mises puts it,

> Here the roundabout processes of production are many and each is very lengthy; here the conditions necessary for the success of the enterprises which are to be initiated are diverse, so that one cannot apply mere vague valuations, but requires rather more exact estimates and some judgment of the economic issues actually involved.[7]

His point is that economic calculation in a complex industrial society seems to require an objective, homogeneous standard capable of indicating in precise terms the values of all goods and all factors in all stages of production. For Mises, free-market prices provide such a standard.

The Role Of Objective Exchange Ratios

Free-market prices are the objective exchange ratios established among traded goods or factors; they are the objective consequence of subjective valuation, ranking and exchange. Free-market money prices are the exchange ratios expressed in divisible, measurable units of a universal medium of exchange. Free-market money prices make economic calculation possible because they provide a homogeneous method of comparing the costs of different factor inputs to each other, and to the gains of different outputs. Money prices, therefore, become the economic link between alternative means and ends, and allow—through monetary comparisons of the respective costs of different factors and different factor combinations with the respective revenues or gains from different commodities—the adoption of the most efficient techniques of production for realizing any desired end.

---

[6] *Ibid.*
[7] *Ibid.*

Objective Money Prices and Private Ownership

Objective money prices arise, Mises emphasizes, only where factors and goods are privately owned and exchanged, that is, in the context of a free, private market. Goods or factors not privately owned or exchanged —while possessing subjective value—could have no objective money prices since such prices are exchange ratios, and goods or factors not exchanged could not have exchange ratios. Private ownership is necessary, he believes, since the process of subjective valuation presupposes that men have full control of the services derived from traded commodities or factors.[8] Otherwise, any subsequent "exchange" would be artificial and any consequent "price" would be arbitrary, that is, not fully related to a personal gain or loss of utility. Hence, it is Mises' conclusion that objective money prices are impossible without private ownership and exchange and that economic calculation is impossible without objective money prices.[9]

The Insufficiency of Physical Formulas Alone

Mises rejects the notion that engineering formulas which detail the physical quantities in which resources might be combined to achieve given ends are any substitute for objective money prices and economic calculation.[10] Technical formulas might be enough to solve the problem of efficient resource allocation if factors were specific and had no alternative uses. But factors have alternative uses and may be substituted, more or less easily, in the production of a wide variety of capital and consumer goods. Thus the problem of efficient production is more than purely technical. Since man has a limited number of factors at his disposal and a host of alternative uses for these factors, he is burdened with the additional problem of attempting to decide which possible combination of factors will deliver the greatest amount of net satisfaction, in order that no unit of any factor shall be used to satisfy a need less urgent than the one it is presently satisfying. And the solution of this problem, according to Mises, requires objective money prices.

As an example, Mises suggests that the science of engineering can establish how a bridge might be constructed to span a river at a given point with a specific load stress. But engineering could not answer the question of whether building the bridge might withdraw material factors of production and labor from an alternative employment (road, canal,

---

[8]Mises, *Human Action*, p. 682.
[9]Mises, "Economic Calculation in the Socialist Commonwealth," in *Collectivist Economic Planning*, pp. 92, 98-110.
[10]*Ibid.*, p. 129.

or home building) in which they could be satisfying needs more urgently felt. No purely physical formulas could determine whether the bridge should be built at all, where it should be built, what capacity for bearing burdens it should have, and which of the variety of alternative plans for its construction should be adopted. Only a comparison of the money costs of the diverse factors with the expected money gains to be realized from the bridge could provide a rational solution to the allocation problem. Only money prices make the multitude of technical combinations comparable and allow the determination of the most efficient means—the cheapest—for achieving any specific end.

The Insufficiency of the "Labor Hour"

Mises also rejects the idea that the "labor hour" can be used as an objective calculating device instead of objective money prices.[11] In the first place, valuation in terms of labor time neglects the contribution of land and capital goods. Secondly, valuation in labor hours ignores the fact that "there exists among men varying degrees of capacity and dexterity, which cause the products and services of labor to have varying qualities."[12] Mises concludes that any theory of value which ignores material contributions to production and fails to provide a common denominator to make diverse labor quality comparable cannot possibly lend itself to rational economic calculation.

Mises' Arguments Against Socialism

With the preceding comments on value, prices, and economic calculation as a theoretical background, Mises' arguments concerning the economic rationality of resource allocation in a socialist community can now be developed more formally. Socialism, for Mises, is the public ownership and control of the means of production or, as he puts it, "all the means of production are the property of the community. It is the community alone that can dispose of them and which determines their use in production."[13] The essence of socialism, therefore, is that all land and all capital goods are owned and employed by the community—the state.

Consumer-goods markets are free to the extent that consumers can purchase what they want with their income. Mises does not claim that socialism will necessarily coerce the consumer into purchasing certain commodities, or that socialism will purposely generate an arbitrary amount of commodities that no one cares to purchase. In fact, Mises takes pains

[11]*Ibid.*, pp. 113-116.
[12]*Ibid.*, p. 114.
[13]*Ibid.*, p. 89.

to point out that the state will attempt to produce in accordance with "the systems of exchanges between the commrades";[14] goods in greater demand will have to be produced in greater quantities while those in less demand will have to be reduced in supply. What he does specifically and unequivocally deny, however, is the notion that socialism can accomplish any of its production in an efficient and economical manner.

Mises' reasoning here is deductive and based firmly on his theories of value and economic calculation reviewed above. A brief summary of his arguments will illustrate his thinking. Since, in socialism, the material means of production are exclusively owned and controlled by the state and are never traded or exchanged, there can be no free market for these factors of production. And because these goods or factors are not exchanged in free markets, they will not have exchange ratios or objective money prices. Since these factors are not objectively priced in terms of money, no rational economic calculations concerning them are possible. Without economic calculations, no efficient allocation of these scarce factors can be made. Without an efficient allocation of scarce resources, no "economy" is possible.[15]

An Illustration of Mises' Basic Argument

Mises' reasoning may be illustrated by imagining a socialist director who decides that the state should build a power plant, or who decides that the consumers wish the state to build a power plant. Each alternative method of plant construction would offer certain advantages and disadvantages, and each would require different combinations of diverse factors and different production periods. For example, either atomic or fossil fuel might be utilized as an energy source; either one large generator or a series of smaller ones might be adopted for the generation of electricity. But which *specific* technique of production using which specific factors should rationally be adopted? Since all the material means of production are owned by one agency—the state—and are not exchanged or priced in free markets, and since without objective money prices they cannot be reduced to a common denominator for economic comparison, the socialist director is at a loss to compare the economic advantages to be gained by the utilization of one set of factors *vis-a-vis* another. What he needs to know is whether the adoption of a specific factor mix will increase net well-being without impairing the fulfillment of other ends that might be considered more valuable. What he requires is a method for contrasting the expected costs of the investment with the expected gains. But objective money prices and, consequently, economic

---

[14]*Ibid.*, p. 93.
[15]*Ibid.*, p. 111.

calculation are not available to the director in a socialist state. Hence, in Mises' terminology, he cannot make a rational economic decision. If and when the power plant is built at a particular point with particular resources, it will represent an "arbitrary" and not an economic decision. It will certainly be production—since production is a technical problem— but it will not necessarily be economic production or production carried through in the most efficient manner.

Irrelevancy of Calculations in Equilibrium for Disequilibrium Conditions

Professor Mises discusses other issues associated with resource alloca- tion in a socialist community. He notes, for example, that economic cal- culation ceases to be a problem in the stationary state or in equilibrium. But he considers this fact to be quite irrelevant to the problem of eco- nomic calculation under socialism, since "equilibrium" is an imaginary construct and certainly not obtainable in a real world where economic data change and uncertainty exists.[16] Besides, the transition from capital- ism to socialism is likely to disrupt any link between the previous state of economic affairs and its hypothetical equilibrium position.[17] In a later work, Mises takes the position that information concerning an imaginary state of rest is useless to proper economic decision making in the present since it does not describe how, by successive steps, the given state of economic affairs can be transformed—in the most efficient manner—into the equilibrium sought.[18] Equations describing an equilibrium position in the future can hardly, Mises claims, teach man how to economize scarce resources in the present.

Mises on Initiative and Responsibility Under Socialism

Mises also feels, as did Aristotle centuries earlier, that it is likely that the economic virtues of initiative and responsibility will decline under a system of common ownership of the means of production.[19] He specifically denies the socialist argument that it will make no difference whether managers work for the state or for private corporations and indirectly for stockholders. For Mises, the property relationship makes all the dif- ference in the world. Business managers and entrepreneurs, he claims, are not similar to civil servants, nor are successful private firms operated in the same manner as the civil service. Successful business action involves

---

[16]*Ibid.*, p. 109.
[17]*Ibid.*, p. 110.
[18]Mises, *Human Action*, pp. 710-715.
[19]Mises, "Economic Calculation in the Socialist Commonwealth," in *Collectivist Eco- nomic Planning*, pp. 118-122.

the independence of risk taking and the consequent gain or loss with one's own property; it involves speculation, trading in futures and in the commodity and stock markets and a whole host of other exclusively capitalistic economic activities and institutions that would almost certainly be absent under any system of state socialism.

Pretense of a Competitive Market Will Not Provide Efficiency

Placing former businessmen or commercial school graduates in charge of socialist production would not change the problem of efficiency significantly, since community ownership of the means of production precludes all essential aspects of a truly competitive market system. Mises holds that production and resource allocation would not be efficient where bureaucrats or former businessmen are asked to pretend that there is a competitive market when there is not, or are asked to make believe that they are speculating with and investing their own funds when they are not. Also, any socialistic system which attempted to induce competition by parceling out the ownership and employment of specific factors would cease to be a system of state socialism, and would become instead a form of syndicalism or fascism.[20] Thus, state socialism with economic efficiency remains an impossibility from Mises' viewpoint.

As a final thought, Mises cites the economic confusion in Soviet Russia at the time of his writing, not as a practical demonstration of his comments, but simply to indicate that most of the Russian intellectuals—particularly Lenin—had not even begun to comprehend the fundamental problem of economic calculation in a socialist community.[21]

Other Critics of the Economic Rationality of Socialism

Other neoclassical commentaries concerning resource allocation under socialism followed the Mises article, though none of them broke significant new ground. Sociologist Max Weber, for example, in a work published posthumously in 1921, re-emphasized the contention that socialism made rational economic calculation impossible since it lacked money prices for the means of production.[22] The same charge, raised in the context of actual Soviet planning experiences, was made by Russian economics professor, Boris Brutzkus, in 1922.[23] Interest was again drawn

[20]*Ibid.*, p. 112.

[21]*Ibid.*, pp. 122-128.

[22]Max Weber, *Wirtschaft und Gesellschaft*, (Tubingen: J. C. B. Mohr (P. Siebeck, 1922), pp. 55-56. See also Max Weber, *The Theory of Social and Economic Organization* (New York: The Free Press, 1947), pp. 194, 207.

[23]Boris Brutzkus, "Problems of Social Economy Under Socialism," *Ekonomist*, Winter 1921-22, cited in *Collectivist Economic Planning*, p. 35.

to the same issue a decade later when economists Lionel Robbins, Georg Halm, and Frederick von Hayek published material in which they argued, among other things, that socialism or social planning was incapable of rational, efficient operation. Since these later authors added interesting footnotes to the dialogue concerning the feasibility of achieving economic efficiency under socialism, their comments are examined briefly below.

Professor Robbins on Socialism's Resource Allocation Problem

The interesting aspect of Professor Robbins' comments concerning the efficiency of social planning is his contention that the problem of rational resource allocation cannot be solved by a series of mathematical calculations.[24] Although he admits that the problem can be formulated by a series of mathematical equations, he holds that the fluidity of the data, the time factor, and the number of equations combine to condemn this method as unworkable in actual practice. Robbins concludes by noting that those who suggest the equation method as a practical solution to the problem of social planning, indicate that they do not, in fact, comprehend what the equation method really involves.[25]

Professor Halm on Efficiency Under Liberal Socialism

Professor Halm begins his essay concerning the problem of resource allocation in a socialist community[26] by distinguishing the socialism he will be debating from other types of economic systems. For Halm, socialism implies an economic community within which all capital goods and all land are owned and employed by the state. It also implies an economic system which attempts to preserve consumer choice and occupational freedom;[27] in fact, consumer choice is expected to provide direction for socialist production through a market-like system of consumer-goods price movements. In essence, Halm defines a variety of democratic socialism which is similar in all important respects to the system outlined and debated by Mises in the analysis above.

Before Halm attempts to discuss the problem of efficiency under socialism, he notes that the terms *planning* and *consumer choice*, as used in a socialist context, seem to imply conflicting methods for determining the direction of state production. Planning suggests that consumer and capital goods will be produced in accordance with a social blueprint developed and executed by the state. Consumer choice, on the other hand, implies that commodities will be produced in accordance with the

---

[24]Lionel Robbins, *The Great Depression* (New York: The Macmillan Company, 1934), p. 151.

[25]*Ibid.*

[26]Georg Halm, "Further Considerations on the Possibility of Adequate Calculation in a Socialist Community," in *Collectivist Economic Planning*, pp. 132-200.

[27]*Ibid.*, p. 137.

demands of consumers as indicated by final-goods price movements. For Halm, these two theories are irreconcilable. A socialism which uses planning will eliminate or reduce the scope of consumer choice and any system which adopts full consumer choice must reject planning.[28] Halm holds that any proposal which attempts to integrate both ideas is misconceived and headed for failure.[29]

Though presumably consumers will exercise free choice and attempt to direct production under socialism, Halm maintains that the state will find it impossible to allocate the factors of production so that supply is efficiently and rationally accommodated to consumer demand. It is not enough, he indicates, to suggest that state production will be guided by the price movements of consumer goods; price movements alone are an insufficient guide to rational production.[30] It is the movement of final prices with relation to the costs of production which permits rational economic calculation. It is the monetary comparisons of final-goods prices with intermediate-goods costs which allow the selection of the most efficient techniques of production. Since Halm holds that intermediate-goods prices cannot be discovered in an economic system where all land and capital are nationalized, he concludes that socialism will not be able to operate in a rational and efficient manner.[31]

Professor Halm's argument concerning the inability of socialism to price objectively the factors of production is deeply rooted in the Mises notion that objective factor pricing is impossible without private factor ownership and free, competitive factor markets. Halm claims that capital goods cannot be objectively priced when they are neither bought nor sold; by definition, all capital goods are already in the hands of their intended user, the state. Accordingly, since free, competitive capital and money markets do not exist, the determination of objective capital-goods prices or interest rates becomes impossible. Halm explicitly refuses to admit that the adoption of some fictitious rate of interest by the state will solve the pricing or allocation problem; since new capital goods are produced with the aid of older capital goods, and since all capital goods are owned and controlled by one agency, the costs of the old capital as well as the prices of the new capital must be indeterminate and, hence, arbitrary.[32]

In addition, units of labor cannot be objectively priced because the state will find it extremely difficult to generate a rational demand for factors whose value cannot be measured or separated from the contributions of land and capital goods.[33]

---

[28]*Ibid.*, p. 149.
[29]*Ibid.*, p. 150.
[30]*Ibid.*, pp. 150-151.
[31]*Ibid.*, p. 173.
[32]*Ibid.*, p. 164.
[33]*Ibid.*, p. 168.

In summation, Halm concludes that arbitrary costs of capital, land and labor on the one hand, and monopolistically determined consumer-goods prices on the other, appear to make any sort of rational economic calculation out of the question. Any money differential between price and cost could hardly be used as a guide to rational production since this "profit" might simply be the consequence of arbitrarily low factor costs and not efficiency, or arbitrarily high consumer-goods prices brought about by a decrease in monopolistic supply and not by an increase in effective consumer demand. Hence for Halm, as for Mises, it is the absence of objectively determined factor prices which makes an economic and rational socialism impossible.

Professor Hayek on the Mathematical Approach to Resource Allocation

Professor Hayek's major contribution to the discussion concerning resource allocation under socialism involves his analysis of the so-called mathematical solution, or the idea that a rational allocation of factors can be discovered by solving a set of simultaneous equations. While he notes that such a solution is not "logically contradictory," he would rule out the method as being "humanly impractical and impossible."[34] Just the assembling of the statistical data and the quantification of technical knowledge necessary to formulate the correct equations for such a solution would probably be a "task beyond human capacity."[35] Even if the data were accumulated, thousands of simultaneous equations would have to be reset and resolved for every change in the economic data, and the new solutions continuously fed to a socialist director who would, in turn, attempt to execute them. But all this is "an absurd idea" since these activities "could not be carried out in a lifetime."[36] Hence for Hayek, as for Robbins, the mathematical solution is really no solution at all.

Professor Hayek on Socialism's Use of the Competitive Market

Hayek's other contribution to the controversy is his claim that most serious socialists have recognized the logic of the Mises and Halm criticism and have, therefore, attempted to re-introduce the competitive market into their plans for an efficient socialism. While Hayek considers it pure illusion to believe that a competitive market mechanism can be successfully grafted onto state socialism,[37] his significant comment is to

---

[34]Frederick A. von Hayek, "The Present State of the Debate," in *Collectivist Economic Planning*, p. 207.
[35]*Ibid.*, p. 211.
[36]*Ibid.*, p. 212.
[37]*Ibid.*, p. 237.

point out that any socialist system that adopts competition must, thereby, abandon almost all of its socialistic principles.[38] What would become, Hayek asks, of the supposed superior productivity of state socialism if it is forced to adopt the capitalistic pricing mechanism? What would be left of the argument that the wage system must be abolished under socialism? And what real meaning could be attached to the phrase "social planning" in a system which attempted to use competition to allocate the factors of production efficiently? Thus, Hayek concludes that the socialists appear to relinquish almost their entire platform in their desperate quest for an efficient economic rudder. The only plank of any significance that they might retain is the notion that socialism—since it will abolish rental and interest income—will raise the relative economic position of the working class and, hence, their living conditions. But even this "advantage" depends on the potential productivity of the new hybrid market-socialism, a system which Hayek, as well as Mises and Halm, feels would surely be less efficient than full, free-market capitalism.[39]

As one would imagine, these strongly stated economic arguments against socialism in time stimulated rebuttals from those who believed that a socialist system could achieve efficiency in allocating its resources. Some of these counter-arguments are considered in the next chapter.

---

[38] *Ibid.*, p. 238.
[39] *Ibid.*, pp. 238-243.

Socialist Thought: Liberal and Authoritarian Socialism

9

Reactions to Mises' Arguments

Professor Mises' vigorous attack on socialism was so clearly stated that socialist thinkers could no longer ignore his basic contention that a rational allocation of productive resources would not be possible where capital goods were socially owned. Though, as has been noted, he was not the first to be concerned with the problem of decision making under socialism, he dealt with the question with a directness that amounted in effect to a challenge to the entire concept of socialism. If his central point could not be refuted, a practical case for socialism could not be argued effectively. Thus, once he had published his thesis on the impracticability of socialism, the question could no longer be skirted or lightly brushed aside as being of little relevance.

The Challenge Posed by Mises' Position

The typically Marxian idea that the practical problems of socialism could only be dealt with effectively when this system had actually come into being through the inevitable dialectical process had made it easy for socialists to pay little attention to the practicality question. In the face of Mises' criticisms such a cavalier attitude could no longer be taken. Also, since his systematic attack on socialism began about 1920, when the new communist regime in Russia was struggling to establish itself and to introduce a new socialist order, an added urgency was given to the basic question which he raised. If Mises' claims could not be refuted satisfactorily, then there could be little hope for the long-run success of Russian communism or for the spread of socialist systems to other countries. Mises had, in effect, sounded the call to arms for socialist theoreticians.

Professor Taylor's Solution

The first important step toward answering the Mises-type criticism was made by Professor Fred M. Taylor in his Presidential Address delivered at the 1928 meeting of the American Economic Association.[1] In this address he developed in somewhat more detail the concept of a trial-and-error or shadow-pricing solution to the resource allocation problem under socialism than Barone had done in his much earlier work. Professor Taylor pointed out that the basic problem in a socialist system is the determination of proper values for the primary factors of production. His solution was disarmingly simple. He suggested that a provisional price be assigned to each factor and that the managers of the socialized industries be directed to act as though these provisional prices were accurate and would be continued. There would be a surplus supply of any factor whose provisional price had been set too high and a shortage of any factor assigned too low a price.

Shortages and surpluses of the various productive factors at the end of an accounting period would provide guides to the authorities for revisions in factor prices. Through a process of trial and error, Professor Taylor stated that, over time, appropriate prices for the various factors could be determined. It should be added that he was discussing a liberal socialist system in which consumer demand would give direction to production and in which the prices of commodities would be set by the authorities at levels which would cover their costs of production. The pattern of income distribution would be determined by the state.

Professor Taylor concluded his address by affirming that in his opinion the economic authorities in a socialist state could solve effectively and practically the resource allocation problem.

Problems of Socialism as Viewed by Hayek and Robbins

The simplicity and practicality of Professor Taylor's briefly stated solution to the problem of resource allocation under socialism apparently was not fully understood or appreciated by his professional colleagues.

---

[1]Fred M. Taylor, "The Guidance of Production in a Socialist State," *American Economic Review*, Vol. 19, No. I, March 1929.

For example, Professor Hayek and Professor Robbins, both eminent economists, in works published several years after the appearance of Professor Taylor's trial-and-error solution, directed their critical comments to the type of analysis developed by Pareto and Barone. While accepting the theoretical validity of Barone's proof that accounting prices could be used in place of market prices to achieve a rational resource allocation in a socialist system, Hayek and Robbins concluded that this approach would not provide a practical solution to the problem. Barone had formalized his proof by using a system of simultaneous equations, and Hayek and Robbins pointed out that any attempt to use this technique in an actual socialist economy would be doomed to failure because the number of variables, relationships, and equations would be extremely large and quite unmanageable.

Though their practical objections to Barone's solution had validity, they did not acknowledge the fact that Professor Taylor's solution was much simpler and more readily applicable in actual practice. Using Taylor's approach, a newly-established socialist system would begin initially with the price structure which had last prevailed in the preceding capitalistic system. New prices for individual primary factors of production set on a trial-and-error basis would be introduced over time in response to observed shortages or surpluses of these factors. The prices of consumer goods would be set to cover fully their costs of production, and direction to the production of these goods would be given by consumer demand freely expressed in the market. The pattern of income distribution would reflect in part the social objectives of the system.

Here the number of decisions to be made by the central authorities would be relatively small. No complex and almost infinitely large system of simultaneous equations would have to be constructed and solved. Instead, it would only be necessary for the government to make a limited number of observations concerning the supply-and-demand situation for primary factors and to institute trial-and-error price adjustments based upon these observations. Managers of industries producing consumer goods would react to consumer demand as expressed in the market and follow the imposed convention that the price of any good must be established at a level which would cover the full cost of production. The only other decisions to be centrally made would be concerned with determining the broad social and political objectives of the system. Having determined these, the government of such a socialist system would then have to institute an income distribution pattern consistent with their attainment.

Professor Lange's Case for Socialism

In view of the continuing doubts expressed by Mises and others concerning the ability of a socialist system to achieve in practice an efficient use of its resources, Professor Oscar Lange developed a strong attack on their position in his well-known article, the first part of which was published in the fall of 1936, with the remainder appearing in the winter of 1937.[2] In this article, Professor Lange developed in considerably more detail and somewhat more formally the trial-and-error approach introduced by Professor Taylor.

Lange first gave attention to the argument developed by Mises concerning the impossibility of achieving a rational allocation of resources under socialism. He pointed out that Mises had based his case on the narrow concept of market prices. That is, Mises had said that with no free market for capital goods under socialism, there would be no way to determine relative market prices for them and hence no rational way to determine their appropriate allocation in the various lines of production using them.

Prices as the Terms for Alternatives

In rebutting Mises' contention, Lange used the point made by Wicksteed that prices can be considered either in the market-determined sense or in the broader sense of the terms on which alternatives are available.[3] It is prices in this more general context that are relevant for a socialist system. Barone had appreciated this, but Professor Mises did not acknowledge its validity. Lange indicates that Mises is wrong in contending that only where capital is privately owned and the prices of capital goods are determined by market forces can there be a rational allocation of resources. All that is needed, Lange maintains, is the establishment of the terms on which various capital goods are available. This can be done by administrative decree and does not have to be done by free-market forces. In establishing the relative prices of capital goods under socialism, production functions would have to be taken into account, and Lange points out that the price administrators under socialism would know just as much about these functions as would the executives in capitalistic enterprises.

Lange next turned his attention to the arguments of Hayek and Robbins who, unlike Mises, accepted the theoretical possibility of Barone's approach, but who concluded that it did not provide a practical solution to the resource allocation problem under socialism because of the excessively large number of equations which would have to be formulated and solved. Lange indicated that Hayek and Robbins had missed the

---

[2]See Oscar Lange, "On the Economic Theory of Socialism," *Review of Economic Studies*, Vol. IV, No. 1, October 1936, and No. 2, February 1937. This article is reprinted with some revisions in Oscar Lange and Fred M. Taylor, *On the Economic Theory of Socialism*, ed. Benjamin E. Lippincott (Minneapolis: The University of Minnesota Press, 1938), pp. 57-142.

[3]P. H. Wicksteed, *The Common Sense of Political Economy* (2nd ed.; London: G. Routledge and Sons, Ltd., 1933), p. 28.

significance of Professor Taylor's solution which showed how simply Barone's trial-and-error techniques could be applied in a socialist economy. Lange then proceeded in his article to develop the concept of the trial-and-error approach in detail. It is not possible to reproduce Lange's analysis in full here, but it will be useful to note a few of his basic points.

Market Prices as Parameters Under Capitalism

Lange points out that in a capitalistic system prices are established as a result of the collective actions of all individuals in the system, yet each person in viewing the market accepts the existing market prices as given and bases his market behavior on them. Under capitalism, then, market prices at any time are parameters to which individuals react. Through a succession of reactions over time—that is, through a succession of trials and errors—an equilibrium set of parameters (prices) is approached. This is the process of successive *tâtonnements* described by Walras.[4]

Accounting Prices Under Liberal Socialism

Having shown how equilibrium conditions are approached through a process of successive approximation under capitalism with market prices serving as parameters, Lange then turned his attention to the allocation problem in a liberal socialist system. His liberal socialist system is characterized by a free labor market and a free market for consumer goods. Consumer preferences as expressed in the market give direction to production and to resource allocation. So far, these are the same conditions which exist under capitalism. The difference between the two systems stems from the fact that capital goods are owned by the state in Lange's liberal socialist model, so there is no free market for them. The prices of capital goods in this case are set by the state and are thus accounting prices rather than free-market determined ones.

Rules for Managerial Decision Making Under Socialism

Consumers in spending their incomes confront prices of consumer goods which they view as given or fixed, and they allocate their incomes among these goods in the manner which will maximize their satisfactions. In reacting to consumer demand, firms do not follow the profit-maximizing criterion of capitalism, but instead must conform to certain conventions established by the central authorities. For example, production managers under liberal socialism must follow the principle of minimizing average cost in deciding in what proportions to combine the various factors of production. This simply means that managers are required to combine

---

[4]Léon Walras, *Elements d' économie politique pure* (Paris: 1926 ed.).

the factors of production in such fashion that the marginal physical product of each factor divided by the marginal outlay for it is the same. This convention provides a solution to the problem of determining the factor mix, but there remains the problem of determining the scale of output. Here Lange introduces a second convention which directs managers both of plants and industries to push output to the point at which marginal cost equals price or average revenue.

As Lange points out, this second convention when applied at the individual plant level is the liberal socialist counterpart of the efforts of individual firms to maximize profits under capitalism. When applied at the industry level, it provides guidance for the expansion or contraction of industries as a counterpart to the free entry and exit of firms in industries under capitalism. Or, expressed in slightly different terms, this second convention tells both plant and industry managers how to adjust their scales of output. The second convention must be followed, Lange says, even if average costs are not covered in individual plants or in an industry as a whole. The appearance of "profits" or "losses" would indicate the need for expansion or contraction in various lines of production.

Accounting Prices as Parameters Under Liberal Socialism

To make it possible to follow these two conventions successfully, the managers must confront given prices of both the products which they produce and the factors of production. Under Lange's liberal socialist assumptions, the prices of consumer goods and of labor are determined in free markets while the prices of all capital goods would be fixed on a trial-and-error basis by the central authorities. This means that prices could perform the same parametric function in Lange's model as they do under capitalism. For them to do so effectively, it would be necessary for the managers of plants and industries to make their current decisions on the basis of the existing prices established by the central authorities. Managers would simply be required to follow this further convention also.

Lange points out that the necessary conditions for progress toward an equilibrium position have now been established. Wherever the prices set by the central authorities were too low, there would be physical shortages of the capital goods or resources concerned, and where the prices were set too high, there would be surplus supplies. On the basis of the shortages and surpluses noted at the end of the accounting period, a revised set of prices would be established by the central authorities, and so the system could progress toward equilibrium through this trial-and-error process. In starting with the historically given prices of a preceding capitalistic system, Lange says a newly instituted socialist system should not find this trial-and-error process difficult to follow. It could work even more effectively under socialism than it does under capitalism, he thinks, because the central authorities would have a broader view of the economy than the individual business firms under capitalism. Lange adds optimistically that this might mean the trial-and-error path to equilibrium would be shorter under liberal socialism than under capitalism where the process of decision making is more diffused.

The Distribution of the Social Dividend

Two further points which would have to be taken into account in a liberal socialist system are mentioned by Lange. The first is concerned with the distribution of the social dividend. He emphasizes that, given the free labor market assumed for this system, it is important that the social dividend be distributed in neutral fashion in relation to occupational decisions. That is, the technique chosen for the distribution of this dividend must be one that will not exert any impact on the choice of occupations made by those in the labor market. If this policy were not followed, the payment of the social dividend would interfere with the attainment of objective equilibrium conditions.

The Rate of Capital Accumulation

A second fact which Lange considers is that the rate of capital accumulation would be determined arbitrarily by the central authorities. This is an infringement on consumer sovereignty, but one that is consistent with the objectives of a socialist system, Lange emphasizes. His presumption is that the central authorities would choose a higher rate of capital accumulation and hence a higher growth rate for the economy than would be realized in a capitalistic system where these rates are in large part the collective result of the savings decisions of the public.

Lange's Case for Authoritarian Socialism

Having developed his case for use of the process of successive approximation to achieve efficiency in the allocation of resources under a liberal socialist system characterized by a free labor market and a free market for consumer goods, Lange next turns to the question of whether or not the same approach could be used successfully in a system of full or authoritarian socialism. In this latter form of socialism, allocation of resources is determined by the objectives of the central authorities rather than by consumer preference, and there is not freedom of occupational choice. In this most extreme case, the central authorities would determine the types and quantities of goods to be produced, the basis for the distribution of consumer goods to the public through rationing, and the assignment of individuals to jobs.

Here, too, Lange concludes that it would be possible to achieve a rational use of resources; only in this case it would be within the context of the preference scale established by the central authorities rather than the preference scales expressed by consumers and those seeking employment. All prices would now be accounting prices set by the central authorities. As under liberal socialism, individual plants and industries would be required to follow the convention of combining the factors of production in the proportions which would minimize their average costs. Similarly, each would be required to expand production to the point at which the accounting price set for its product would be equal to its marginal cost.

As under liberal socialism, prices would be viewed as parameters, and the central authorities would have to adjust them through trial and error as necessary to achieve equality between the quantity demanded and supplied of each commodity. Again, where prices were set too low, shortages would develop during the accounting period, and where they were set too high, surpluses would result. The appearance of shortages and surpluses would provide guidance to the central authorities in revising the accounting prices which they would establish for the next accounting period.

Lange's Preference for Liberal Socialism

Lange makes it clear that in demonstrating the possibility of achieving economic efficiency in a system of authoritarian socialism in which there is neither a free labor market nor a free market for consumer goods, he is not expressing personal approval of such a system. As a socialist, he prefers freedom of consumption and occupation in a socialist system. He further makes the point that even under the communist regime in Russia, the early experiments with distributing consumer goods very largely by rationing were abandoned as the supply of these goods increased beyond the initial, virtually subsistence level of output. He also observes that there has always been a considerable degree of freedom of occupation under Russian communism.

The Need for an Interest Rate Under Socialism

Under both liberal and authoritarian socialism the central authorities would have to set the interest rate at which investment funds would be available to firms and industries. This rate would have the effect of allocating investment funds where they could be most effectively used, which would be in those firms and industries which could cover all of their costs, including interest charges out of the receipts from the sale of their products. Without an interest charge for investment funds, or something approximating this, it would be impossible in a socialist system to determine whether an increase in the output of electricity should be accomplished by means of a hydroelectric, a fossil-fuel or an atomic reactor system. Each would involve different amounts of initial capital investment and different operating costs for the same volume of electrical output. Without an interest charge to indicate the relative scarcity of capital, the full cost of producing electricity by each method could not be estimated and a rational investment decision could not be made.

In this connection it should be noted that the communist regime in Russia in following Marx's criticisms of the concept of interest under capitalism tried to operate without an interest charge for funds for capital investment. It became evident that this made it impossible to arrive at rational investment decisions and a substitute for the rate of interest referred to as the coefficient of relative effectiveness of capital was used. More recently, this subterfuge is being abandoned in favor of a more direct application of a rate of interest itself as an instrument for the attainment of rational resource allocation.

In the models of liberal and authoritarian socialism discussed by Lange, a trial-and-error setting of the interest rate by the central authorities would have to be followed in order to equate the total demand for investment funds with the quantity of such funds that the authorities have decided to make available in attempting to realize the rate of investment which they have set as a goal for the economy. If the rate were set too low, the demand for investment funds would exceed the supply which had been set by the authorities; if it were set too high, a relative deficiency in the demand for investment funds would result.

From this rather sketchy outline of the arguments which Lange developed in support of his thesis that an effective theoretical case can be made for the attainment of economic efficiency in the allocation of resources in both liberal and authoritarian socialist models through the relatively simple process of trial-and-error price setting by the central authorities, it becomes evident that he has developed a strong rebuttal to the criticism of Mises, Hayek, Robbins and others who followed their line of reasoning. In working toward equilibrium, the central authorities would not have to contend with an impossibly large system of simultaneous equations. Also, by using a trial-and-error interest rate, he argues that an economic allocation of capital goods could be realized even though they were publicly owned.

Other Arguments Concerning Socialism and Capitalism

Lange's arguments were so strong that they effected a radical shift in the nature of the discussion concerning the relative advantages and disadvantages of capitalism and socialism. No longer did attention focus on the elemental question of whether or not socialism was an economically feasible system from a theoretical point of view. Now the discussion turned to questions of how the two systems would compare in

practical operation. This greatly widened the area of discussion and introduced political, sociological and other considerations in addition to purely
economic ones. Space does not permit a review of the many arguments
which have been raised in debating the merits of capitalism versus socialism, but a few of them will be noted briefly.

The Pattern of Income Distribution

Lange expressed the view that the distribution of income in a manner
that will maximize social welfare can only be realized in a socialist
system.[5] He bases his claim on the grounds that in systems characterized
by private ownership of capital goods, the distribution of income is a
function of the distribution of the ownership of such goods. The ownership distribution of capital goods, in turn, he considers to be a result of
historical development which is not necessarily related to the maximiz-
ing of social welfare. As he views it, the development of capitalism has
concentrated the ownership of capital in the hands of a relatively small
proportion of the population while the vast majority of the people have
only their labor power to offer in the market. The income allocation
stemming from these circumstances, he says, results in a situation in
which some members of the population are starving while others are
enjoying great luxury.

Lange contends that in a socialist system in which the distribution of
income is based on the assumption that everyone has an identical marginal
utility of income curve, a more equitable distribution would result than
in a capitalist system in which the distribution pattern is heavily biased
in favor of the owners of capital. Socialists further claim that the unearned incomes in the form of interest, rent and profits on financial
investments under capitalism would not exist under socialism.

At first glance, the income distribution argument of the socialists seems
rather dramatic and impressive, particularly when they contrast the
expensive antics of the economically idle jet set with the human misery
encountered in the slums of Harlem as well as in the slums of other large
urban communities and some rural areas. On more careful analysis, however, their case loses much of its force. First of all, it should be remembered that there are significant differences in individual ability, and that
great ability is in relatively scarce supply. Also, human nature being
what it still is, people who are more fortunately endowed with ability
and who are able to make relatively greater contributions to society are
not willing to provide their services for the same rewards that are
extended to their less gifted fellow citizens. Though human nature may
eventually evolve to the point at which this will no longer be true, it is

---

[5]*On the Economic Theory of Socialism*, pp. 99-103.

now and will undoubtedly continue to be for a very long time to come a fact of life which must be taken into account by any type of economic system. Indeed, all existing socialist systems do recognize it, for they all have significant wage and salary differentials based upon skill and ability. The basic question, then, is whether or not the unequal income distribution pattern under socialism is likely to be both more equitable and more significant in its contribution to economic growth and development than that under capitalism. This is far too complex a question to be settled here, but a few relevant points will be mentioned briefly.

Equality of Opportunity

Given the factor of differences in natural ability, which is not related to family income levels, it is highly important that a society offer true equality of opportunity for education and personal development if it is to capitalize in optimal fashion on its human resources. This is a matter which is well recognized in contemporary capitalistic and socialistic states alike. There would seem to be no inherent theoretical reason why one system could provide any greater equality of opportunity than the other.

It is sometimes claimed that attendance at the more exclusive private preparatory schools and colleges and universities in capitalistic countries confers a competitive advantage not directly related to ability. The old school tie is said to provide an easier entree to the business and financial world. Though there is an element of truth in such assertions, this factor is becoming increasingly less significant since public higher education is attaining relatively more importance in the advanced capitalistic countries. It may also be pointed out that a socialist country like Russia is not immune from a degree of inequality of opportunity. The children of upper echelon officials enjoy significant differential advantages in regard to education and to employment opportunities.

If there is no inherent reason why a capitalistic system cannot provide essentially as much equality of opportunity for education and the development of labor skills as a socialistic one, can it also provide similarly favorable employment and income opportunities for its citizens after their education and training have been completed? Here again the answer would seem to be yes. In a competitive capitalistic system, individuals should be able to capitalize effectively upon their ability and the effort which they are willing to exert. No longer in highly developed capitalistic countries can it be claimed that labor is at a marked disadvantage in bargaining with employers; for the growth of strong unions has done much to equalize the bargaining strength of the two groups. As a result, wages today tend to be reasonably reflective of worker productivity in these countries.

Socialist writers sometimes point to the high salaries of top business executives in advanced capitalistic countries as evidence of excessive income differentials. Here, too, it can be argued that competition for outstanding executives has helped to establish their economic rewards. Were the supply of such talent greater, the differentials would certainly be smaller. As a corollary, socialists claim that such executives would work just as hard for less money and that the difference could be diverted to the advancement of the general social welfare. Though there may well be an element of truth in this, it should also be remembered that given the highly progressive income tax structure in most advanced capitalistic countries, the real income differential may be substantially less than the nominal one.

As part of their general inequality argument as applied to capitalistic systems, socialist critics have stated that inequality of income distribution based upon the private ownership of capital prevents equality of opportunity in the establishment of new business firms. It is quite true that the capital requirements for entry into some large-scale lines of production such as the steel and automobile industries make it extremely difficult for new firms to enter them, even given the corporate form of organization which makes it possible to tap the investment funds of large numbers of individuals and institutions. This does not mean that, in general, it is necessarily extremely difficult for those with ability to establish new enterprises under capitalism. In the United States, for example, special assistance is made available by the government to help small businessmen get started and continue successfully in business. The Small Business Administration is an agency which is concerned with these matters.

Rentier Incomes

Socialist writers emphasize the fact that incomes in the form of economic rent, interest and dividends from the ownership of corporate shares would not be present under socialism. The absence of such unearned income would make for a more equitable income distribution, it is argued, and by keeping such income in the hands of the state, a higher level of social services could be provided. It is true that eliminating *rentier* incomes would provide the state with funds which could be used for other purposes including social services. At the same time, it is worth noting that the share of national income accruing in the form of *rentier* incomes in an advanced capitalistic country like the United States has declined noticeably over the past forty years. In addition, a significant part of rent, interest and dividend receipts is probably being used for retirement living, medical expenses and other social services which would have to be provided by the state under socialism.

Social Services and Social Welfare

It also is said by socialist writers that the more equal income distribution of socialism would make possible a much higher level of social services for the public as a whole. Socialized health services would give all citizens equal access to medical and dental care regardless of family income; free public education at all levels would provide equality of educational opportunity for all; and comprehensive programs of social welfare would provide income for workers during periods of sickness and disability and for older people in retirement. Finally, programs of public construction would provide reasonable standards of comfort in housing for all. In short, socialists claim that through reducing income inequality and eliminating *rentier* incomes, more equal opportunities and a higher degree of social security will be provided for all citizens than will be the case under capitalism.

In evaluating these socialist arguments, it should be noted that the more mature capitalistic economies have given increasing attention to the matter of general social welfare. In the United States, for example, there is a highly developed system of public education through the university level. Extensive financial assistance and loan programs currently make it possible for virtually all who qualify academically to acquire a college education. An extensive system of social security provides unemployment, disability, retirement and survivorship benefits. The recent Medicare program helps to relieve the financial burden of serious illness in old age. Other social programs include those for slum clearance, low-rental housing construction for poorer families, urban renewal projects, and a number of programs directed toward the relief of poverty. Though this is by no means an exhaustive listing, it does indicate that concern for social welfare has also developed under mature capitalism.

As a final comment on the matter of the distribution of income under socialism and capitalism, it should be noted that the trend toward highly progressive income taxes and high inheritance taxes in some capitalistic countries has considerably reduced the extent of income inequality.

Social Costs

Lange, who supports the foregoing socialist arguments, also states that under a socialist system a much broader range of factors would be taken into account in the establishment of prices. He distinguishes here between capitalism in which only the cost of the capital, labor and materials used by business firms enter into cost calculations, and socialism in which the social costs of production would also be taken into account in the price determination process. Among the social costs which he feels are not taken into account by individual firms under capitalism are the provision for workers who are discharged during periods of cutbacks in output, and the care of workers who have been disabled by occupational diseases or accidents while on the job. Though Lange does not refer to them, it would also be appropriate to include the social costs of production in the form of air and water pollution, and noise and traffic nuisances caused by industrial production. With a little imagination the reader can add to the list.

These social costs of production, Lange says, are not taken into account in the determination of market prices under capitalism but would be given full consideration in the economic accounting of a socialist system. He is simply making the claim here that what remain as uncompensated social overhead costs under capitalism would be included in the accounting of prime costs under socialism. As a result, he feels that socialism would eliminate most of the social waste associated with the operation of private enterprises under capitalism.

How valid is this claim? It seems reasonable to say that most of these social costs of production either already have been, or could be taken into account effectively under capitalism. In the case of workers who are discharged by firms during periods of declining demand for their products, there is now the protection of unemployment compensation programs. Lange was writing on this while the mass unemployment of the 1930's depression was still a serious problem and when programs of unemployment compensation had not become well developed in the United States. The protection provided unemployed workers in this country is much better at the present time, and employers are required to contribute to the funds available for the payment of unemployment compensation. To the extent that they do so, there is a transfer of this social cost under capitalism to the prime costs of individual firms.

It should not be concluded from the foregoing discussion that there are no social costs of unemployment in the United States at the present time. Unemployment compensation payments cover only a portion of the wage received by the worker while he was employed and they normally are extended for only a limited number of weeks. The unemployed worker thus still suffers an income loss and this could be considered as an uncompensated social cost under capitalism. To the extent that capitalistic systems can manage to operate at or near full-employment levels of output over time, this social cost can be kept to a minimum.

A related social cost associated with unemployment under capitalism stems from the process of automation. The technological unemployment which results from the spread of automation can be overcome, at least in part, by job-retraining programs. Some individual firms in the United States have introduced retraining programs and governmental programs have also been established. So far, only somewhat limited results have been realized, and more remains to be done in this area of unemployment in the future.

Much has been done in the United States in the way of adopting legislation to protect workers from occupational diseases and the risk of industrial accidents. Occupational disease can no longer be considered a serious problem in this country and this social cost is now relatively insignificant. Industrial accidents do still occur with some frequency in spite of the protective measures taken by firms voluntarily as well as under the pressure of legislation. Though the accident insurance protection which workers have in the United States provides helpful benefits, such insurance does not solve the problem entirely by any means. An uncompensated social cost remains in this area.

The large social costs in the United States in the form of air and water pollution are just beginning to receive major attention. The critical nature of these problems is such that they will almost certainly be pursued more rigorously in the future. Already pressure is being put on individual firms to take remedial action where they are contributing excessively to air or water pollution. It seems likely that these social costs will increasingly be converted to prime costs of production for the firms concerned.

Though Lange admits that the waste represented by social costs can be overcome in capitalistic systems, he claims that this would be done much more thoroughly under socialism. Given the growing concern for such costs in mature capitalistic economies, the differences between the two systems in this matter may be considerably less important than Lange believed would be the case.

The Rate of Capital Accumulation

The rate of capital accumulation under both socialism and capitalism is considered by Lange. He admits that the rate of capital accumulation under socialism would be arbitrary since it would be decided by the central authorities and would not therefore represent consumer preferences. He recognizes that this infringement upon consumer sovereignty would represent a reduction in social welfare, but he feels that the overall advantages of socialism outweigh this shortcoming. In addition, he makes the point that under capitalism the public's desired rate of saving at a full-employment level of income may be frustrated if the rate of investment is too low to support this level of income, and savings and investment are equated at some lower income position. To the extent that capitalistic systems can use monetary and fiscal policies effectively to maintain full or nearly full-employment income levels over time, Lange's argument loses force.

Bureaucracy and Managerial Efficiency

Lange was also concerned with the argument against socialism which held that the management of production by public officials would be less efficient than the private management of production under capitalism. In fact he regarded the possibility of an excessive bureaucratization of the economy under socialism as the most serious danger inherent in this system. He glosses over this point rather too quickly in suggesting that a similar or even greater danger would prevail under mature capitalism. On balance he concludes that socialist officials who, as he puts it, would be subject to democratic control would be more desirable than private corporate executives ". . . who practically are responsible to nobody."[6]

Lange is basing his criticism of corporate executives under capitalism on the assumption that competition is severely limited and that monopolistic conditions prevail. While the argument might have some validity in these circumstances, it does not seem to be highly significant in the case of the contemporary capitalistic system in the United States. Though most of the U. S. economy is characterized by monopolistically and oligopolistically competitive industries, this does not mean that competition within each particular industry is absent. The extent of competition among the firms in the automobile industry is a case in point. Bureaucratic managerial inefficiency may well be held within reasonable limits where such competition prevails. Though illustrations of Lange's point can be found—perhaps some of the industries in England may have lagged behind because of bureaucratic managerial problems—it does not seem reasonable to conclude that such managerial inefficiency is an inevitable accompaniment of capitalism.

On the other hand, it is difficult to see how a bureaucratization of management can be avoided under socialism. The socialist plant manager is not a free agent who can react immediately to changing market conditions. He must operate within constraints imposed by the management of his industry, and the industry managers must take their guidance from the central planning authorities. There is thus a hierarchical managerial structure which tends to make the process of economic adjustment under socialism a somewhat slow and cumbrous one. That this is a serious problem for socialist economies can be seen from the pressures in Russia to reduce bureaucratic inefficiency. The Liberman proposals were designed in part to achieve a closer orientation of individual firms with market conditions and to reduce their dependence upon directives from above.

In a system of liberal socialism, the problem of managerial bureaucracy would be less serious than under full authoritarian socialism, but here, too, a certain amount of bureaucratic inefficiency would still be present.

---

[6]Lange and Taylor, *op. cit.*, p. 110.

The Introduction of Innovations

In Lange's comparison of capitalism and socialism his most important point is concerned with the question of whether or not the continuation of capitalistic systems in the future will be consistent with economic progress. Like Marx, he gives capitalism credit for having brought great progress in the past, but he questions whether the private enterprise system will continue to provide such progress in the future. He bases his skepticism on the argument that as the size of firms becomes too large in a number of industries for easy entry of new firms, the existing firms in those industries will try to hold back on the introduction of innovations until existing capital has been amortized. Of course, if the expected cost saving of the innovation is great enough to offset or more than offset the loss of value that its introduction would impose upon already invested capital, Lange recognizes that the innovation would be adopted. He thinks, however, that in a mature capitalistic system there would be an extensive withholding of innovations and that the result would be a marked slowing down of the rate of economic growth. In his opinion, this stage had already been reached at the time when he was writing these articles, which was in 1936 and 1937.

It is perhaps not surprising that Lange would have been impressed by the problem of economic growth under capitalism in this period, for the United States was still recovering from the depression of the 1930's. In fact, Lange considered depressions in capitalistic countries to be a result of the impact of innovations, when they could no longer be withheld, upon the values of existing investments. The efforts to preserve existing values which would retard economic development in alternation with the sharp fall in these values when widespread innovations could no longer be resisted, represented for Lange a basic source of instability in capitalistic systems. Lange seems further to have accepted the stagnation thesis, for he took the position that a shortage of profitable investment opportunities would develop in mature capitalistic systems. Writing in the context of the 1930's depression, it is easy to see why Lange was so pessimistic in his evaluation of the prospects for capitalism. Since he could see no practical solution to the problems of serious instability and stagnation under capitalism, he concluded that socialism represented the only effective alternative.

In evaluating Lange's conclusion, it can be said that he tended to overgeneralize from the extremely bad conditions of the 1930's depression. For one thing, he appears to have underestimated the extent of competition among firms in monopolistically and oligopolistically competitive industries. Though there is undoubtedly concern among such firms in regard to the timing of the introduction of new innovations, it seems clear that there is not the massive tendency among them to withhold investments which Lange describes. The growth rate achieved by the United States in the period since World War II, and particularly during the more recent decade of the 1960's, could not have been realized if Lange's contention had been applicable over this period. In short, the experience of the postwar period indicates that the problem of growth with reasonable stability can be handled effectively within the framework of an adaptable mixed-capitalistic system.

Scientific Research

In addition to the points which Lange offered in support of his contention that socialism is a more effective economic system than capitalism, other arguments have also been introduced. It has been said, for example, that the scientific research required for continued technological progress has become so expensive that it cannot be adequately financed by the individual firms in a private enterprise system. It is claimed that only under socialism can such research be adequately coordinated and financed.[7] The remarkable growth of research in private industry and in educational institutions in the United States since World War II strongly suggests that research constraints have not yet become a serious problem in this country. The marked increases in governmental funds made available for research have helped to counter any tendency for limitations on private financing to retard the pace of research in the private sector.

Sweezy has stated that governmental financing in capitalistic systems is only likely to be helpful in financing the large-scale research projects which are directly related to military needs.[8] The great proliferation of research not closely connected with military requirements which is financed through government contracts in the United States suggests that Sweezy did not foresee the extent to which the supporting role of government in peacetime research would develop in this country.

Advertising and Salesmanship

Sweezy has also been critical of the economic waste involved in advertising and salesmanship under capitalism.[9] He regards the expenditures directed by firms to induce consumers to buy their products to be a waste of resources. Though certainly not all advertising is defensible under capitalism, much of it is, nonetheless, directly involved in the competitive process of matching goods to consumer tastes. Firms with products which do not appeal to consumers cannot long survive in spite of advertising efforts.

---

[7]This point is made by Sweezy, for example, in *Socialism* (New York: McGraw-Hill Book Company, 1949), pp. 212-213.

[8]*Ibid.*, p. 213.

[9]*Ibid.*, p. 214.

It is also significant that Russia has more recently begun to appreciate the role which advertising can play in promoting a more effective satisfaction of consumer wants by firms in the consumer goods industries. The limited encouragement now given to consumer goods advertising by Russia's economic planners seems likely to expand over the course of time.

Individual Freedom

The points considered so far are illustrative but by no means exhaustive of those which have been raised in discussions concerned with economic comparisons of socialism and capitalism. In addition to the purely economic points so far described, there is one mixed economic and non-economic consideration which is widely raised in discussions of these two systems. This is the question of relative individual freedom under capitalism and socialism. Since this is a very broad question, and since our main concern is with the essentially economic aspects of systems, no attempt will be made to deal with it in detail here. Some brief comments may be useful, however, in indicating the nature of the arguments that have been developed on the subject of freedom as related to the two systems of capitalism and socialism.

Hayek and other critics of socialism have pointed out that though socialist systems wish to promote the common good, they cannot do so since the central planners will inevitably impose their scale of values and preferences on society in formulating and implementing their economic plans.[10] In addition to deciding what consumer goods will be produced and in what quantities, the planners in full authoritarian socialist systems will correspondingly have to decide where and how long individual workers will work, it is claimed.

The socialist rebuttal holds that central planners can effectively direct production in line with free consumer demand. It is stated that if the planners have good data concerning population, total consumer income and the pattern of income distribution, and the typical expenditure pattern of consumers in each income grouping, they will be able to determine with reasonable accuracy the demand for and proper production levels of the various consumer goods to be produced. Though this may seem to be a simple process, in practice it is likely to be quite difficult to carry out smoothly. The problems which Russia has experienced in gearing the output of consumer goods to match the public's demand is a case in point.

In regard to criticisms concerning restrictions on freedom of choice of occupation under socialism, proponents of this system contend that this

---

[10]F. A. Hayek, *The Road to Serfdom* (Chicago: University of Chicago Press, 1944), pp. 42-43.

would not be a serious problem. They point out that planning only indicates the number of persons needed in each occupation, and considerable leeway could be given to individual occupational choices within the global employment requirements. At present, however, there appears to be significantly less occupational freedom in the socialist economies than in the capitalistic ones.

The argument concerning relative freedom under capitalism and socialism has also included the matter of such basic civil liberties as freedom of assembly, freedom of speech, freedom of the press, freedom from arbitrary arrest, and other freedoms of this type. Some critics of socialism have said that if the economic life of the individual is to be controlled, it will be necessary to limit all of his freedoms as well.[11] This argument is sometimes extended to include the point that it is fundamental to socialism that personal freedoms be restricted in order to achieve the social benefits of the system.

Against these arguments, socialist writers have replied that there is nothing in socialism or communism that makes it inevitable that personal freedoms must always be limited or curtailed. While admitting that these freedoms have been severely restricted under Russian communism, they reject the contention that this one experience justifies the generalization to all communist or socialist systems. Supporters of socialism add in this connection that capitalistic systems have not yet extended full personal freedom to all citizens. They cite the plight of Negroes, Puerto Ricans and other minority groups whose constitutionally guaranteed freedoms have been seriously infringed upon in a country like the United States. Socialists ask whether the generalization should be drawn from this that personal freedom can never be experienced by all citizens under capitalism.

This socialist counter-argument misses the point that a democratic capitalistic country tends to start from a higher plateau of personal freedom than does a socialist system which from the outset inevitably involves a higher degree of centralized control. A capitalistic system would seem to have a considerably shorter distance to go to achieve personal freedom for all. The growing concern for the rights of minority groups in the United States is evidence of the desire in this country to correct past abuses.

It is also true that Russia has shown some liberalization tendencies in the period since Stalin. The gap in personal freedoms between such countries as Russia and the United States is still so great, however, that one may well ask whether any real convergence between the two countries in this area is likely unless there is a marked change in the nature of the economic system in one or the other, or both.

In attempting to defend socialism against charges of restrictions on

---

[11]For example, see Hayek, *op. cit.*, p. 68.

freedom, socialist writers also point out that freedom under capitalism really has significant meaning only for those who have adequate jobs and incomes. Those who are unemployed and impoverished, though they may have freedom in a civil sense, do not have the freedom to live decent, self-respecting lives. These writers further claim that a socialist system with its greater concern for the general welfare would not have an economically downtrodden class of "have nots."

It is true that the problem of pockets of poverty is a difficult one for capitalistic countries. In the United States with its exceptional prosperity of the 1960's, there has still been a major poverty problem to overcome in urban slums, in the Appalachian region, in parts of the rural South, and among migrant farm workers in the West. The great concern of the American people for this problem gives reason to believe that major progress toward its solution will be made in the years ahead. Had it not been for the financial drain imposed upon the country by the war in Viet Nam, significantly greater progress might already have been made.

Differences in Ability

In the light of present concern over the impoverished groups in the United States, the socialists' claim that capitalism by its nature will inevitably result in a society characterized by those who have benefited by the system and those who have been exploited by it tends to lose force. An increasing trend toward equality of opportunity seems evident in the United States. With perfect equality of opportunity, however, there would still be marked differences in economic accomplishment reflecting differences in individual abilities and goals. The most that could be hoped for under any economic system would seem to be reasonable equality of opportunity and a system of income distribution which will provide all citizens with at least a decent level of living. Theoretically both would seem to be attainable within the framework of capitalism. The negative income tax that has been proposed in the United States would be one means of modifying the income distribution pattern in favor of the most impoverished segment of society.

Imperialism

Sweezy, as well as a number of other socialist writers, speaks of the monopolistic and imperialistic stage of capitalism.[12] In his opinion, this stage began in the latter part of the nineteenth century, and it has developed at a faster pace in the present century. Basically, the shift as he sees it has been from conditions of competition and relative freedom of trade to monopolistic conditions and imperialism; and this later stage of capitalism has been characterized by violence and major wars.

---

[12]Sweezy, *op. cit.*, pp. 259-262.

He accepts Hilferding's comment that in this later stage of capitalism the bourgeois class loses its peaceful and humanitarian outlook and becomes highly nationalistic.

Though certainly the twentieth century has seen savage warfare among major powers, it has, nonetheless, brought an end to the policy of colonialism on the part of the capitalistic countries. Sweezy's comments on this subject which are referred to here were made before the post-World War II breakup of the British, French and Dutch colonial empires. Indeed, at the present time, policies of colonialism or quasi-colonialism seem more evident among the communist countries as these seek actively to extend their spheres of influence and control.

Socialism as a Secular Outlet for Religious Fervor

Professor David Wright pointed out an advantage which socialism may have over capitalism, but he hastened to add that this is likely to be only a temporary phenomenon.[13] His point is that socialism may initially serve as a secular outlet for the religious fervor of those who are not attracted to existing formal religions. In an era of weakening faith in religious traditionalism, socialism may represent for many an attractive alternative for the expression of their faith. This appeal which socialism may have is likely to be only a temporary and transitory manifestation, Wright thought, for the excitement and idealistic fervor which may be present during the establishment of a new socialistic state will be likely to be replaced by boredom and the realization that changing from a position as an administrator or worker in a capitalistic business firm to a similar position in a state-owned enterprise does not represent such a significant change after all.

A few additional comments are necessary in bringing this lengthy discussion of the theoretical case for socialism to a close. The Lange and Taylor analysis which has been described in some detail in this chapter develops a strong set of arguments in support of the thesis that a socialist system can achieve economic efficiency in the use of its resources. Others, such as Professor Abba Lerner, have elaborated upon various aspects of the socialist model.[14] There are, however, still some theoretical problems and questions other than those already mentioned which have not yet been fully answered.

The Problem of Equilibrium Under Socialism

In using a system of centrally imposed shadow prices as parameters, are the basic functional relationships in the economy such that at any

---

[13]See David McCord Wright, *Capitalism* (New York: McGraw-Hill Book Company, 1951), pp. 236-238.

[14]Abba Lerner, *Economics of Control* (New York: The Macmillan Company, 1944).

point in time only one determinate equilibrium position will exist toward which the economy will progress through use of the process of successive approximation? Or may not the basic functional relationships in the system define several possible equilibrium solutions rather than a single one? If there is no unique solution, serious problems would be posed for socialist models in which little scope is left for the exercise of economic direction through free markets for consumer goods and for labor. The more centralized the decision-making process, the greater is likely to be the problem of attaining consistency and of progressing toward an optional equilibrium position.

The Determination of the Social Welfare Function

Another theoretical problem which must be solved in the socialist model is the determination of the social welfare function. On what bases should the rate of capital accumulation, the rate of aggregate current consumption including the provision of social services, and the pattern of income distribution be decided? The more centrally directed the system, the more arbitrary in some senses these decisions become. What assumptions are appropriate for use in making social welfare decisions by the central authorities? These are difficult questions to answer, and yet rational answers must be found if socialism's case is to be convincing.

Though a few additional problems have also been raised more recently in connection with the theoretical case for socialism, space does not permit consideration of them here.[15]

Concluding Comments

In concluding this review of the theoretical case for socialism, it should be emphasized that the various points and arguments presented are by no means exhaustive. An attempt has been made to select the more important ones, but even in presenting these, it has been necessary to discuss them in summary form. A later chapter will develop an empirical analysis of the growth rates achieved by a selected group of countries having different economic systems. There it can be seen how certain socialist economies have fared in practice.

Socialist thoughts concerning various problems faced by mature capitalistic systems were summarized briefly in the latter part of the current chapter. The comments made in connection with the socialist criticisms of capitalism suggest that there is no inherent theoretical reason why a mature capitalistic system cannot solve satisfactorily the variety of problems which it faces. Whether in practice these problems will be solved

---

[15]For a more complete listing and discussion of these problems, see Benjamin N. Ward, *The Socialist Economy* (New York: Random House, Inc., 1967).

sufficiently well to insure the successful continuation of this type of system indefinitely into the future can only be determined over the course of time.

From this discussion of socialism and socialist criticisms of capitalism, we turn now to a consideration of corporatism, which includes that form of capitalism known as authoritarian capitalism, or fascism.

Corporatism and Fascism   **10**

The Nature of Corporatism

Corporatism is a rather broad concept which refers to those economic, social and political systems which emphasize organization on the basis of occupation. The principle of private ownership of productive capital is an inherent aspect of corporatism, but it is distinguished from capitalism in its traditional form by the stress placed upon cooperation and mutuality of interests between employers and employees. At one time or another, corporatism has been associated with religious movements, with capitalistic attempts to reduce the spread of socialism, and with highly nationalistic movements. There is thus no one unique set of forces which can be said to give rise to corporatism, but, instead, there are several different sets of stimuli which have contributed to corporatist movements in the past.

Corporatism Prior to World War I

An interesting expression of the philosophy of corporatism occurred in the early nineteenth century in Western Europe.[1] The impact of the

---

[1] For an excellent discussion of the historical development of corporatist thought, see Eugene O. Golob, *The "Isms": A History and Evaluation* (New York: Harper & Row, Publishers, 1954), pp. 541-598.

French Revolution and the Napoleonic wars upon the established social and political structure was viewed with alarm by those conservative religious elements in society that regarded such movements as attempts to overthrow the supposedly divinely inspired order which had previously prevailed. Romantic political thinkers in both France and Germany began to advance the thought that man could only find a way of life consistent with Christian principles within a society which was oriented toward the established Catholic Church. These thoughts were put forth in opposition to the concepts of rationalism and individualism which had contributed to the overthrow of existing orders.

Romantic Political Thought

Such thinkers as Johann Fichte and Friedrich Schlegel rejected the notion of individualism on the grounds that it promoted disruptive influences in society such as excessive greed and ambition. To them, proper social harmony could only be achieved within the framework of strong and well-organized states. The idea that the state must foster a structuring of society which would be conducive to Christian morality led to the conclusion that the organization of society on the basis of occupational groupings was the proper approach. Their objective was to achieve the social harmony of the medieval period within the framework of nineteenth-century capitalism. The system of corporatism sponsored by strong national states seemed to them to be the best approach.

Fichte, for example, held that the state should be the supervisor of a host of contracts between producers and workers. The state would also be responsible for assigning markets and for the fixing of prices in various lines of production. To provide further assurance of internal economic harmony and stability, he would have foreign trade carried on only by the government and not by private enterprise.

These early nineteenth-century corporatist thinkers had little influence. Their objective of returning to the social order which had existed prior to the Revolution did not appeal to the masses, and their advocacy of a modern elaboration of the guild system did not lead to any substantial accomplishments along these lines. In short, the early romantic efforts to introduce corporatism in the immediate post-Napoleonic period, linked as they were with the notion of restoring the pre-Revolutionary hierarchical structure, were marked by failure as far as practical accomplishments were concerned.

The Shift from a Political to an Economic and Social Emphasis

Having failed in its early objective of turning back the political clock to the kind of political structure which had existed prior to the French

Revolution, the spirit of corporatism was next manifested in efforts to provide better economic and social conditions for workers within the framework of the capitalistic system. Here, too, an important driving force came through religious groups which viewed with concern the unfavorable position of workers, particularly in England, during the first half of the nineteenth century. Efforts to encourage workers to organize and to establish cooperatives in order to improve their condition were not limited to any one denomination. In England, encouragement was given by Protestant groups, while in France, as would be expected, such efforts were Catholic inspired.

The Social Catholic Movement

During the latter half of the nineteenth century, the improving economic position of workers in England made it less necessary for religious groups to concern themselves with social welfare problems, but in France and Germany the Social Catholic movement became an important force in working for corporatist objectives. This movement was strongly religiously oriented, and its adherents were concerned about the poor condition of workers which virtually precluded their being able to live in decent circumstances and to provide a favorable Christian home life for their families. The proper solution, they thought, was for workers and employers to join together in organizations designed to encourage better understanding and greater cooperation between the two groups. They stressed the mutuality of interests of workers and employers, and it was thought that through the development of confederations of such employer-employee organizations, substantial progress could be made in improving the lot of workers.

For such improvement to occur, workers would have to recognize and accept their obligation to work honestly and conscientiously. Employers, in turn, would have to recognize their responsibility to provide their workers with decent working conditions and with a fair wage which would enable them to live with their families in simple comfort. The Social Catholic movement, in short, was attempting to introduce the concepts of the older guild system to the system of industrial capitalism. The form of corporatism proposed was limited to the economic structure only, and did not include the objective of reinstituting the political structure of the pre-French Revolution period as advocated by the earlier romantic political thinkers.

The Philosophy of Social Catholicism

The corporatism advocated by the Social Catholics was an economic doctrine which occupied a position between the extremes of Marxism and classical capitalism. In contrast to the Marxian concepts of class conflict and the ultimate proletarian revolution, Social Catholicism emphasized the basic harmony of interest between employers and employees, and through confederations of employer-employee unions, the members of this movement held that effective pressures for social improvement could be realized.

Social Catholics also rejected the concept of classical capitalism because they thought that its doctrine of unbridled competition would result in poor conditions for the working class since its members would be in a weak bargaining position relative to their employers. In conditions such as these the Social Catholics considered that the Christian social harmony which they advocated could not be realized. They did not anticipate the improved relative competitive position which workers would in time achieve in capitalistic systems not characterized by strong corporatist elements.

The philosophy of the movement of Social Catholicism which developed in France and Germany in the latter half of the nineteenth century was incorporated near the end of the century in Pope Leo XIII's encyclical, *Rerum Novarum*. The economic doctrine expressed in this encyclical is that of an enlightened and humane capitalism. The Catholic Church reaffirmed its doctrine of economic corporatism when Pope Pius XI restated the philosophy of *Rerum Novarum* in his encyclical, *Quadrigesimo Anno*, issued in 1931.

Though Protestant groups also worked for improvements in the economic and social conditions of workers during the latter part of the nineteenth and first half of the twentieth century, their efforts were less well organized and their corporatist approach less formalized than was the case with Social Catholicism.

Assessing Catholic and Protestant Corporatist Efforts

It is difficult to assess the accomplishments of Catholic and Protestant corporatist efforts in the period since 1850, for they have not resulted in sudden dramatic changes in economic conditions and institutions. Certainly it can be said that they have contributed to the development of social consciousness and concern in capitalistic countries. In this context, they have undoubtedly made an important contribution. It is important to recognize, however, that they did not give rise to the twentieth century political fascist movements which developed in Italy and Germany. These fascist regimes developed corporatist systems more from political expediency than from religious and social conviction. In addition, the corporatism which they sponsored was introduced primarily as a means of strengthening the political power of the state rather than of improving the economic and social conditions of the working class. Under the

fascist form of corporatism it is the state which assumes the responsibility for promoting economic and social harmony. To achieve this, the
state must see that employers and employees are organized along lines
which emphasize class cooperation rather than class conflict. Such
cooperation is necessary for the realization of the nationalistic objectives
of fascist states.

Corporatism in the Post-World War I Period

Corporatism in its most flagrantly fascist form developed after World
War I, first in Italy and then in Germany. Since German national socialism is treated in detail in the volume in this series contributed by Professor Knauerhase, Italy will be used here to illustrate briefly some of
the basic elements of fascism.

Fascism in Italy

Italy was economically a relatively poor country when it became involved in World War I, and the effort which it was forced to make to
confine the fighting to its northern provinces left the economy seriously
weakened when the war ended. The production, trade, communications,
and financial sectors of the economy were badly disrupted, and inflation
and unemployment had reached serious proportions. When the sociological, political and psychological strains caused by the war are considered in conjunction with the economic dislocations which had resulted,
it is easy to understand why the masses of the people were in a recep-
tive mood for a system which would improve their lot.

The Growth of Radical Movements in Italy Following World War I

It was in this disturbed political and economic situation that communist
and socialist movements began to gain significant strength in the period
immediately following the end of hostilities. By 1920, the socialist-led
General Confederation of Labor had a membership of some 2,300,000,
while the Christian-Democratic Italian Confederation of Workers num-
bered only about 1,800,000. In addition, the Italian Syndicalist Union,
led by revolutionary syndicalists and anarchists, and the Italian Union
of Labor, controlled by nationalistically oriented socialists and syndicalists, had memberships of some 500,000 and 200,000 respectively.[2]

---

[2]Estimates made by Gaetano Salvemini in his *Under the Axe of Fascism* (New York: The
Viking Press, Inc., 1936).

Italian Fascism and the "Red Peril"

Strikes and lockouts were frequent during this period, and a succession of weak governments proved unable to furnish the leadership needed to restore more settled conditions in agriculture and industry. The strikes, violence and activities of radical political groups in the early postwar period caused many outside Italy to conclude that Italian fascism developed in opposition to communist and socialist movements and saved Italy from the "Red Peril." This line of thought was encouraged by the Fascists to justify their usurpation of power; but both Volpe, the official historian of Italian fascism, and Mussolini made statements which show the falseness of such propaganda. Volpe wrote:

> We must acknowledge that during the second half of 1921 and much more during 1922 conditions in Italy, or some of them, had begun to show improvement. There were encouraging signs of economic recovery. The people of Italy were back at work. Infatuation for Russia and its Bolshevism was disappearing . . . .[3]

And Mussolini, himself, stated in the party newspaper of July 2, 1921:

> To say that there still exists a Bolshevist peril in Italy is to substitute certain insincere fears for the reality. Bolshevism is vanquished. Nay, more, it has been disowned by the leaders and by the masses. The Italy of 1921 is fundamentally different from that of 1919. This has been said and proved a thousand times.

The early efforts of the Fascists to combat the radical movements of the left thus no longer seemed to be needed by 1921, even according to statements made by fascist leaders. Volpe said in speaking of this period that:

> Many even among the Fascist sympathizers thought the time had come for Fascism to disarm . . . . Fascism, to the contrary pushed forward the mobilization of its forces. The main target was now the government, or, we may say, the parliamentary regime.[4]

Thus Italian fascism, which had begun as a somewhat idealistic movement to protect Italian nationalism from the inroads of foreign ideologies, had by 1921 largely accomplished this objective. The Fascists had received financial and moral support from laborers and capitalists alike—from capitalists to insure the continuation of the institution of private ownership of productive capital, and from laborers to support a movement which was seeking to better the conditions of a laboring class disheartened by the early postwar economic maladjustments. When the initial objectives of fascism had been realized, as they were by the latter part of

---

[3]Gioacchino Volpe, *Storia del Movimento Fascista* (1932), p. 81.
[4]Quoted in Salvemini, *op cit.*, p. VII.

1921, the Fascists should have been content to dissolve their militant organization. That they were not was a reflection of the growing political ambitions of their leaders.[5]

The Consolidation of Fascist Political Power in Italy

During the early years of Italian fascism, the importance of political events overshadowed economic developments. Having obtained power by the questionable means of the famous "March on Rome," Mussolini's immediate concern was that of maintaining his party's political control. He was able to get from the Italian Chamber of Deputies a grant of full powers for his government for one year. This made it easier for the new regime to deal positively with the problems facing the country.

As a further step in assuring the continuation of his government, Mussolini was able to get Parliament to vote a change in the electoral law. This change, known as the Acerbo Reform, would give the party which received the most electoral votes—if more than 25 per cent of the total vote—two-thirds of the seats in the Chamber of Deputies. The existing Chamber was dissolved in January 1924, and the Acerbo reform was used for the first and last time in the new election held on April 6, 1924. The Fascist party used force and other strong persuasive tactics during the campaign, and succeeded in polling approximately 65 per cent of the vote. This gave the Fascists a very substantial majority in the Chamber even without use of the Acerbo reform.

Strong criticisms were raised against the deplorable methods which had helped the Fascists to their victory. Outstanding among the critics was Giacomo Matteotti who disappeared mysteriously on June 10, 1924, and was finally found buried in a remote part of the Roman countryside, the victim of a violent murder. The "Matteoti Affair" led to the withdrawal of the opposition as a bloc from the Chamber of Deputies in a move that was expected to lead to the fall of the fascist government. Though the withdrawal was nearly successful in its purpose, Mussolini finally reacted by assuming dictatorial power on January 3, 1925. This marked the end of democratic government in Italy until after World War II. The Chamber of Deputies became a rubber stamp, and elections in the following years, as a result of further electoral changes, became simply formal votes of confidence in the regime.

The Philosophy of Italian Fascism

This brief outline of the political development of fascism in Italy provides a perspective for consideration of the broad question of just

---

[5]For an interesting discussion of the mentality, ambitions and personality of Mussolini and other key figures in Italy during this period, see G. A. Borgese, *Goliath* (New York: The Viking Press, Inc., 1938).

what was the philosophy of this particular form of corporatism. This is not an easy question to answer because fascism did not begin with a fully developed philosophy and plan of action; these were developed as time passed. From the very beginning, however, it was a nationalistic movement. As Mussolini put it,

> The foundation of Fascist doctrine is the conception of the State,—of its essence, tasks and purposes. For Fascism, the State is the absolute, in relation to which all individuals and groups are relative.

And later, in a speech delivered on March 10, 1929, he stated:

> The Fascist State is not a nightwatchman, solicitous only of the personal safety of its citizens; nor is it organized exclusively for the purpose of guaranteeing a certain degree of material prosperity and relatively peaceful conditions of life. . . . Neither is it exclusively political, divorced from practical realities and holding itself aloof from the multifarious activities of the citizens and the nation. The State, as conceived and realized by Fascism, is a spiritual and ethical entity for securing the political, juridical, and economic organization of the nation. . . . The State is not only the present, it is also the past and, above all, the future. Transcending the individual's brief spell of life, the State stands for the imminent conscience of the nation.

The Pragmatism of Italian Fascism

Fascism in Italy was rather opportunistic and pragmatic in its approach, and this accounts for the fact that Mussolini, upon gaining power, did not immediately alter the relatively *laissez-faire* policy of the preceding government. The institutions of private property, individual freedom of initiative, and freedom of competition were preserved, not because they were regarded by the Fascists with any innate sanctity, but because it was felt that they would contribute most to the strengthening of the state at the time. When conditions changed, so could—and did—the government's attitude toward the policy of *laissez-faire*. Alfredo Rocco, one of the principal doctrinal spokesmen for Italian fascism, stated the matter quite plainly when he wrote:

> Fascism does not look upon the Doctrine of economic liberty as an absolute dogma. It does not refer economic problems to individual needs, to individual interests, to individual solutions. On the contrary it considers the economic development, and especially the production of wealth, as an eminently social concern, wealth being for society an essential element of power and prosperity. But Fascism maintains that in the ordinary run of events economic liberty serves the social purposes best; that it is profitable to entrust to individual initiative the task of economic development both as to production and as to distribution; that in the economic world individual ambition is the

most effective means for obtaining the best social results with the least effort. Therefore, on the question also of economic liberty the Fascists differ fundamentally from the Liberals, the latter see in liberty a principle, the Fascists accept it as a method. By the Liberals freedom is recognized in the interest of the citizens; the Fascists grant it in the interest of society. In other terms, Fascists make of the individual an economic instrument for the advancement of society, an instrument which they use so long as it functions and which they subordinate when no longer serviceable. In this guise Fascism solves the eternal problem of economic freedom and of state interference, considering both as mere methods which may or may not be employed in accordance with the social needs of the moment.[6]

In the light of later developments, this seems to have been a rather accurate statement of fascist doctrine.

When Mussolini assumed dictatorial power after the furor caused by the murder of Matteotti, he quickly took stringent measures to preserve his position as head of the state. Opposition political parties were suppressed, and freedom to criticize the regime in the press, cinema, speeches or conversation was revoked. Such strong penalties for violations were prescribed that all formal opposition soon ceased to exist. In addition to this self-evident expansion in the control exercised by the government, a more subtle movement for increasing its power was also developing. This was the development of the so-called corporative system.

Italian Fascism and the Concept of Corporatism

So much propaganda was put forth by Mussolini's government about fascist corporatism that it is somewhat difficult to develop a clear picture of what this doctrine was intended to be. Finer was probably correct in his belief that the word "corporative" was chosen by the Fascists to mislead the public and to veil the true extent of the assumption of dictatorial powers by the government.[7] As he put it:

> The fundamental truth . . . is that the Fascist State claims the right to regulate economic as well as other aspects of life, and has aimed at accomplishing the former through the Corporate organization.[8]

The development of the fascist corporative system extended over a number of years. One of the first steps was the agreement by the national

---

[6]*International Conciliation* (New York: Carnegie Endowment for World Peace, October, 1926), p. 404.

[7]For substantially the same interpretation, see Salvemini, *op. cit.*; and for a full technical treatment of the corporative development, see Fausto Pitigliani, *The Italian Corporative State* (New York: The Macmillan Company, 1934).

[8]Herman Finer, *Mussolini's Italy* (New York: Holt, Rinehart & Winston, Inc., 1935), p. 499.

council of the National Confederation of Fascist Syndical Corporations in June 1923, that labor contracts should be the result of a careful appraisal of all the circumstances involved and not the result of harmful class struggles. This was a pledge that agreement on labor contracts should be reached without resort to strikes and other forceful means. A similar pledge was obtained from fascist employer and employee representatives at a Rome meeting in December 1923. It was also decided at this same meeting that employers and employees would be grouped into separate organizations.[9]

From this point events moved rapidly toward the organization of all workers and employers into groups based upon occupation or type of business. Further, under legislation passed on April 3, 1926, fascist employee and employer organizations were recognized as the sole legal representatives of labor and capital. This law, in effect, dealt a death blow to all labor and employer organizations other than the legally recognized fascist ones. In addition, the wastefulness of strikes and lockouts was eliminated, since they were made illegal and punishable under law; collective agreements negotiated by the fascist organizations were made binding upon non-members as well; and a labor court system was established to handle employee-employer disputes which could not be settled by syndical bargaining.

The general pattern of the Italian Corporate State was clearly indicated by these early developments. Many changes and improvements in the Corporative system were made as time went by, but they were primarily designed to increase the organizational effectiveness of the system.[10] By 1934, the Fascist government had not only outlawed strikes and lockouts and eliminated all except the fascist organizations of workers and employers, but it had also carried out such an elaborate development of fascist worker and employer organizations that its potential control over production was quite extensive.

In 1934, a formal reorganization of the whole system of fascist employee and employer groupings was completed. This constituted the change from what Mussolini termed the "syndical" to the "corporate" phase of fascist development. What it really amounted to was a further tightening of the reins of government control over employers, employees, and production, so that the powers of the Fascist party became virtually absolute in the economic as well as in the political sphere.

The Syndicalism and Corporatism of Italian Fascism in Perspective

The true nature of Italian syndicalism and corporatism was carefully concealed from the Italian people and from the world at large. Instead

---

[9]For a good discussion of this, see William G. Welk, *Fascist Economic Policy* (Cambridge, Mass.: Harvard University Press, 1938), pp. 49-50.

[10]For a more complete discussion of these developments, see Welk, *op. cit.*, pp. 54-55.

of emphasizing the dictatorial aspects of these developments and pointing out the great advantage to be gained in time of war from such centralization of control, fascist propaganda gave a misleading impression
by dwelling continuously upon the supposedly new type of relationship
which had been developed between labor and capital under fascism. This
so-called new relationship was said to be a peaceful blending of the
interests of employers and employees in a manner which would maximize
the well-being of the state. The Fascists claimed that the great revival
of nationalistic spirit which they had brought about had raised labor
and capital above the level of class warfare which still existed in the
democratic capitalistic countries. Much was made of the fact that this
had been accomplished without destroying the institutions of private
property, competition, and freedom of initiative. These results were contrasted in fascist propaganda with those under Russian communism.

On the surface, these favorable results did seem to have been realized
in Italy under fascism. What was not generally realized until the
approach of World War II was that the truce between labor and capital
had been achieved less through the appeal to nationalism than by major
infringements upon individual freedom and initiative. It is true that the
strong revival of nationalistic spirit contributed to the labor-capital
peace, but primarily in the sense that this revival facilitated the fascist
substitution of dictatorial absolutism for the traditional democratic
laissez-faire government.[11]

The Militaristic Adventures of Italy's Fascist Government

The nationalistic ambitions of the Fascist government led Italy into
the Ethiopian adventure, which shocked and aroused the moral indigna-
tion of the world in 1936. At the conclusion of the Ethiopian War,
Mussolini gave active military support to General Franco in Spain's
Civil War. Hopes for an early fascist victory in Spain were thwarted,
and Italy's military machine showed up poorly. Participation in these
two military adventures placed severe strains upon Italy's economy. It
became clear during this period, however, that the corporatist elements
which had previously been imposed upon the economy by the Fascists
did enable the government to gear the economy to conditions of wartime
operation with relatively little difficulty and without disruptive disagree-
ments between employers and employees. The government's final military
gamble in siding with Germany in World War II brought an end to the
fascist era in Italy.

Though the two major fascist experiments in Germany and Italy did
not survive World War II, fascist regimes have prevailed in Spain and
Portugal during the postwar period, and elements of fascism have been

---

[11]For an excellent critical survey of Italian corporatism, see Salvemini, *op. cit.*

present at one time or another in Argentina and some other countries as well since the war.

Conclusions on Fascism in the Interwar Period

In concluding this discussion of fascism in the period between the two world wars, it should be noted that this system has been characterized by the blending of a strong spirit of nationalism with elements of corporatism. In practice, fascist systems in the period since World War I have developed in dictatorial regimes which have preserved the private ownership of capital. To insure that these private enterprise economies would function in a manner which would promote the nationalistic objectives of the dictatorial governments, corporatist elements were introduced in each case as a means of giving the government greater control over the operation of the economy. The nationalistic form of corporatism which is fascism has not proved to be a particularly enduring system in practice. Though the fascist regimes in Spain and Portugal have continued in force throughout the post-World War II period, both seem likely to experience significant changes as a result of the passing of power from Franco and Salizar respectively.

Corporatism After World War II

Christian Democratic Parties

Elements of a religiously motivated corporatism reappeared in some countries after World War II. In Germany and Italy, for example, Christian Democratic parties became the major political force. These parties occupied middle-of-the-road positions between the no longer acceptable fascism of the extreme right and the objectives of the left-wing socialist and communist groups. Though relatively little progress toward the development of corporatism has been achieved by the Christian Democratic parties when in power or when sharing power in coalition governments, this has been in part a result of the pressure of other problems which have required attention. Their philosophical orientation includes corporatist elements.

Secular Corporatist Trends

There has also been a revival of corporatist concepts in mature capitalistic countries where there was no religiously-based political party to provide the impetus. In the United States, for example, the checks and balances which have developed within the framework of large business units, powerful labor unions and a national government which has accepted an important measure of responsibility for the manner in which the economy functions can be viewed as a secular corporatist trend. The important role of these "countervailing powers" in promoting economic stability, and hence the well-being of both laborers and capitalists, has been interestingly described by Professor Galbraith.[12]

If capitalism is to survive as an effective economic system, it seems reasonable to conclude that it will be necessary for it to find workable solutions for such basic economic and social problems as maintaining high employment levels of operation without excessive inflation; providing for a favorable rate of economic growth; providing adequate social security against the risks of unemployment, loss of work-time from accident and sickness, premature death, and sickness in old age; providing adequate retirement benefits; developing techniques for settling labor-management disputes without strikes which would be damaging to the economy; providing favorable educational and employment opportunities for all citizens regardless of race or creed; and providing a favorable esthetic environment through slum clearance and low-cost housing projects, and through air and water anti-pollution programs.

This listing is suggestive rather than complete, but it does indicate clearly that capitalism must move in the direction of corporatism if it is to remain a viable and vigorous system in the face of contemporary problems. There must, in short, be a concern for the interests of all groups in society and a blending together of these interests in a manner that will provide reasonable stability and adequate growth. If capitalism cannot accomplish this, socialism is waiting to take up the challenge.

[12]See John Kenneth Galbraith, *American Capitalism: The Concept of Countervailing Power* (Boston, Mass.: Houghton Mifflin Company, 1952).

Economic Systems and Growth

11

By Professor Morris Singer

Growth, Inequity and Economic Systems

The question at hand is a momentous and exciting one. It concerns the relationship between the desire for higher incomes and the type of political and economic system best designed to attain that objective. Few other issues so involve the peoples of the contemporary world.

In a sense, this concern with economic activity and economic organization is an outgrowth of earlier expressions regarding this problem. Now, as before, many of those who would revise their institutions to improve upon economic performance are interested largely in the modification of inequity. Past and present views differ, however, in that the earlier revisionists and revolutionaries sought greater economic and social justice primarily through the redistribution of the existing level of income. In more recent years the reduction of inequity has been identified much more with the need for growth. This has been recognized within nations as social scientists have increasingly come to realize that growth constitutes a major vehicle for attacking and mitigating poverty. To an even greater extent, growth has been advocated to reduce inequities among nations. The peoples of the developing countries—and for that matter, of the poorer countries within the more economically advanced group—regard their lower plane of living together with the relatively low prestige and power that typically accompany such low per capita incomes as intensely unfair. Confronted by the pressing need to develop, they search persistently for a, or *the*, mode of organization which will spur their economies. Collectively they have not tended to grow more rapidly than the economically advanced nations. This has led them to further agonizing reappraisals of their systems, particularly when the aid forthcoming from the more advanced countries has been insufficient for the growth targets which they would like to attain. For diverse reasons the richer nations, too, have searched for modes of organization which would intensify their growth rates. This is illustrated by France's adoption of a system of "indicative planning" in which representatives from the private sector participate in the planning process.

Factors Reducing the Dependence of Growth Upon Systems

The significance of the foregoing problems is at least matched by their complexity. Growth, it has thus far been suggested, may be a function of the mode of economic organization. Yet one nation may have become hardened to a particular set of dogmas while another, ostensibly of the same type of economic system, may remain flexible and grow more rapidly. Again, any given system is designed to do much more than affect the rate of economic expansion. It possesses other objectives and functions as well, and these can at different times and places either impinge or react favorably upon the growth rate. Probably even more to the point, growth cannot be explained by a simple pairing of two sets of variables; advances in income depend upon a host of considerations other than the type of economic system. Finally, the nature of the economic system may itself serve as a dependent variable. There is some evidence that the kind of economic system adopted by a community depends partially upon the level of its national income. Since the latter is subject to change through growth, then over the long run growth rates may affect systems as well as conversely. Each of these propositions reduces the dependence of growth upon systems. Each requires elaboration.

Institutional Flexibility and Growth

Assume, first, that a nation greatly modifies its economic system in some fashion. How can this affect its growth rates? Some generalizations seem possible.

The change in institutions can of course immediately disrupt economic activity, particularly if it happens to be accompanied by violence. The initial impact may then be one of a lower, perhaps even a negative, growth rate. This may well be followed, however, by a period of buoyancy as the latent forces of the pre-reform and possibly the transitional period are released. The society may then be imbued with hope and vitality as institutions more appropriate for its needs emerge. A change in organization is often a sufficient condition for reasonably satisfactory growth.

Similarly, a new ideology can greatly affect growth rates. Fresh ideas may of course impart spirit and fire to otherwise routine procedures and so animate an economy in its daily tasks. Yet the views about society must not be permitted to assume apocryphal forms; they cannot be permitted to be distorted into dogmas, stubbornly adhered to and bearing little relation to the world at large. If they do degenerate into myths, they can seriously affect the rate of economic advancement and perhaps even the very fabric of society itself. Illustrations abound. Thus communist countries have recognized the importance of investment for industrial growth, but in the process they have at times neglected agriculture, an important source of consumer goods, to the point of endangering their overall growth. Fascistic nations have suffered losses, economic and otherwise, through their persecutions of minorities. The emphasis upon the values of private initiative and minimal governmental interference in economic affairs in the more capitalistic societies has until recently been associated with the idea of balanced budgets, presumably in order to restrict governmental expenditures to the revenues at hand. Thus the retarded growth rates in the United States economy from 1957 through 1963 can be attributed largely to insufficient government outlays and to tax structures which were siphoning off too much purchasing power in the range of full employment—that is, to a fear of deficit financing and an adherence to the myth of the balanced budget. It is hoped that the tax cuts which occurred in 1964 witnessed the end of this fiscal orthodoxy in the United States; since the enactment of reduced taxes occurred within the atmosphere of a presidential assassination, one cannot be sure.

In similar fashion, the underdeveloped world must retain a flexibility in its organization and ideology if it is to attain the progress it seeks. This has, for example, been realized and urged by Julius Nyerere, President of Tanzania. Although enough of a socialist to have nationalized a considerable segment of his country's economy, he has warned of "theologies" of the Left as well as the Right. In his speeches he has called for pragmatism in socialism and for an acceptance of economic and political diversity among the African nations.[1]

It is precisely this sort of flexibility which *all* systems must possess if they are to lead to satisfactory economic growth. A nation—be it socialis-

---

[1]Jack Shideler, "New Voice for Unity in Africa," *Christian Science Monitor*, April 14, 1967, p. 4.

tic, fascistic, capitalistic, middle way or whatever—cannot advance properly if it permits itself to be encumbered by the rigidity of its institutions and ideology. In sum, a country's growth depends in part upon its ability to adjust to change realistically, and yet its particular economic system does not uniquely determine the degree of its adaptability.

The Diversity of the Objectives

Another explanation of the limited relationship between a nation's growth rate and its mode of organization has to do with the wide variety of functions any economic system is called upon to perform. An economic system must do considerably more than merely provide for growth. It somehow has to find solutions for the daily, pressing problems of the what, how, and for whom of production. Its decision makers may be called upon to focus upon the problem of unemployment. In the poorer countries this certainly tends to conflict with the objectives of growth and extensive improvements in productivity. The richer nations, also, do not experience a one-to-one relation between growth and stability; note, for example, that a low capital output ratio is to be preferred for the former but not necessarily for high employment. Problems of inflation and a deteriorating balance of payments position frequently force a reduction in growth rates. Frequently the authorities may find it necessary to mitigate various types of inequities and injustices, as in modifying regional imbalances. Nations may be forced to turn away from growth to these and other objectives, which are not always compatible with growth. One cannot assume that the pursuit of objectives other than growth is dominated rigorously by the type of economic system that a nation possesses.

In addition, growth itself constitutes an ambiguous objective. The concept has been employed to indicate advances both in national income and in per capita income. The terminology is far from standardized, but the relatively rich nations as well as those otherwise large enough to make a serious dent in the world's power politics are frequently assumed to be interested in their national incomes. For them, population increases are either an advantage or presumably do not matter seriously. When their incomes advance, they are typically deemed to be "growing." The poorer nations tend to be concerned with rising per capita incomes. If they are successful, and in the process they necessarily introduce qualitative changes into their societies, they "develop." For literary purposes the terms must often be employed interchangeably, but data on both "growth" and "development" as just defined will be offered below.[2]

The objective of economic advancement is further vague with respect to its time dimension. Does an attachment to growth or development imply the most rapid rates of advance now, or at the end of a decade,

[2]See the second section of this chapter as well as the following chapter.

or after a quarter of a century? Does it involve the terminal year alone or the sums of incomes and outputs over the time spans in question? The longer the period, the less eager the authorities should be to concentrate on projects with brief gestation periods, so that the specific growth goals reflect the fundamental growth strategy. Nations typically hope to increase the sums of their incomes over relatively short periods in the near future, but such is not universally the case. Moreover, precisely what major components of output are supposed to highlight the growth? Is the stress to be on agriculture, or on manufacturing? If it is to be on manufacturing, then should it be on the light or heavy components? What is the attitude toward the development of the consumer goods industries? Are added expenditures for the military needed or desired?

Thus a nation does not merely desire growth in the abstract; it also tends to set some specific growth objectives for itself. The specifics in turn affect the aggregate growth rate, particularly when these objectives happen to be rather seriously out of line with the nation's productive services. As in the case of the non-growth economic objectives, these various aspects of growth are not uniquely correlated with a nation's economic system. True, communist countries are particularly inclined to promote industry over agriculture, but most of the developing countries tend to equate development with industrialization; frequently they do so with justification, but some of them also err as do the communist nations. Totalitarian and authoritarian systems are likely to allocate resources to "national defense," but so must a more democratic community if its geography and history so influence its politics. Nor is the impact of militarization on growth completely predictable.

In sum, a nation pursues various economic goals, only some of which are related to growth; and these goals are not uniquely determined by the nature of its economic system. The nations which grow most convincingly are those which are committed and dedicated to growth and which are not precluded by external circumstances from pursuing their objective. This has been found to be true, for example, in studies of effective foreign aid. For aid to work it needs first to be sufficient— which is to say that the donors must be seriously committed to growth and must not permit it to be diluted by other considerations. Beyond this, the recipients must be prepared to respond to it and to act forcefully, even if this often results in errors; they need to be "briskly opportunist" about their development plans. Their governments, typically authoritarian in character, must not hesitate to come to grips with political obstacles to development. "The key fact is simply that their governments seem to want to give real priority to economic development and are stable enough to face the political difficulties this entails.[3]

---

[3]"Aid That Works," *The Economist*, 222, March 11, 1967, 908. The countries examined were Pakistan (February 4, pp. 411-412), Formosa and South Korea (February 11, pp. 508 and 511) and Kenya (March 4, p. 819).

The Complexity of the Growth Process

Greatly complicating any discussion of the relationships between growth and systems is the wide diversity of factors affecting the former. Economic development very much depends upon many variables other than the mode of economic organization. While economists do not have, and may never have, a single general theory of growth or development, they have long grappled with the challenge of explaining economic advancement. In the process they have certainly managed to enumerate the factors which may have a bearing in any particular instance, and they have on many occasions proposed functional relationships among the variables in question.

To note what economists have had to say about explaining and promoting economic development, let us appeal initially to the classical approach, particularly as it is reflected in the names of Smith, Ricardo, Malthus and John Stuart Mill.[4] These writers were concerned with functions rather than the mere enumerations of factors, and their views were comprehensive, a property which is useful here in that it minimizes the elaborations which follow. Further, this group of economists lived and wrote at a time when, as is true today, paramount interest centered both on development and on economic organization. The questions which they posed, as well as many of their points of view, meet very well the test of modern day relevance.

The classical writers had a generalized production function in which output depended upon four types of productive services: land, labor, capital and technology. Insofar as all of these could be expanded, national output also tended to rise. Implicit in these relationships was the role of private entrepreneurship. Heads of firms, governed by the profit motive, brought these various factors together and supervised productive activity. Most importantly, they engaged in acts of capital formation which frequently embodied new and higher levels of technology, and in this fashion they particularly contributed to economic development.

Unfortunately, not all of the productive services could expand at similar rates. The prime difficulty lay in a growing population combined with limited quantities of land. Rising agricultural output, responding to the population growth, was subject to diminishing returns per unit of labor and capital. These spelled higher unit costs in agriculture, which were transferred to industry in the form of higher prices for raw materials as well as the higher money wages which were attributable to the rising prices of food. While industrialists could thus enjoy profits and engage in capital formation in the short run, their long-run prospects were dim.

---

[4] Their general economic views have been summarized in earlier chapters. For a further review of the classical position on growth see Benjamin Higgins, *Economic Development* (New York: W. W. Norton & Company, Inc., 1959), Chap. 3.

Eventually the high prices brought about by population increases and agricultural bottlenecks would depress profit *rates* and discourage further capital formation. *Aggregate* profits would deteriorate relative to their earlier prosperity levels, wages would fall to subsistence levels as a result of the rise in population, and landlords would live in states of comparative luxury because of the high prices of food and the rents which they would be able to exact.

There were some short-run recourses in the face of these dismal and gloomy predictions of ultimate stagnation. The nefarious long run could be postponed through two major types of measures designed to increase the supply and reduce the prices of agricultural commodities. One, particularly advocated by Ricardo, was the extension of foreign trade and the importation of food. The other, perhaps most associated with the name of Malthus, was the encouragement of technological progress in agriculture.

Here, then, are the several kernels of the theory of economic development. National output, the various productive services, population increases, an agricultural sector and an industrial sector together with their specific conditions of production, and the distributional share of wages, profits and rents all play their respective roles in contemporary thinking about the problems of economic development.

On the other hand, the classical system evidently constitutes only a point of departure. The richer countries of today, contrary to the classical predictions, have thus far not stagnated at some given level of income. Moreover, the presently poorer countries for the most part experience some development. In today's world, population increases do not tend to drive per capita incomes back to some initial level but rather *dissipate* the increases in the gross product. That per capita incomes do advance at all is the consequence of the factors which the classical writers emphasized—capital formation and technological change in both industry and agriculture, together with the international transactions that affect each. In sum, the first critical point regarding the classical writers is that the major variables which they included in their system must today yield a *different quantitative significance*—possibly, as in the case of trade, because of the arguments which they themselves pursued. The forces making for growth have thus far been more potent than those making for retardation.

A second major point has to do with their advocacy of a near *laissez-faire* policy on the part of government. Their view regarding this issue goes abegging almost everywhere in today's world, for reasons which will be discussed in the following chapter.

Finally, one must note the many *omissions* in their arguments. Important as it is to understand the classical variables, no one would today accept them as the sum total of development theory. What major additions, then, have taken place over time? The following stand out as the most significant.

(a) The years since the late 1950's have witnessed a tendency to add a fifth type of productive service, the quality of the work force. This may be broadly defined to include private and public administrative expertise, professional services, productive skills, the health of the work force, and even the political awareness of the citizenry. It is sometimes approximated by the expenditures on education and training, and there is a growing awareness that such outlays may yield a rate of return at least as high as that forthcoming from investment in fixed capital.[5]

(b) Contemporary growth analysis frequently utilizes a rather celebrated growth formula which focuses on the contribution of capital to economic growth.[6] This simple but widely employed equation can be derived in a variety of ways. For example, let Y and K stand for income and capital respectively, while Δ designates an increment. Then the value of $\Delta Y / Y$, the relative rate of growth, is not altered if it is multiplied by $\Delta K / \Delta K$. That is,

$$\frac{\Delta Y}{Y} = \frac{\Delta Y}{Y} \cdot \frac{\Delta K}{\Delta K}$$

or rearranging,

$$\frac{\Delta Y}{Y} = \frac{\Delta K}{Y} \cdot \frac{\Delta Y}{\Delta K}$$

Further, ΔK, capital formation, can be written as I, or investment, so that the growth formula assumes the form:

$$\frac{\Delta Y}{Y} = \frac{I}{Y} \cdot \frac{\Delta Y}{\Delta K}$$

The first factor on the right side may be dubbed the investment coefficient; the second, the incremental output-capital ratio. As customarily employed, the latter is not a *ceteris paribus* concept like the marginal productivity of capital, but rather it refers to the productivity of fixed capital used in combination with the remaining productive services. If it assumes a value of one-third, for example, this signifies that the increase in income of *all* the participating productive services aggregate to one-third of the value of the capital formation.

Given the continually expanding focus on the quality of the work force noted above, one might wish to think of investment not merely as fixed

[5]For illustrations of the views on human investment, see Theodore W. Schultz, "Investment in Human Capital," *American Economic Review*, 51, March 1961, 1-17; and Gary S. Becker, "Underinvestment in College Education?" *Idem*, 50, May 1960, 346-354.

[6]The names conventionally associated with this approach are Roy F. Harrod and Evsey D. Domar. See Harrod's *Towards a Dynamic Economics* (London: Macmillan & Company, 1948), and Domar's *Essays in the Theory of Economic Growth* (New York: Oxford Book Co., Inc., 1957).

capital formation alone but as the employment of resources in any fashion, be it education, training, or research and development, that yields a social return sometime in the future. The purpose of this would simply be that of incorporating the newer thinking about human investment into a familiar way of describing the growth process, and it would meet one of the criticisms levied against "growth economics," namely that it stresses fixed capital formation unduly. Note that the broader definition of investment reduces the magnitude of $\Delta Y/\Delta K$, since it increases the denominator without affecting the increase in income.

(c) A further recent innovation in the thinking about growth has to do with the wisdom of overthrowing the old monarch, capital, and of replacing it with a new ruler, technological change. This view has followed closely upon the discovery that mere increases in the supply of capital and labor have not contributed extensively to advances in per capita income unless they have also been accompanied by improvements in quality.[7] The proposed coup d'etat has not materialized, however, in part because of a reconsideration by some of the people who initially proposed it. For one thing, once the contributions of increases in capital and labor to higher incomes have been deducted, the difference is not the contribution of technological change alone but "the residual." The latter also includes the effects of the aforementioned improved quality of the work force, economies of scale, institutional changes such as tariff modification, and so on. Moreover, not only does technological change constitute a fraction (albeit a significant one) of the residual, but in addition the weight of its alleged contribution depends in part upon a particular assumption, namely that it can be divorced from, or occur independently of, capital formation. It is assumed to be "disembodied," to use the favorite jargon. While this characterizes some innovations, as in the case of scientific management, the more probable occurrence is that technological change must be embodied in acts of capital formation. Generally, any coup d'etat that seeks to establish a single monarch to preside over growth theory is bound to fail. Thus far in our review it would be more realistic to speak of a triumvirate composed of fixed capital formation, human investment, and technological change.

(d) Economic growth evidently requires sufficient demand as well as an expanding supply. The classical writers of course emphasized the latter, but it does not do them justice to assert that they ignored demand completely. After all, Smith built his ideas regarding economic growth around the concept of the division of labor, and this in turn depended upon the extent of the market; while Malthus, more than any other classicist,

---

[7]This finding is particularly associated with the work of Robert M. Solow in his "Technical Change and the Aggregate Production Function," *Review of Economics and Statistics*, 39, August 1937, 312-320, and of John W. Kendrick in *Productivity Trends in the United States* (Princeton, N. J.: Princeton University Press, 1961).

realized that weaknesses in demand might cause cyclical downturns which would retard the process of development. Yet it has taken modern writers, under the influence of John Maynard Keynes, to recognize the significance of aggregate demand in maintaining and advancing national income. Among other reasons, poor countries are poor because they have weak markets. In turn, the richer countries have been plagued by the inability of their actual output to keep pace with their potential output—that is, they have been troubled by fluctuations in actual output associated with weaknesses in demand. The supply function therefore must be supplemented by a demand equation in which income appears as the sum of four components of aggregate demand: consumption, investment, governmental spending on new goods and services, and net foreign investment as measured by export proceeds minus expenditures on imports.

This introduction of aggregate demand invites a reconsideration of the growth formula discussed under (b). One of the factors there used to account for a growth rate was the investment coefficient I/Y, since capital formation, however narrowly or broadly conceived, is a contributing factor to growth. Given the assumption of a closed economy, however, it is more usual to substitute the average propensity to save for the investment function and to employ the form:

$$\frac{\Delta Y}{Y} = \frac{S}{Y} \cdot \frac{\Delta Y}{\Delta K}$$

In what senses may I/Y equal S/Y? The two are certainly identical *ex post*. Looking back, all expenditures are composed of either consumption or investment and all income allocations may be classified as consumption or saving; and since income equals expenditures (including net additions to inventories), saving equals investment. The two concepts may also equal each other in *ex ante* terms. Given the propensity to save, the community must invest sufficiently to fill the gap created by its failure to spend on consumption in order to prevent its income from declining. Paradoxically, a nation may experience a higher saving ratio in either sense and grow more rapidly if it spends more and enjoys a high and rising aggregate demand and full employment. The growth formula in question is in fact an offshoot of Keynesian economics. When applied to the richer communities, its cardinal tenet is that aggregate demand, particularly investment, must be high enough not to interfere with the rate of growth. When the growth formula is adapted to the poor countries, it is true that limitations in capital and income are likely to make for a low propensity to save and thereby retard the growth rate. Even in these instances, however, markets are not to be taken for granted. In part, the capital of these countries has not been built up because of inadequate *inducements* to invest.

(e) A major explanation of the significance of demand for the developing nations is to be found in their export situation. Much concern has been expressed over the relatively weak position of the developing countries in the world economy. This is too involved and complex to summarize in several sentences. Included among the problems are allegedly deteriorating terms of trade; and among the various types of the worsening terms of trade, the kind most commonly alluded to (because of the readier availability of the data) are the unit terms of trade, which compare changes in export prices with changes in import prices. Some have argued that the data do not take account of quality changes, that they do not distinguish between f.o.b. and c.i.f. prices, and so on. However, the representatives of the poor countries are convinced that the developing nations typically, though not always, suffer from adverse price trends. The problem is seen to be one of inflexibility in the structure of production of the poorer countries combined with an insufficiently advancing demand on the part of the richer countries. These difficulties have given rise to proposals for compensatory capital assistance, which are little heeded, or for controls over the prices of the exports of the poorer countries, which have proved difficult to implement and administer.

Of course the poorer countries are not alone in experiencing balance of payments difficulties. The relatively rich but small states continue to be highly vulnerable to the demands for their exports. Further, richer nations may find, and in fact have on occasion found, their balance of payments and their domestic demand to be weak simultaneously. In such cases, the credit ease desirable for stimulating a revival and a more rapid growth rate would conflict with the higher interest rates desirable for strengthening the balance of payments. At full employment and with some inflation the conflict should be less severe, in that credit tightening reduces inflation and maintains the ability to compete abroad and attract foreign assets. Even in this range, however, the problem remains a serious one.

(f) While equations of aggregate supply and aggregate demand provide a broad framework for analyzing the factors contributing to growth they offer little specific guidance for the promotion of economic advancement. Beyond these we require microeconomics—the economics of particular firms and industries. Since the firms in a developing nation do not enjoy a wide variety of services offered by other firms in the economy, the mechanisms for promoting inter-firm and inter-industry relations particularly require the attention of the governments of the poor countries.

Some of the literature in this area is concerned with the deliberate, although presumably limited, unbalancing of economic change. According to this view, short-term pressures and tensions tend to result in long-run development gains. This argument can apply at many levels; for example, inflation, urban overcrowding, or regional disparities may lead to demands for correction. On a more technical level, imbalances in the outputs of goods at different stages of production can create pressures for further action, as with imbalances in the output of steel and the coke used to produce that steel. Either the buyer or the seller of the common good—in this case, coke—may move ahead of the other, but it has been argued that the *buyer* should be encouraged to assume the lead more frequently. Then he places pressure upon his supplier to produce more, whereas if the coke producer were to be relatively prolific this would merely encourage, not compel, the buyer of his product to purchase additional units. Even in this microeconomic approach, demand emerges as a strong factor in development.[8]

There is a more conventional solution to the problem of assigning priorities to particular acts of capital formation. According to this view, investors, whether private or public, should for purposes of expanding the national income be encouraged to seek the investment with the highest social marginal product. However, the rate of return formula is difficult to apply with precision because of the problems of identifying and measuring all of the benefits and costs involved. These include the external economies and diseconomies—that is, the benefits and costs beyond the immediate industry in which an act of investment occurs. Thus there may be effects on related industries, employment, health, overall incentives and *esprit de corps*, and so on.

Since externalities and interdependence are so significant in affecting rates of return, it may be possible to combine the previous short-term imbalance approach, which does take account of inter-industry relations, with the concept of the highest social rates of return. One can plan initially on the basis of inter-industry imbalances and then permit the most efficient firms in a given complex of industries to carry out much of the investment. If all goes as it should and real unit costs can actually be determined, the efficient firms should generally realize the highest profit rates. However, this approach still fails to embrace many of the externalities involved. Because of this, and because even many of the immediate benefits of investments are not subject to measurement, the assignment of priorities to acts of capital formation remains an art as well as a science.

(g) Along with the contributions in the areas of aggregate supply, aggregate demand, and microeconomics, much work has also been done in the realm of values and institutions since the days of the classicists. Marx, as we all know, erroneously predicted the course of capitalism in the richer countries, but so for that matter did Malthus—at least until the

---

[8]See Albert O. Hirschman, *The Strategy of Economic Development* (New Haven, Conn.: Yale University Press, 1958), especially Chaps. 4 and 5.

present. The great achievement of Marx in the area of economic development was to focus on the power structure and dualistic class relations in the poor feudalistic countries, and to show that change could not be initiated until the major decision makers in a society favored it. This yields rewarding insights into backwardness, as in the case of many Latin American countries. Equally impressed with the decision making of the elite, though in a considerably different vein, was Joseph A. Schumpeter.[9] To Schumpeter the investment that mattered for development was the type that embodied new techniques of production or that brought forth new products. Since such investment was highly uncertain, Schumpeter emphasized the importance of a socioeconomic climate that would reduce risk and uncertainty. Unless this were done, he felt, the rate of innovational investment would be severely impaired.

Generally, it is when one delves into the institutional arrangements that affect development that diverse opinions and differences in emphasis particularly come to the fore. Views become more personal at this point, although the scientific ideal still shines through. The present writer's position is that the following institutional factors contribute in no small measure to economic development: contacts with foreign cultures that are continuous, quantitatively significant and largely devoid of authoritarian and repressive features; a reasonably stable, predictable and dynamic government that is committed to economic change; and the "right" degree of equality or inequality in the social-economic-political structure. These have in common the property of playing upon the wills of people, of motivating them to behave in growth-promoting fashion, and of helping to make economic change widespread.

The foregoing comments on the nature of development and growth have been designed to call attention to the multi-faceted aspects of economic advancement. Technically, they suggest that the relationships among the many variables associated with growth tend to be complementary. While substitutability among the many factors is certainly feasible, it tends to be limited to a fairly narrow range. Thus the poorer countries frequently strive for more labor-intensive modes of production, but they cannot indefinitely substitute labor for capital formation and the superior technology the latter is likely to embody. Conversely, the richer nations may not manage to overcome the ultimate constraint upon a cyclical expansion, that of a labor shortage. Governments may adopt policies to enhance domestic demand, but these may still fail to offset the declining planes of living brought about by decreases in exports. Reforms may remove some very severe institutional restraints upon economic advancement, as in the case of land tenure, but limitations in technology or trained manpower may still retard the rates of growth.

---

[9]See previous discussion, pp. 84-96.

The problems of economic expansion simply are not to be solved by panaceas.

In sum, since economic growth is such an exceedingly complex phenomenon, we cannot expect a single set of factors, including the mode of economic organization, to account for it.

The Dependence of Systems Upon the Level of Income

For a final commentary on the factors limiting the dependence of growth upon systems, let us survey the period since World War I (when the Bolsheviks came into power in Russia), in order to take note of the fairly marked relationships between the *levels* of per capita income and the modes of economic organization.

Communist regimes tend to come into existence in low income nations, typically with per capita incomes of less than $300 per year. The reasons for this are simple and yet monumental. Communist regimes, with their concentrated leadership and acute sense of direction, are particularly well adapted for assuming control of the development process. Viewed economically, the function of communism is to mobilize resources for economic development.

Nevertheless, the proposition that communism tends to appear in poor countries needs to be restated in order to avoid a faulty impression. Or, to phrase it alternately, the reaction against Marx needs to be modified. In examining the sweep of history, Marx believed he detected a sequence of stages, namely primitive communism, empire building with its slavery, feudalism with its serfdom, capitalism with its proletariat and socialism with its classless society. Since the highly centralized form of socialism which we designate as communism tends to appear in poorer countries, observers have suggested that Marx erred in his stage thesis and that communism actually follows directly on the heels of feudalism, or oligarchy, or old-time dictatorship, call it what one will. Yet the nations which have adopted communist regimes have often not been completely devoid of capitalistic development. Russia experienced considerable growth under the Czars, particularly during the decade of the 1890's; China had its bourgeois revolution under Sun Yat-Sen in 1911; Cuba was a relatively high per capita income country within the underdeveloped world when Castro assumed power. Marx may thus have to be revised to read feudalism, an abortive capitalism, and then communism. Communism is, after all, a rather sophisticated system. Among other things it requires a fair amount of literacy and a rather intricate organization. The most economically retarded countries tend to be dominated not by Communists but by the old-time change-resisting "elites."

The reference to an "abortive capitalism" contains some implications which merit at least passing attention. The term conjures up images of a society dominated by government officials who are subject to corruption and by businessmen who derive many of their gains from activities unrelated to growth, while the frustrated masses experience much less improvement in their lot then they had hoped for. This is a society ripe for communism. It is one which the more democratic societies should refrain from supporting, through economic assistance or otherwise, until the introduction of some reforms which will permit the use of aid primarily for its intended purposes. Without such revisions aid might just as well be withheld, since the identification of the hated "elite" with the foreigner may fan the flames of revolution all the more. On the other hand, nations which have moved relatively far in their degree of governmental participation in economic affairs and in the process have given promise of fairly rapid and sustained development may well be deserving of considerable support. The kinds of systems which other nations adopt, and the private-public mix which they prefer, would not seem to be the richer countries' affair. As long as systems elsewhere do not directly threaten their national security, the proper concern of the richer states is the effective employment of their treasure. While they may be relatively rich, they have not yet managed to abrogate the law of scarcity.

If relatively low per capita income countries have sometimes found communism appealing, middle income countries have on occasion embraced fascism. One or two of these countries, notably Nazi Germany, have possessed a highly advanced technology for their era.

Since fascistic nations frequently defy generalization, it is difficult to explain this particular relation between systems and levels of per capita income. Given their individual histories and cultures, several of the countries in question embraced warfare as an instrument of national policy and in fact sought world military supremacy. Such vast ambitions require a relatively advanced economic machine. On the other hand, their aggressiveness was partially motivated by their failure to attain the income levels of the very rich countries of the world; in fact, they were often referred to as the "have not" nations. (There is a disquieting analogy to the behavior of the middle class in all this.) Internal factors may also help to account for this association of fascism with a middle income status. Nations roughly in the range of $500 to $1,000 of annual per capita income tend to require various reforms to achieve further advances. Some changes which were impractical when the country was poorer may now become feasible. Many of these, such as the progressive income tax, tend to be levelling or equalizing in their nature. As a consequence, the powerful (big business), the insecure (the non-professional white-collar workers and petty shopkeepers, and, in Argentina, union labor), and the culturally conservative (the peasants) may in some societies respond to articulate conservatives who call for a preservation of the *status quo* or even a return to some prior arrangements. These internal forces are evidently strengthened in an atmosphere of a highly militant nationalism.

Finally, democratic societies and mixed economies tend to characterize the highest per capita income nations. Some cynics and/or idealists are likely to question the degree of democracy, while others may wryly suggest that only rich countries can afford it. Be that as it may, a higher level of wealth brings with it more pressures for personal freedom and for greater equality. Similarly it promotes greater literacy and political participation. Further, the relationship between democracy and a high per capita income is probably reciprocal. At relatively high income levels, a society's course is no longer as simple and certain as in the days of lower incomes when a sheer quantitative increase in goods and services was the prime economic objective. The economically advanced societies need to examine the nature of their goals more carefully and to exercise greater concern over the qualitative aspects of their living. Public dialogue and decentralized decision making commend themselves for these purposes.

Many of the poorer countries also view themselves as democracies, and they similarly tend to possess mixed economies. Their claims regarding democracy are both difficult to assess and touchy. Much depends upon definitions. Here let us merely content ourselves by asserting that the poor countries are frequently democratic within the framework of their particular needs and circumstances. Very often, for example, they may for practical purposes possess a single party and yet permit maximum free discussion within that organization. The matter of their mixed economies is a less sensitive one. In the next chapter it will be argued that the mixed economies of the poor and of the more economically advanced countries tend to, and should, perform considerably different functions. Certainly a relatively high proportion of the modern sectors of the developing economies is subject to public control.

Systems, then, are to an extent correlated with, and in part dependent upon, levels of per capita income. This proposition of course also implies that systems are eventually affected by growth rates. The characteristics of systems tend to alter as they develop and attain new income levels.

Nonetheless this relationship does tend to be a reciprocal one. That is, granted that many factors weaken the effects of systems upon growth, it is still possible to assert that certain regimes tend, *ceteris paribus*, to promote growth more readily than do others. Support for this proposition is to be found in the next section as well as in the following chapter.

Totalitarian Systems and Economic Growth

Growth Rates Under Communism

On *a priori* grounds one would expect the communist countries as a whole to perform relatively well in the area of income growth, but at the expense of improved planes of living for consumers. The communist nations have been less encumbered by a multiplicity of economic objectives,[10] and they have generally managed to establish organizations in keeping with their relatively well defined and somewhat more restricted goals. To phrase it alternately, the communist regimes have not concerned themselves unduly with the costs of growth.

Thus the authorities tend to mute demands for increased consumption on the part of the citizenry, particularly during the earlier years of the regime. Open unemployment tends to be a less serious problem than in other poor countries because of greater control over the mobility of labor—and also, one might add, because of the strength in aggregate demand associated with governmental investment. The balance of payments constraint upon economic development, so potent a limitation for other poor nations, assumes less seriousness for the communist nations because of attempts at autarchy and "operation bootstrap"; of course, the greater the nation's size the greater the feasibility of this approach. If the economy becomes closed, then inflation also matters less. In brief, the communist countries tend to devote themselves more seriously and effectively to the objective of economic development, as opposed to other poor nations which must temper their very genuine interest in growth because of their need to pursue other goals, economic as well as non-economic. This is of course not to assert that other matters never intrude under communism. They can and they do, as in the case of Red China's concern with ideologies. Thereupon communist growth rates can also decline.

When other developing nations place a greater value upon personal freedom than do the communist countries, this implies more than a mere dilution of economic goals or objectives. It similarly affects the methods which can be pursued. In very many of the poor countries, growth is evidently hampered by a change-resisting elite, who may or may not be directly associated with the government. Not only may communist leaders be dedicated to change but they are in a superior position to eliminate resistance to it.

The data seemingly lend support to these *a priori* expectations. Difficulties do abound, however, in the collection and use of the statistics in question. Ideologies may assume command over national income con-

---

[10]As discussed under (2) in the preceding section.

cepts, as when in the true Physiocratic-Smithian spirit the Russians exclude services from the national output or (since altered) when in true Marxian spirit they neglect the contribution of capital in computing the value of a commodity. Similarly, of what worth is the aggregate national product datum of Czechoslovakia, for example, if no relatively free markets determine the values of the commodities and prices take on a highly arbitrary quality? The nations in question may be too poor to yield adequate output statistics; this has tended to be true of Rumania. Mainland China illustrates the secrecy which may attend the economic performance of a communist nation. All things considered, the data thus contain a considerable margin of error. Nevertheless, at least two considerations render them more credible: (a) It is always helpful to receive support from theory, and such is of course true in this instance. (b) The reported communist figures have received the severest scrutiny from noncommunist experts who have been bent upon what might genteelly be called objectivity, and who have often revised the official data considerably.

The Soviet Union has been highly adept at growing, so much so that care must be taken not to generalize about growth under communism on the basis of its particular experience. According to one source, the *industrial* growth rate of the U.S.S.R. bordered on 7.5 per cent per year during its formative and peace-time years, 1928-1940 and 1950-1955.[11] This figure is a conservative one relative to others that have been cited. Some data, for example, have industrial production growing at 8.9 per cent or at 12.5 per cent annually between 1927-1928 and 1950, a period which also covers the war years.[12] The Net National Product probably advanced about 6.5 or 7.0 per cent between 1928 and 1937,[13] while the G.N.P. grew at an average annual rate of some 7.1 per cent from 1950 through 1958 and at 5.3 per cent even during the relatively retarded years from 1958 through 1964.[14] A further indication of the statistical discrepancies involved appears in the data offered by the United Nations, which cannot tamper with the figures presented to it by sovereign nations.

---

[11]Warren G. Nutter, "The Structure and Growth of Soviet Industry: A Comparison With the United States," in *Soviet Economic Growth: A Comparison with the United States*, Part I, Joint Economic Committee, 86th Cong., 1st sess. (Washington, D.C.: Government Printing Office, 1959), p. 105.

[12]The first of these rates is based on the work of Donald R. Hodgman, while the second is derived from the official index of the U.S.S.R. See Harry Schwartz, *Russia's Soviet Economy* (2nd ed.; New York: Prentice-Hall, Inc., 1954), p. 136.

[13]Gregory Grossman, "Soviet National Income and Product: Trends and Prospectives" (Cambridge, Mass.: Russian Research Center, Harvard University, 1952), pp. 7 and 8 ff.; cited in N. S. Buchanan and H. S. Ellis, *Approaches to Economic Development* (New York: Twentieth Century Fund, 1955), p. 210.

[14]Joint Economic Committee, *New Directions in the Soviet Economy*, Part II-A, 89th Cong., 2nd sess. (Washington, D.C.: Government Printing Office, 1966), p. 105.

It has reported that the GNP per capita alone grew by as much as 8.7 per cent a year in the U.S.S.R. from 1950 to 1959.[15]

The issue at hand is neither the lack of reliability of the figures nor the discrepancies in their interpretations. Each of these is immediately granted, and some of the reasons for the existence of these problems have already been noted. The point is simply that the most conservative estimates indicate a strong growth performance while the more charitable ones suggest growth rates bordering on the spectacular. As Buchanan and Ellis write of the 1928-1937 upward surge of output:

> Whatever the 'true' rate, if any such can be firmly established, the expansion was certainly a rapid one and one which has rarely, if ever, been matched by other countries even for short periods.[16]

When we turn our attention to Eastern Europe we find that the same disparities and suggestions of rapid growth appear with respect to Yugoslavia. The more conservative source indicates that the GNP of this relatively decentralized socialist nation advanced at an impressive rate of 6.5 per cent a year from 1950 to 1959.[17] In turn the United Nations reports its GNP per capita as growing at a rather phenomenal 9.2 per cent from 1952 through 1959.[18] Table 1 summarizes the growth rates of the remaining East European communist nations during the 1950's and first half of the 1960's. Their representative growth rate approached 5 per cent a year, or about one-half of 1 per cent above the average rates achieved by the non-communist countries during the same period. Theirs was not a remarkable performance but a relatively strong one nevertheless—particularly when viewed in the light of their satellite status. Some

TABLE 1. GNP Growth Rates in Eastern Europe, 1951-1964°

Country	Annual Percentage Increases in GNP			
	1951-1955	*1956-1960*	*1961-1964*	*1951-1964*
Bulgaria	5.9	7.3	4.3	5.9
Czechoslovakia	3.6	6.6	1.3	4.0
East Germany	7.2	4.9	2.7	5.1
Hungary	5.5	4.2	4.6	4.8
Poland	4.8	5.0	5.0	4.9
Rumania	8.6	3.5	4.9	5.7

°Source: Joint Economic Committee, *New Directions in the Soviet Economy*, Part IV, 89th Cong., 2nd sess. (Washington, D.C.: Government Printing Office), p. 880.

[15]United Nations, Department of Economic and Social Affairs, *Yearbook of National Accounts Statistics* (1960), p. 268.

[16]*Approaches to Economic Development*, p. 210.

[17]Wilcox *et al.*, *Economies of the World Toady*, p. 20.

[18]United Nations, *Yearbook of National Accounts Statistics* (1960), p. 268.

of the policies which the eastern European countries were called upon
to adopt, such as those pertaining to their exports of food to the U.S.S.R.,
presumably hampered their attempts at growth.

The more economically advanced nations, especially the United States,
have only belatedly reacted to the powerful influence Mainland China
is sure to exert upon world politics in the foreseeable future. This attitude is reflected in our seriously inadequate knowledge about the Chinese
economy. According to one of the best available estimates, the Chinese
GNP in real terms grew at a high average annual rate of 8.6 per cent
from 1952 through 1957.[19] Thereupon an ideology other than that pertaining to economic development interfered. The regime attempted a
"great leap forward" through various measures designed to enhance the
degree of collectivization, but it proceeded to gyrate backward instead.
The damage brought about by this ideological intrusion (as well as by
some uncooperative weather from 1958 through 1960) was so severe that
the economy may have declined as much as 20 per cent by 1962, and
it probably did not regain its peak of the late fifties until 1966. Its overall growth rate thereby fell to approximately four or five per cent over
the entire period, 1952-1966.[20] Over the longer time span, China may
thus have done a shade better than the approximate 4.2 per cent regis-
tered by India from 1950 through 1964[21]—to make the inevitable comparison. It was in the earlier part of this period that China particularly
outshone India. During the 1950's India could manage a rate of increase
in its national income of only 3.5 per cent per year,[22] although it apparently received more foreign assistance than did China. Given their marked
population increases, both nations evidently performed poorly in per
capita terms over the entire period in question.

Generally, then, communist nations have been relatively successful in
developing their economies—though perhaps not nearly so much as their
propagandists would have the rest of the world believe. The many other
factors notwithstanding, here is an indication that systems do affect
growth rates. The modes of economic organization can influence the
many factors making for growth and as such they can stimulate or retard
growth rates.

---

[19]A. Doak Barnett, *Communist Economic Strategy: The Rise of Mainland China* (Washington, D.C.: National Planning Association, 1959), p. 11. In turn, Barnett has taken his
data from William W. Hollister, *China's Gross National Product and Social Accounts,
1950-1957* (New York: The Free Press, 1958).

[20]Joint Economic Committee, "Mainland China in the World Economy," 90th Cong.,
1st sess. (Washington, D.C.: Government Printing Office, June 19, 1967), p. 12. These figures
of course do not reflect the influence of the "Cultural Revolution" and the Red Guards
in 1967.

[21]Committee for Economic Development, *How Low Income Countries Can Advance
Their Own Growth* (New York: September, 1966), table two, p. 67.

[22]B. R. Shenoy, *Indian Planning and Economic Development* (New York: Asia Publishing House, 1963), p. 20.

A convenient way of analyzing the development experienced under communism is given by the growth formula introduced in 3(b) and 3(d) of the preceding section, that is

$$\frac{\Delta Y}{Y} = \frac{S}{Y} \cdot \frac{\Delta Y}{\Delta K}$$

The key to the relatively rapid growth under communism is to be found in the exceedingly high saving ratio, S/Y. The communist countries have on occasion benefited from assistance, and some, such as Cuba, have probably received a rather considerable proportion of their capital from abroad. Nevertheless, as a group, the communist countries—particularly the prototype, the U.S.S.R.—represent a model of growth in which foreign capital assistance is minimized and major reliance is placed upon domestic efforts. To assert that the economic function of communism is to promote economic growth is in effect to state that the system can allocate its resources to the production of consumption goods sparingly and can then mobilize its savings for investments that expand the national product. It is not at all unusual for communist governments to force their citizens into savings rates of 25 or 30 per cent. An expert on Rumania, for example, has estimated that country's average saving ratio to be 30 per cent, while its marginal ratio has perhaps reached as high as 40 per cent.[23]

The means of promoting these high savings rates are familiar from the U.S.S.R. experience. The evident technique is to eliminate the price system as a guide to the production of particular goods and services, and instead to employ prices in accord with a central plan. The state planning organization first establishes its production goals largely on the basis of non-price criteria and then proceeds to assign prices that are compatible with the output decisions already taken. While it may set relatively low prices for some staples as well as a few quasi-luxury goods directed to the urban worker, its general practice is to price consumer goods at high levels to discourage purchases and to clear the market of the relatively small number of goods produced. In the U.S.S.R. experience, these poor terms of trade confronting the consumer were associated with excises, or "turnover" taxes. The "turnover" taxes exacted relatively high proportions of consumers' incomes; when they attained their peak in the U.S.S.R. in 1935 they represented in the aggregate 175 per cent of the values of the goods to which they were applied![24] In any event, the effect of the inflated costs of the goods is to reduce the purchasing power of the households irrespective of whether the price officially embraces a tax. Further discrimination is exercised against the peasants. The low prices which they receive for their commodities are designed

---

[23]John M. Montias, in a lecture delivered at the University of Connecticut during the spring of 1967.

[24]Paul Alpert, *Economic Development* (New York: The Free Press, 1963), p. 29.

both to reduce their consumption and to promote occupational mobility on their part. On the other hand, considerable inducements in the form of favorable prices may frequently be offered to the managers of industrial firms. In short, the decision to force the citizenry to engage in widespread real saving must have its pecuniary counterpart.

What, however, of the incremental output-capital ratio? Under communism does this also tend to reach fairly high magnitudes that are conducive to growth?

At best, the capital concept and its mode of measurement are difficult issues; consider the problem of appropriate depreciation procedures, for example. They become most challenging indeed for countries that are both poor and resorting to socialist pricing. Beyond this, an economy's output and capital formation are exceedingly broad categories, subject to myriads of influences. Hence *a priori* hunches prove almost as difficult in this area as do the collection of data. Very many factors may be enumerated, but what weights should we assign to them?

As is to be expected, one can identify factors making for both relatively high and relatively low incremental output-capital ratios in communist regimes. A favorable factor for economic growth, though hardly for the comfort of the average citizen, is the relatively low proportion of investment in infra-structure or social overhead capital, such as transportation or housing. The latter in particular has a very low ratio because of its durability and its low productivity. Moreover, the communist countries have tended to place a rather high value on education and training. Since output-capital ratios normally do not include these in the denominator, this type of resource allocation also leads to a higher $\Delta Y/\Delta K$. Other types of allocation exercise a converse effect. This would be particularly true of the tendency to favor industry over agriculture, since this policy evidently directs resources to the more capital-intensive sector. Similarly, the fundamental communist strategy calls for a stress upon heavy industry and the adoption of the more capital-intensive techniques of production when alternative modes of production present themselves. Finally, communist production has often been woefully inefficient. Hungary presents one illustration out of many of the failure to coordinate the deliveries of intermediate goods and to idle the remaining productive services until the arrival of the missing components of the production mix.

All things considered, it would seem that the incremental output-capital ratios have tended to be fairly low in the communist countries. The various factors cited above suggest as much. This conclusion also follows from the growth formula if their savings ratios have indeed been exceedingly high while their growth rates have generally been moderately higher than elsewhere. In effect their high saving and investment ratios have more than compensated for the shorter-term inefficiencies of their systems.

Growth Rates Under Fascism

Fascism probably offers the most severe obstacles to any generalizations. Here, more than for the other categories, the uniqueness of each country's experiences seems to predominate. At the very least the nations designated as fascistic need to be separated into two major categories: the one type associated with an industrial-military complex and bent upon warfare as a means of achieving national goals; the other dominated by a dictator, lacking a dynamism, and no more associated with external aggression than most sovereign nations. Into the first group fall Germany, Italy and Japan during the 1930's and early 1940's. (During the twenties, Germany and Japan toyed with liberalism, while Mussolini had not yet adopted a warlike stance). In the second group appear Portugal under Salazar and Spain under Franco, as well as Argentina under Péron.[25]

One might expect Germany, Italy and Japan to have performed like the communist nations in several respects. They also would have tended to restrict consumption and make its enhancement subservient to other goals. Then too, their incremental output-capital ratios could be expected to have been somewhat lower than in less totalitarian societies because of certain inefficiencies. At the economic level, the inefficiencies would embrace the allocation of resources to military goods and an approach to autarchy. In addition, in at least one instance they included genocide, and thereby provided yet another illustration of the workings of ideology in the extreme. That amoral being, the economist *qua* economist, would presumably describe the effects of this policy in terms of a depletion of skills, or a disinvestment in human beings, which served to reduce the system's productivity and degree of economic advance. In any event, it would appear that the savings and investment rates and the incremental output-capital ratios in the three fascist countries would combine to yield growth rates of fairly average magnitude.

The rates of economic advance exhibited by the fascistic nations were, however, subject to at least two major extraneous influences. One revolved around the presence of Japan. This nation has exhibited a remarkable capacity for growth since 1868, and it has done so irrespective of its system. Its growth record since World War II has, if anything, been more spectacular than during the days of its domination by the Emperor and the top military officers and business families. The inclusion of Japan thus tends to bias the growth results in favor of fascism.

The other intrusive factor had to do with the period during which fascism flourished. The beginning of the decade of the thirties was of course characterized by exceedingly severe unemployment; in fact, this extensive waste of human resources undoubtedly contributed significantly

---

[25]At the time of writing, Greece was showing signs of becoming another middle-income country to join this category.

to the appearance of nazism in Germany. While nations work their way out of severe unemployment they tend to experience abnormally high growth rates. Such economic advances are largely cyclical or short term in nature; they are more associated with eliminating the slack in idle resources than with the major factors responsible for secular growth. The United States, for example, experienced striking growth rates from 1933 into World War II (9.7 per cent per year from 1933 to 1937) without embracing extreme doctrines of either the Left or Right.

Given these considerations regarding employment, it is useful to resort to an atypical growth concept along with a more usual one in order to examine the growth records of the more advanced nations during the 1930's. The measure in question is the rate of increase in national product per man year. It refers to the rate of growth in real national product per unit of *employed* labor. If O and N respectively indicate the national product and the total annually employed work force, the measure may be represented as

$$\frac{\Delta \left(\dfrac{O}{N} \right)}{\left(\dfrac{O}{N} \right)}$$

It reduces but does not eliminate the more obvious effects of rising employment upon growth, since productivity tends to advance during the expansionary phase of economic fluctuations. Table 2 employs this concept as well as that of total output to indicate the economic advances of the countries in question. Additional information is supplied for comparative purposes.

The data indicate a somewhat more rapid rate of increase for the three fascistic nations than for other economically advanced nations in a comparable period of recovery from unemployment. The case is not terribly convincing, however. If France is removed from consideration on the grounds that it experienced depression throughout the years in question and that its negative growth rates influenced the average unduly, the remaining non-totalitarian advanced economies just match the three totalitarian countries in the rate of increase in product per man year and slightly exceed the fascistic nations in the rate of growth of total product. Moreover, as already noted in the case of Japan, these same totalitarian countries often performed better under more liberal systems than when identified with fascism. Thus the somewhat liberalized Japan of the 1920's outshone the more militaristic Japan of the 1930's in its advances in both total product and productivity. Germany advanced more rapidly with respect to total product when dominated by Hitler, but it experienced higher rates of improvement in productivity as a republic in the late 1920's. Italy never attained any impressive growth record during this period. However, this was probably as much, or more, a reflection of such other factors as Southern Italy's lack of capital or Sicily's culture as it was a consequence of Mussolini's policies.

The other three fascistic nations may be discussed more quickly. Péron of Argentina, Salazer of Portugal and Franco of Spain have approximated the elites of the quasi-feudalistic regimes in their attempts to maintain, and capitalize upon, the *status quo*. What distinguishes them from, let us say, Trujillo of the Dominican Republic and Duvalier of Haiti is the superior economic power of their countries. When Péron assumed control in the mid-forties, Argentina had advanced to a middle income status and it ranked very high among Latin American nations in its per capita income. Portugal under Salazar and Spain under Franco have been among the poorest of the European nations, but they have nevertheless enjoyed relatively high incomes for underdeveloped countries.

TABLE 2.   Rates of Increase in Total Product and Product per Man Year for Germany, Italy, Japan and Selected Countries *

| Nation(s) | Period | Annual Per Cent Increases | |
		Total Product	Product per Man Year
Germany	1925-1929	5.7	6.0
	1928-1937	2.8	2.1
	1932-1937	8.8	3.5
Italy	1922-1938	1.9	1.7
	1922-1929	2.3	2.2
	1930-1937	3.0	2.7
Japan	1922-1929	6.5	5.9
	1929-1937	3.6	2.4
	1933-1938	4.8	3.7
The three fascist nations	Recovery(a) from depression	5.5(b)	3.3(b)
Eight Non-totalitarian nations(c)	Recovery from depression through 1937	4.9(b)	2.7(b)
Seven non-totalitarian nations(d)		5.9(b)	3.3(b)

*Adapted from Deborah C. Paige, *et al.*, "Economic Growth: The Last Hundred Years," *National Institute Economic Review*, July 1961, table 4; reprinted in Edmund S. Phelps, ed., *The Goal of Economic Growth* (New York: W. W. Norton & Company, 1962), p. 79.
(a)From lines (3), (6) and (9) of this table.
(b)Unweighted average.
(c)The countries include Denmark, Norway, Sweden, France, The Netherlands, The United Kingdom, Canada, and the United States.
(d)The above nations less France.

In addition, Portugal has possessed an empire, particularly in Africa. In their impact upon growth, however, Franco, Salazar and Péron have often appeared closely related to Trujillo, Duvalier and others. Franco and Salazar made stability, including stability of prices and output, the key to their economic policies. Péron squandered Argentina's wealth, notably the exchange his country had earned during World War II. As a consequence, none of these countries has been known for its growth rate.

According to one source, Argentina's GNP grew at an average annual rate of approximately 3.5 per cent from 1950 through 1957, a span which runs two years beyond Péron's deposition.[26] Another estimate has the nation's Gross Domestic Product growing at an annual rate of 2.1 per cent per year from 1950 through 1955.[27] Over the period 1948-1960, Portugal may have advanced at an average rate of 4.6 per cent per year.[28] The available data further suggest that Spain also grew at about 4.6 per cent per year from 1940 through 1946 and then advanced at rates somewhat above four per cent from 1952 through 1957.[29] The evidence also indicates that in more recent years Portugal and Spain alike have awakened to the more rapid economic movements around them. During 1957-1964, the GNP's of Spain and Portugal, respectively, grew at average annual rates of 7.2 per cent and 5.5 per cent.[30] These growth performances exceeded the world average, but that of Spain was not unusually strong given the slower advance of the preceding period. As a group, the three countries in question have not tended to grow as rapidly as the world's remaining nations.

The conclusion seems inescapable. Relatively free and democratic societies which have managed to escape from the lowest income, underdeveloped status are not well advised to surrender their freedoms and to turn to fascism if their major objective is to enhance their economic growth.

---

[26]Committee for Economic Development, *How Low Income Countries Can Advance Their Own Growth*, table two, p. 68.

[27]Computed on the basis of income data in the United Nations, Department of Economic and Social Affairs, *Yearbook of National Accounts Statistics* (1957), p. 1.

[28]For 1953-1960: United Nations, Department of Economic and Social Affairs, *Yearbook of National Accounts Statistics* (1965), p. 472; for 1948-1953: United Nations, Statistical Office, *Statistical Yearbook* (1954), p. 411. (The author is responsible for the computations).

[29]For 1952-1957: United Nations, Department of Economic and Social Affairs, *Yearbook of National Accounts Statistics* (1958), p. 205; for 1940-1946: United Nations, Statistical Office, *National Income Statistics, 1938-1948* (1950), p. 242. (The author is responsible for the computations).

[30]Both growth rates are from Committee for Economic Development, *How Low Income Countries Can Advance Their Own Growth*, table two, p. 68.

Government's Role in the Growth of Non-Totalitarian Economies

12

By Professor Morris Singer

This chapter is concerned with the growth records of the non-totalitarian economies and with the organization which may affect the rates of their economic advancement. It particularly directs attention to governmental involvement at the microeconomic level within the poorer countries.

The Relation of Government Intervention to Growth and Freedom

While there may be no clear lines of division, it is possible to distinguish three alternative growth paths, depending upon the degree of participation of the government in economic affairs. At one extreme is a system approaching *laissez-faire*. The government may subsidize the shipping industry, as it did in the eighteenth-century United Kingdom, or grant land to the railway companies, as in the case of the nineteenth-century United States, but for the most part the private sector provides the sources of growth. At the other end of the scale lies socialism, under which the government owns and controls the lion's share of the means of production. While such a system can be reasonably democratic, this is not likely. The authorities tend to be interested in compelling their citizens to behave in ways that increase the national product, and hence the government is likely to be totalitarian in intent and at least authoritarian in practice. In between, though frequently closer to the business approach, lies a composite of governmental and private activities, designated by such phrases as "the mixed economy" and the "middle way." Since the particular combinations of public and private economic involvements are exceedingly numerous, individual countries frequently take great pride in the alleged uniqueness of their own specific arrangements. They may in fact invent terms to direct attention to the distinguishing features of their development.

As noted, the data apparently show that as a group the communist countries have been able to grow fairly rapidly, despite their relative inefficiency in combining the various productive services. If the most rapid rate of development over time were the only social objective, a centralized socialism would tend to provide it. Intent as many societies are on economic development, however, rapid growth rates evidently do not comprise their only aim. Most peoples also tend to value some modicum of freedom and liberty, so that freedom would not seem to be an overrated virtue. Most of the richer countries have long committed themselves to relatively democratic ways, while many of the developing countries may approach authoritarianism but have stopped short of seeking totalitarian solutions to their economic problems.

On the other hand, the prime illustration of a *laissez-faire* approach to economic development—the United Kingdom during the eighteenth and nineteenth centuries—could not manage to increase its GNP at an average annual rate of 3 per cent. Even the United States, blessed though it was with institutional and natural advantages and adopting an approach not quite as *laissez-faire* as the British, experienced annual rates of increase in the GNP of 3.5 per cent and in per capita income of approximately 1.7 per cent from the mid-nineteenth century on. Growth rates of these magnitudes are not at all satisfactory to the countries of today. In particular, growth rates in the national product of 4 per cent or less are not regarded as sufficient by today's poorer countries anxious for economic development. If the richer countries are often motivated by considerations of power as well as interests in higher planes of living, the poorer ones are spurred not only by their desire to overcome poverty and occasionally by considerations of power but also by their intent to reduce the gap between the economically advanced countries and themselves.

They have not been successful in their pursuit of this last goal. True, their GNP's have grown somewhat more rapidly than those of the richer communities. From 1950 through 1964, the national products of the low income, non-communist nations increased at average rates of 4.7 per cent a year, while the richer countries managed growth rates of 4.3 per cent a year. The poor countries did not fare so well in per capita terms, however. Their populations expanded so rapidly that their incomes per head could increase at annual rates of only 2.4 per cent per year. At the same time the per capita incomes of richer countries were advancing at rates of 3.1 per cent.[1] On occasion, the prospects for the poorer countries appear bleak indeed. Some international statisticians have warned that unless there is a pronounced increase in the aid rendered by the richer nations the world will no longer be able to content itself with the fact that the poorer countries "are at least making some progress." According to the experts in question, average income per head in the underdeveloped world may decline from some $130 in the early 1960's to as low as $80 in 1980.[2] This is probably the most pessimistic projection made in recent years. The economic prospects of the poor countries may not be quite so dim, and as heretofore they may continue to advance at slower per capita rates than the more economically advanced countries. Behind this, however, dwells the "inexorable logic of mathematics" to further frustrate the developing nations. Even if they should muster such high rates of increase in per capita incomes as the richer countries, their increases in absolute terms (that is, in number of dollars per head) will still fall short of the richer communities. An equal percentage growth rate applied to a lower base unfortunately yields less of an absolute increase in income per head. With identical percentage growth rates (not very likely), the gap between the planes of living in the rich and poor nations still widens.

In these circumstances, the poor or developing nations are assuredly in no mood to tolerate the relatively low growth rates which they associate with near *laissez-faire* models. Hence they have tended to turn to the mixed economy which one authority in the development field has described as a system in which ". . . both government and private enterprise undertake parallel and combined efforts for the over-all economic growth of the nation." He then goes on to write:

> This pattern of cooperation and division of functions is appropriate to developing countries, because an underdeveloped economy cannot afford

---

[1]Committee for Economic Development, *How Low Income Countries Can Advance Their Own Growth*, table two, p. 20. For a detailed presentation of these trends see the United Nations *Statistical Yearbook* for 1965.

[2]Paul Bouteille, "The Civil Service and Economic Development," in *Government Organization and Economic Development*, ed. Graeme C. Moodie (Paris: The Organization for Economic Cooperation and Development, 1966), p. 146.

to be doctrinaire. It faces serious shortages of all kinds and it must, in order to experience economic growth, confront the serious business of getting things done—getting capital accumulated and invested in the most useful directions for economic growth. Given widespread backwardness among large masses of the population and urgent desire for economic development, the leadership of the government is essential to an economy which otherwise might remain almost completely stationary.[3]

Despite this, it is pointless to seek to demonstrate that within the non-communist developing world the economies with the greater government-mix grow more rapidly. This would not be rewarding for a variety of reasons. (a) The poor countries have almost universally turned to their governments to assist them with their development. (b) The degree of government involvement is a subtle matter, and one that is highly resistant to measurement. Governments perform so diverse and pervasive functions that some simple measure, such as the percentage contributed to the GNP, does not do justice to the matter. (c) Governments are often called upon to act precisely where the private sector is weak. Hence any attempt to relate the extent of government involvement in economic activity to the degree of economic growth might well yield a negative, albeit spurious, correlation.

In sum, the majority of the world's nations has sought to pursue at least two sets of objectives, and in so doing they have hit upon some middle way. In the range of *laissez-faire* they can gain a great deal in income with very modest, if any, sacrifices in freedom if they move toward a mixture of private and public activity. In the range of socialism, they can gain a great deal of personal freedom with only a moderate reduction in income growth (and probably none at all in the case of the richer countries) if they similarly move toward the center. The middle way thus tends to represent the least foregone in income growth and personal freedom, and at least approaches an optimum solution.

Governmental Contributions to Growth in the Richer and in the Developing Nations

The next question concerns the precise contributions of government to economic advancement. Why should government involvement raise the growth rate? Why does the mixed economy tend to yield superior economic results relative to *laissez-faire?*

The answer is to a large extent to be couched in terms of timing—of the particular phase of development in which a country finds itself. This,

---

[3]Bert F. Hoselitz, "The Entrepreneurial Element," in *The Challenge of Development,* ed. Richard J. Ward (Chicago: Aldine Publishing Company, 1967), p. 131.

it would seem, is the important point to make. *The appropriate functions of government tend to alter as the economy advances.* While this occurs along a continuum, for purposes of analysis it appears legitimate to simplify and again to draw a distinction between the economically advanced countries and the poorer ones. Despite some permissible exceptions, in the richer nations the governmental functions tend to be—and *should* be—more macroeconomic in character. They tend to be more general, across the board, less selective. The activities of the government are designed to minimize business fluctuations, add to overall investment, alter income distribution, correct the balance of payments, weaken monopolistic practices, and provide for whatever collective consumption (such as education or national defense) the community as a whole prefers. This is not to assert that the government in a richer economy is never selective or that it never involves itself in particular activities; it may regulate public utilities, influence the stock market for cyclical control, subsidize one industry for national defense, and assist another because of strong lobbies.[4] But in relative terms the government now tends to be less involved in particularized activities, whether it be as a percentage of its own economic affairs or as a fraction of the total decisions concerning specific commodities. To a large extent, in the richer mixed economies, prices in their totality act in fairly systematic fashion to indicate the particular consumer and investment goods to be produced, as well as the quantities of each.

The governments of the poorer countries evidently also engage in activities of a macroeconomic nature, as when they depreciate their currencies to strengthen their balance of payments position. Much of their behavior, however, tends to be microeconomic—that is, selective and discriminatory among industries, although hopefully not between firms in the same industry. This is because their prices are not systematic and, as a consequence, fail to allocate resources in efficient fashion. This failure can be attributed to two types of shortcomings: *(a) the conditions required for a price system are frequently not present; and (b) to the extent they do exist, they often direct decision makers along lines that retard economic growth.* These propositions require extensive elaboration.

The Underdevelopment of Price Systems in the Poorer Countries

While tomes could be devoted to the subject of how a price system is supposed to function, the fundamental aspect, briefly, is that prices reflect underlying changes in the demands for and costs of particular goods and

---

[4]Refer to pages 29-30 for a fuller list of governmental activities.

services, including producers' services. Prices thereby attract people to particular lines and repel them from others. An increase in the demand for some good, for example, should increase the price and direct firms to a greater production of the commodity in question. By the same token, a rise in unit cost and then in price should discourage buyers, who can then turn their attention to a good which utilizes less of the economy's resources per unit of expenditures. To the extent that the demand and supply functions do not shift, the economy approaches a state of general equilibrium in which consumer satisfaction is optimized subject to the constraints of resource availability and use. Thus an economy can be a going concern with a minimum of deliberate central direction.

The foregoing argument implies a number of necessary conditions, however, and it is only when these are approached that prices can perform their allocative duties. The conditions in question are discussed in the following paragraphs.

(a) Prices must be free to move. Unless prices possess this property, the various economic agents have no change to which they can react when the underlying demand and cost functions alter. In addition, price flexibility is required if commodities are to be priced at unit cost and prices of services are to reflect their marginal products. At least two reasons for the failure of prices to move freely are monopoly power and the existence of customary prices.

(b) Knowledge of price movements is a necessary condition. If people are isolated, for example, and do not possess sufficient information about price changes, there can obviously be no response.

(c) The value system must be appropriate. Producers and consumers must behave like economic men and attach considerable worth to material gain; otherwise, even if prices move in their favor, they will fail to take advantage of their economic opportunities. They will remain in the same pursuit or with the same good, although they and the remainder of the economy would be better off if they did shift.

(d) Producers and consumers must possess the freedom to react to changing prices. In the everyday world they may be aware of price movements and be interested in reacting to them and yet be prevented from making the necessary adjustments. Any number of interferences may present themselves. Caste, discrimination on the basis of color, apprenticeship rules, hereditary occupations, monopoly power, and insufficient funds for adjustment all suggest themselves as possibilities.

(e) The distribution of income must not be "grossly" unequal. While this last property of an efficient price system possesses less logical rigor than the preceding four, it deserves at least passing attention. When the distribution of income is very uneven, the wealthy can cast so many votes in the overall competition for all goods and services that the national production fails to satisfy the most pressing wants within the economy. It then becomes inefficient in some sense.

Assume that the above conditions are satisfied and prices do act efficiently to determine the allocation of resources. What, one may inquire, does this have to do with the subject of growth per se? Does not price theory concern itself with static problems? These questions raise some exceedingly difficult issues about the relationships between statics and dynamics on the one hand[5] and micro- and macroeconomics on the other. Unfortunately, the theoretical underpinnings are not as firm as one would wish. It can be argued, nevertheless, that a viable price system may influence growth favorably.

For one thing, when prices help economic agents select from the available alternatives the choices in question need not pertain to the same moment in time. The alternatives may well relate to the consumption or the production of like or different goods at different times. The relevant interest rate may be high enough, for example, to encourage a would-be consumer to forego consumption until a later date; or a set of assorted prices, including a premium for uncertainty, may yield a profit rate sufficiently high to encourage a firm to adopt a more capital intensive mode of production. Prices can, when functioning effectively, be bound up with such matters as saving, investment, innovations, and on-the-job training—all of which can evidently have an impact upon economic dynamics. Furthermore, a price system is characterized by competition, for otherwise condition (a), pertaining to the free movement of prices, would not be satisfied. One of the consequences of competition is that producers are forced to be satisfied with normal profits in the long run.[6] In effect, entrepreneurs do not demand an abnormally high rate of return as the price for engaging in investment. By the same token, the fear of loss which characterizes a competitive world may well encourage firms to adopt innovations, so that they will not be outdistanced by their competitors.

Inter-temporal comparisons aside, an efficient allocation of resources at some moment can also affect growth favorably. The existence of a competitive price system implies movements toward the lowest points on long-run average cost functions. In the aggregate this signifies that minimum constraints are being placed upon the expansions of income and employment in the economy. At some given propensity to save, this further implies a relatively high level of saving and investment. Finally,

---

[5]The terms are employed here to contrast stationary and changing economic conditions, not unlagged and lagged relationships between the variables of the system.

[6]This would seem to be consistent with Schumpeter's view regarding the necessity of monopoly profits in order to induce innovations. The longer run in Schumpeter's system is featured by "gales of creative destruction" and "circulating elites."

production in the neighborhoods of the lowest average costs tends to enhance the marginal output-capital ratio, $\Delta Y/\Delta K$, for the economy. This ratio is relatively high in the neighborhood of full capacity because few of the firms' resources are then kept idle, and hence virtually all of the added capital can be utilized to contribute to the firms' output. In similar fashion, interregional and international trade can encourage economic growth in that the greater efficiency raises real income and creates a more substantial basis for expansion.

Note should also be taken of the proposition that a workable price system maximizes consumer welfare. Insofar as the consumer is also a producer, this heightened satisfaction can have a profound, though often immeasurable, effect on the quality of the work force. The poorer the community the more important this source of improved labor productivity tends to be.

So much, then, for the ideal state. To allege that the conditions required for a price system prevail completely in the richer nations is of course to delude oneself with a sophisticated fairy tale. In particular, the widespread incidence of monopoly power greatly reduces the degree of price flexibility in manufacturing and in other major sectors of their economies. On the other hand, the overall departures from these conditions are not so severe as in the poorer nations. In addition, such departures have probably been more serious in affecting the static problems of resource allocation than in retarding growth. As the United States well illustrates, the richer economies have moved beyond the price system to institutionalize the growth process. Their large and medium-sized firms typically set funds aside for research and development and shift cost functions downward, just as they allocate other outlays to the task of influencing consumer wants and thereby shift cost functions outward. When they succeed in thus improving the level of technology and/or advancing consumption, they affect the major inducements to investment and thereby promote capital formation.[7] When the business sectors of the richer countries do not promote technology and consumption sufficiently, their governments have increasingly tended to supplement their efforts. The United States government has supported the research and development activities of industry for some time, to say nothing of its promotion of popular education, but it has lagged in its adoption of policies to stimulate aggregate demand. The converse has been true of many of the Western European countries. Each, however, is becoming increasingly conscious of the area in which it has been delinquent.

In contrast, most of the poor and developing nations not only have yet to build growth into their systems, but they also fail to meet the

---

[7]These views are in accord with those expressed by John Kenneth Galbraith in his *The New Industrial State* (Boston: Houghton Mifflin Company, 1967).

conditions of the price system to a greater degree than do the richer communities.

Many of the poorer peoples live in hinterlands outside the market economy, so that not a single one of the conditions is relevant for them. Beyond that, one or more of the requirements fail to apply to those that do constitute part of the market nexus. Perhaps the condition that comes closest to being realized is that which pertains to the value system; the peoples of the poorer countries are not too far behind those in the richer ones in approaching the status of economic man. Yet even in this instance other values, such as those pertaining to religion, frequently assume a greater role than in the wealthier societies. Knowledge regarding alternative opportunities is not as limited as one might suppose. For example, a great deal of information is conveyed informally in the unskilled labor markets through friends and relatives. Nonetheless, knowledge about alternatives still tends to be quite inadequate, particularly when it involves relatively new and untried ways. The circumstances with respect to monopoly power, customary prices, obstacles to entry, and income distribution certainly tend to discourage a reliance upon a price system and a decentralized organization. As a consequence, the government has a powerful role to play in advancing the nation's economy. When it does not or cannot perform this role, the most probable outcome is a relatively low growth rate.

The Relation of a Price System to Growth in Underdeveloped Countries

Let us now consider a second major argument in favor of governmental participation at the microeconomic level in the poor countries. Assume reasonably free, workably competitive economic men, knowledgeable about current changes in relative prices, and prepared to respond to the price mechanism. Factor prices reflect the underlying real costs of employing the various product services, so that capital and labor as well as foreign exchange are priced to indicate the various scarcities of each in the current period. Since competition prevails, goods and services are priced at unit, or more specifically at marginal, cost. Assume, in brief, that the price system does somehow manage to function within the framework of an underdeveloped economy. The conditions of the price system are approached as much as they can be in the midst of low per capita incomes, little capital, minor abilities to save, a retarded technology, limited aggregate demand, few existent external economies, a relatively large agricultural labor force, a highly specialized export structure, and all the remaining accouterments of underdevelopment. Then the argument to be pursued is that in these circumstances the price system may effectively perform its static function of allocating resources, but from a *dynamic viewpoint* it can still fail to yield satisfactory results. A going price system within a framework of underdevelopment may direct economic resources effectively in the immediate period and yet help retard the long-run growth of the economy.

In short, the question being attacked is whether the government of a poor country ought merely behave like that of a more mature economy. Need it only maintain the conditions of the price system and see to it that firms behave according to the rules of the game? The answer being suggested is that a competitive price system alone probably cannot stimulate the development of a poor country.

Consider the following cases:

(a) The developing nations are highly limited in the inter-industry, inter-firm relationships which promote external economies. Firms in the underdeveloped regions are not likely to engage in growth-promoting acts, partly because they do not have the advantage of a going economy capable of providing them with a wide variety of services at reasonable prices. Foreign investors in the poor countries have experienced this obstacle; when they wish to develop a particular product they themselves often find it necessary to furnish the power, transportation and many additional overhead services. Inadequate facilities of course represent additions to costs, detract from profits, signify a lower productivity of capital than is frequently assumed, and discourage activity to a substantial degree.

(b) In addition, when a firm contemplates the sale of its product, it may find that its market is quite thin because of overall limitations in purchasing power. If it wishes to expand its sales it can often do so only by reducing the price of its commodity rather sharply. Underdevelopment does not logically require price inelasticity, but it renders it more probable. Moreover, when a firm does expand its scale of operations, it cannot readily rely upon similar expansions on the part of other firms which would counter its price inelasticity by shifting its demand function outward. Once again, the behavior of other firms places a constraint upon the growth of a single firm, although in this instance the limitation is associated with weaknesses in demand and markets. Since here, too, the firm cannot benefit from the functioning of other firms, some writers have included this in their discussions of external economies. Not only may a firm be discouraged from investment and expansion because of a current lack of facilities, as already noted, but it may further be deterred in that if it alone acts it provides external economies (sales) to other firms without benefiting from a like expansion on their part. The firm may therefore hold back on added production and employment, aware that much of the income it created would be utilized by its employees in the purchase of the products of other firms.[8]

(c) The price system has a role to play in bringing about the rapid technological change required during the course of development, but it cannot provide a sufficient spur. On the one hand, the prospects of lower unit costs and/or higher commodity prices certainly encourage the adoption of innovations. But the uncertainty associated with the unknown tends to be very marked in the poor countries, so that it is typically difficult to induce the adoption of new techniques and procedures. The price system can of course reflect this attitude. Risk and uncertainty are costs to be passed on to eventual customers in the forms of higher prices and the demands for higher profits. In turn, these respectively restrict purchases and venture capital for growth purposes. The costs of innovation are sufficiently high and the gaps in overall knowledge sufficiently severe to demand action within a broader framework than that of the individual firm or even the individual industry. The training of students overseas, the provision of extension services in agriculture, the promotion of feasibility studies in manufacturing, and the reduction of uncertainty through accelerated depreciation allowances all constitute cases in point.

The last three sets of propositions, (a) through (c), comprise a unit. In each instance the prices reflect the low productivities or the insufficient effective demands within the poor countries. The shapes and the relative positions of the demand and cost curves are such that extensive profits are not likely to be found in growth. A poor economy may thus experience relatively low growth rates when it relies primarily upon the price system to direct it.

(d) The next two cases concern two types of external economies which a competitive price system either cannot reflect or guarantee.[9]

The first type is outside the price system and it involves irrecoverable net gains. Firms cannot depend upon the market to capture all of the social benefits and costs associated with their production and sale of particular goods. They are in no position, for example, to recover all of the gains that accrue to the community when they train their work force for particular skills. Since prices thereby fail to reflect all of the real social benefits and costs accruing to the community, they may readily misdirect the allocation of resources. In addition, a system of competi-

---

[8]This line of argument was first advanced by Paul Rosenstein-Rodan in his "Problems of Industrialization of Eastern and South-Eastern Europe," *Economic Journal*, 53, June-September 1943, 202-211.

[9]These failures of the price system characterize the more economically advanced nations as well as the developing ones.

tive prices cannot allow for economies of scale. If the firms in a given industry experience downward sloping cost curves in the face of a relatively constant market, the most efficient and/or aggressive enterprises can outcompete the others and establish monopoly positions which, if uncorrected, interfere with the optimal results of the system. In effect, when firms with declining cost functions do not pass their decreasing unit costs on to the purchasers of their products, they deny external economies to the system. Both sources of external economies—the irrecoverable net benefits as well as the economies of scale, the one lying beyond the realm of prices and the other beyond the realm of competition—need to be included in decision making to improve upon the results brought about by the price system.

An attempt to embrace these external economies is to be found in the use of what may alternately be dubbed shadow or accounting prices. These prices are fictitious and as such are not really known; in practice they must be estimated from current prices.[10]

Shadow or accounting prices can be designated in various ways. When applied to productive services, they represent the value of the marginal product, or the opportunity cost of employing a given factor. Correspondingly, they are the prices which equate supply and demand. When related to commodities, they are similarly the prices which clear the market and, by the same token, they equal the marginal costs of production. Those who advocate the use of shadow or accounting prices are frequently interested in employing them as tools in the planning process, particularly when determining the priorities to be assigned to investment projects.[11] Not only are the productive services and commodities then priced competitively, but the estimated values of the net social benefits which can be measured are also added to the price of a product. Those who believe in the worth of competitive pricing within the framework of underdevelopment still find it necessary to use shadow prices in a way that reflects the influence of net external economies.

We can now proceed with points (d) and (e) which pertain respectively to irrecoverable gains and economies of scale. If irrecoverable net benefits are relatively extensive, as they are likely to be in the poorer countries, this tends to discourage capital formation. For all practical purposes, a private investor cannot be greatly interested in whether his act of invest-

---

[10]For an indication of the procedures involved, see G. F. Papenek and M. A. Quresni, "The Use of Accounting Prices in Planning," in *The Challenge of Development*, ed. Richard J. Ward (Chicago: Aldine Publishing Company, 1967), especially pp. 46-51. Actually, the use of shadow prices raises several issues of both analysis and feasibility, as will be noted in items (f) and (g) immediately following.

[11]Hollis B. Chenery has employed accounting prices in this fashion. His works on the subject include "The Application of Investment Criteria," *Quarterly Journal of Economics*, 67, February 1953, 76-96; and "The Role of Industrialization in Development Programs," *American Economic Review, Papers and Proceedings*, 45, May 1955, 40-57.

ment benefits the remainder of the economy. The important consideration to him must be his own particular profit rate. If he should find this rate of return to be low, then irrespective of the potential contribution to the economy he would tend to hold back on further activity. The public investor, on the other hand, may or may not be interested in the returns outside a particular industry, depending upon whether he is associated with the general government or a semi-autonomous agency. Even when he adopts the broadest possible approach, he still does not possess adequate information. Nevertheless, he can frequently act with the public benefit in mind. The construction of a few textile plants in the rural hinterland, for example, can yield low returns in the narrow sense and yet be exceedingly fruitful when they conduct a heretofore isolated community into the mainstream of development. This sort of thing has happened in Turkey, where according to one writer:

> The economically unwise industrial locations have turned into social and economic assets. Sivas, Eskişehir, Adana, slumbering centers of rural provincialism initiated into industrial activity by the state enterprises, have developed into important industrial centers today.[12]

(e) A time-honored argument for government involvement, early recognized by the classicists, is given by the infant industry case. This is especially significant for a developing economy with a potential for industrialization.

Assume a young industry in a young economy, for the time being experiencing high unit costs because of its limited output and sales but subject to lower unit costs as it expands production. The decline in costs may be a function of time, as when those who serve and supply the industry become more familiar with its needs and thereby reduce their own costs. This is in effect a learning process that benefits the rest of the economy, and from the point of view of the firms in the industry it constitutes an uncompensated benefit. The infant industry argument thus reflects unrecovered benefits for the industry as well as economies of scale.[13] When decreasing unit costs are a function of size, their behavior is due either to internal economies or to declines in the unit costs of the suppliers. In any event, whatever the explanation, high unit costs over the range of low output and sales may preclude the introduction or expansion of an activity which can ultimately yield a high profitability for a firm and for the economy. If, as is usually the case, like commodities are purchased from other countries, the importers are simply motivated to continue their purchases from abroad and to undersell the

---

[12]Nuri Eren, *Turkey Today—And Tomorrow* (New York: Frederick A. Praeger, Inc., 1963), p. 130.

[13]W. Arthur Lewis, *Development Planning* (New York: Harper & Row, Publishers, 1966), pp. 34-35.

domestic producers. The infant industry requires some protection in the form of a tariff duty or a subsidy which will permit its firms to produce in the neighborhoods of minimum average costs. Otherwise, the industry either perishes, fails to materialize, or at best grows at a considerably retarded rate when the imported commodity is not a perfect substitute for its product.

(f) The set of arguments to be pursued here and under (g) is undoubtedly the most hazardous and controversial of the group. It has to do with time horizons.

Suppose that the shadow prices (read: the prices prevailing under competition) of the productive services do accurately reflect the factor proportions and high degree of risk characteristic of the underdeveloped countries. Even if real costs such as those associated with transfer and training are included, the shadow or accounting prices for unskilled and semi-skilled labor should be relatively low. That is, they tend to lie below the going wages or perhaps even below the subsistence levels because of the very low productivity of labor. Interest rates would tend to be relatively high, reflecting the evident scarcity of capital and the strong preference for present consumption. The shadow price of capital, it is argued, would particularly tend to exceed the going market price in the more advanced sectors of the poor economies, because of the tendency toward governmental interference in the capital market. Since long-term ventures are generally risky, they would as compensation require high profit rates over and above the already high pure interest rates.

In this world in which the productive services are valued at their current shadow prices, let us next assume production functions that permit a reasonable degree of substitutability between the various types of capital on the one hand and the various kinds of labor services on the other. In these circumstances, the relatively high productivity of capital may at times more than offset the higher prices attached to its services and thereby encourage the use of capital in a number of pursuits. In the more usual case, however, the relative prices tend to direct producers to more labor-intensive modes of production within particular industries as well as to goods requiring a greater concentration of labor services. Some writers see this as a necessity because they are intent upon reducing the unemployment in the system.[14] Others view labor-intensive production as a contribution to growth itself. Thereupon they advocate "a tax on credit provided by the organized banking sector"[15] or subsidies to firms for increasing their employment of labor.[16]

---

[14] *Ibid.*, Chapter II, especially sections 1, 3, and 5.
[15] Papanek and Qureshi, *op. cit.*, p. 53.
[16] Henry J. Burton, *Principles of Development Economics* (Englewood Cliffs, N.J.: Prentice-Hall, Inc., 1965), p. 136.

Advice of this sort would seem to be debatable. When the price system decides the issues of the mode of production in favor of more man hours and a lower ratio of fixed capital to working capital, it may well be guiding the economy to slower growth, now and in the future. There is at least a possibility—not necessarily remote—that the husbandry of capital and the thin use of fixed capital, appropriate for the immediate period, may result in the *conservation of capital formation* in the longer run. For purposes of growth, it might instead be advisable to lengthen the time horizon and to employ prices reflecting later periods of time.

Let us listen to one pair of authors, generally inclined to advocate a resort to shadow prices as guides to economic growth:

> If they [the accounting prices] are set to achieve equilibrium at present, this will lead to an efficient allocation of resources at present, but since factor supplies will change in the future, it will lead to increasing inefficiencies over time. On the other hand, setting accounting prices to achieve equilibrium at some future date would mean inefficiencies now.[17]

Given their concern with future weaknesses, they recommend the last year of the current planning period as the time horizon; beyond that, they believe, the planners are not likely to possess sufficiently detailed information about the economy and its factor markets. The number of years in question is of little importance (they suggest four or six), particularly since accounting prices are always governed by a high degree of arbitrariness anyway. The significant point of course is the indication that today's shadow prices may lead to tomorrow's inefficiencies. Should the authorities thereupon decide to employ the factor prices of future years, they would be forced to consider modifications in the factor proportions and to give relatively greater employment to capital.

One other means of raising some doubts about equilibrium couched in terms of current shadow prices is to focus on the price of capital. Prevalent interest rates in the developing countries evidently exceed the rates in the richer countries by a considerable margin. The use of current shadow prices would tend to force interest rates to still higher levels because of the relatively high marginal productivity of capital, and these interest rates would in turn direct entrepreneurs to decisions that would help preserve the relative scarcity of capital goods. The prevalent interest rates also reflect the high individual time preferences—the tendency to discount the future sharply in an environment in which the masses typically struggle through short lives and the wealthy usually pursue their hedonistic philosophies. There is no reason why the community in its entirety should discredit the future in this fashion; quite the contrary.

---

[17]Papanek and Qureshi, *op. cit.*, p. 52.

The social time preference should be considerably lower. This would imply that relatively low rates of interest ought to be applied as costs and for discounting in order to determine the priorities of investment projects.

In short, an adherence to current shadow prices tends to lead to a distorted allocation of resources from a dynamic point of view. Since this conclusion is a negative one, it requires a few comments about the available pricing alternatives.

Given the validity of the above argument, it would be proper to employ the prices applicable for a decade or two hence. The prices would then reflect an economy accustomed to growth. However, such prices would evidently be little more than "questimates"[18] and as such would be quite useless. The alternative is to use the current market prices of labor and capital as points of departure. In part this is because decisions regarding accounting prices are quite arbitrary, as noted, and they tend to be based upon current actual prices in any event.[19] The actual market prices of labor and capital further represent a useful first approximation in that, like shadow prices based on the factor mix in the future, they promote the employment of capital relative to labor, but, like the current shadow prices, they still lead to largely labor-intensive modes of production. This is not to assert, however, that the authorities must accept the wages and interest rates of the moment as sacrosanct. Governments may alter the prices of the productive services in a fashion which is in keeping with their growth objectives. The policy makers certainly should seek to reduce interest rates in the countryside, where monopoly power is often a key factor. Whether interest rates should also be reduced in the advanced sector depends both upon the degree of inflation that has been experienced and that is regarded as tolerable. Whatever reductions in interest rates do occur need not be general but can be discriminatory in favor of certain industries, although typically not in favor of individual firms in those industries. Wage increases for the skilled and semi-skilled in the advanced sector need to be restricted to the improvements in productivity. This is true for a variety of reasons: insofar as the relationships between labor and capital are complementary rather than substitutive, wage restraints encourage capital formation; such a wage policy reduces the degree of inflation, which is likely to occur in any event; limitations upon wage increases mitigate the rise of an elite labor force and reduce the degree of inequality and inequity to be found among workers; and the

---

[18]I owe this "innovation" to the typist of the first draft, who mistook my "g" for a "q". Thus a word has been coined. This apparently supports the hypothesis that many "innovators" have simply erred in their attempts to act as imitators.

[19]For further comments on the "practical limitations in applying the concept" of shadow prices, see the United Nations, Economic Commission for Latin America, *Manual for Economic Development Projects* (E/CN.12/426 Add. 1/Rev. 1), pp. 205, 207.

policy should diminish the excessive flow of migrants from the countryside into the city in the hope of great economic gain.

Nor are there any easy paths to pursue in the pricing of final goods and services, given the objective of economic growth. Public economic enterprises might be prevailed upon to price at marginal cost, insofar as this can be determined, in order to alleviate any idle capacity on their part and to enhance the net external economies for which they may be responsible. Perhaps the most useful approach in the case of private firms is to focus on the spread between producers' prices and costs. The authorities would act to increase business profits where desirable, as in the genuine infant industry case, and reduce them in activities where they are already high and not terribly conducive to growth, as is frequently true in commerce. The techniques for doing so could embrace taxes, subsidies, allowances for accelerated depreciation and the provision of various productive facilities at below cost.

There is little disagreement, finally, over the appropriate policy regarding the price of foreign exchange. In order to reduce the costs of the goods which they must import, and perhaps for reasons of prestige as well, the developing nations typically undervalue other currencies relative to their own. (From their point of view, the exchange rates are low.) This in turn generally necessitates exchange controls to protect balance of payments positions, since the going exchange rates favor imports and tend to discourage exports. It is well known that inadequate foreign exchange very frequently constrains economic development. If the prevalent exchange rates were used as guides in decision making, this would lead to the wasteful use of an exceedingly precious, undervalued resource. In this instance, therefore, shadow prices should definitely be used as much as possible in planning and in assigning priorities to investment projects. An attempt should also be made to raise the everyday prices to the levels of the shadow prices through such techniques as devaluation and charges upon imports.

(g) This last section is in the nature of an addendum to (f). It transfers some of the propositions regarding time horizons and the inadequate facilities associated with poverty to the area of international trade. In this realm, comparative advantage may dictate the production and sales of commodities suffering deteriorating terms of trade. Without governmental assistance, the current specialized facilities may yield such comparatively low unit costs at the moment as to discourage the shifting that would be desirable over the longer period. (Note, for example, the production of cotton in the United States South during the nineteenth century.) On the other hand, the public provision of capital, the establishment of pilot plants, added training, market reorganization, and so on would encourage a shift to other products that could be more beneficial in the longer run. Moreover, what would be the consequences if market prices alone dictated the composition of imports? Given the usual time preferences, would there not be a fairly strong concentration on consumer goods, and hence a misuse of foreign exchange in terms of the growth objective?

In sum, in an underdeveloped country the price system is itself under-developed; this seems crystal clear. The second part of the argument is perhaps less conclusive, namely that where the price system does exhibit signs of strength it nonetheless functions so as to yield fairly good static results but it does not necessarily encourage satisfactory economic growth.

The Nature of Governmental Activities in the Developing Countries

The cases discussed are quite characteristic of underdevelopment. Most of them hamper economic development in most of the poor countries. They certainly impose enough deterrents to growth to justify a rather considerable degree of governmental participation at the microeconomic level. The particular governmental services to be rendered are suggested by the weaknesses of the price system and/or the difficulties confronting prices in their attempts to guide an underdeveloped world. In various ways, the government can promote competition, knowledge, and mobil-ity—as it must indeed continue to do to a lesser degree in the richer nations. Even more, it needs to reduce risk and uncertainty (frequently of its own making), to further investment in human beings, and to promote technological change. These things typically do not have to do with prices but with attacking the conditions of poverty—with shifting the functions—so that the prices can more easily direct the system along the lines of growth. In addition, governments should of course promote capital formation, sometimes directly through their own efforts but more frequently in mixed economies through pecuniary incentives to private firms.

Yet, is not the government itself likely to be underdeveloped? It is most certainly subject to inefficiency as a result of a paucity of adminis-trative skills, and it is likely to be characterized by some favoritism and dishonesty, as in the case of the United States' spoil's system during the nineteenth century. When the hidden payments are fairly uniform, steady, and predictable, and when they are used to compensate government officials whose salaries are otherwise quite low because of inadequate tax revenues, the sums thus exacted can be included in the costs of an enter-prise. These matters are considerably more serious when they bear little relation to growth, thus distorting the allocations of resources for invest-ment purposes. In some instances the government may not be at all inclined toward positive action. Then the immediate prospects for development are indeed dim, since there is really no good substitute for stirring a stagnant economy. The point, after all, is not that a government must necessarily behave well, but that even when its performance is mediocre it plays an indispensable role in fomenting change. If it does not assume the initiative in the currently developing nations, there is typically nothing else to take its place.

One issue that is not to be denied in a work on systems concerns the *form* of governmental involvement in any given industry. The alternatives are considerable. The government may be sole owner; it may permit private participation while itself owning and operating some plants; or it may be content to see ownership and control lodged in private hands, but subject to various regulations. Whether the government furthers investment through its ownership or through inducements to private industry may have as much to do with the community's general attitude toward public ownership as it does with advancing income as such. Typically, government ownership characterizes the activities with extensive external economies, high capital requirements, and long pay-off periods—that is, the social overhead capital, social infrastructure, or public utilities. Industry, mining, agriculture and commerce are more generally delegated to the business sector, although the Japanese frequently employed public ownership as a means of establishing pilot plants which were later sold to private firms. Some industries, such as steel and fertilizers, are borderline candidates for public ownership, since their external economies are stronger than in the case of other industrial ventures. At times, authorities have selected the alternative of public and private sharing of production within a given industry. This arrangement seems desirable in either one of two sets of circumstances, and it calls for a certain condition. It is legitimate, first, as a device for countering monopoly power. If the industry should be reasonably competitive with respect to prices and other matters, then some, or for that matter total, government ownership may still be justified if the industry is old and stagnant and does not yield workably competitive results despite its more competitive structure. When an industry is monopolistic and/or nonprogressive, the device of partial government ownership may thus be an appropriate one. A necessary condition, however, is that the government avoid preferential treatment of the public firms and discrimination against the private ones. Selective treatment within industries does not tend to yield satisfactory economic results. If the government is inclined to discriminate against its private competitors, let it turn instead to complete private or public ownership, depending upon the community's values and the criteria adopted.

The Extensive Role of the Price System in the Economically Advanced Countries

As an economy moves into and beyond a middle-income status and its government has rendered its own singular contributions, it should be prepared to shed most of its interferences at the microeconomic level. Once involved, it will not find it easy to do so, frequently because of the resistance offered by the beneficiaries of its interference. Nevertheless, it should strive to diminish its microeconomic role in the interests of both freedom and economic growth. Most persons do assign high values to the freedoms of consumer and occupational choice. These basic economic liberties are in turn furthered by business freedoms. Decentralized decision making at the producer's level not only provides liberties for firms but assures that no single, large organization possesses enough power to interfere with the freedoms of consumer and occupational choice. Further, a minimum of governmental regulation at the microeconomic level now becomes desirable for growth purposes. The economy by now possesses a momentum. Specific interferences, particularly with prices, could well reduce the flexibility and mobility required of a dynamic economy. Firms continuing under government ownership will, it is hoped, price on a marginal or average cost basis and, as much as possible, meet market competition in attracting the various productive services.

The most difficult period for generalizations about the relative roles of government and the price system in microeconomic affairs occurs during the *transition* from underdeveloped to developed country status, especially since different industries within an economy develop at different rates and at different times. There are no clear criteria, not even per capita incomes, for distinguishing between the rich and the poor countries; there exists a vast middle range which can accommodate both types of communities. The majority of the following questions would have to be answered in the affirmative if a country is to be regarded as relatively advanced and prepared for the price system. Has its per capita income risen to a level of at least several hundred dollars? Has it been developing at an annual rate of at least 2 per cent a year in per capita terms for an extended period, and has it done so without foreign aid? Is there a growing labor shortage? Is the private propensity to save relatively high, say 10 per cent in net terms? Has illiteracy all but been eliminated? Unless the country is specializing in primary commodities, has the proportion of the work force in agriculture been reduced to a range of approximately thirty to forty per cent? Except in the case of an exceedingly marked comparative advantage in one commodity, has the structure of exports been diversified? Are transportation, energy, professional and other social overhead services in sufficient supply to forestall rapidly rising production costs? Have manufacturing concerns reached a point in their development where declining unit costs seem to flow as much or more from technological advance as from economies of scale? As a valid sign of reduced risk and uncertainty, is private foreign capital anxious to invest in a variety of endeavors? No one of these criteria is definitive. If, as a group, they offer some consensus, this would indicate that the time had arrived for a reduction in the government posture toward the private sector. The economy should now be more price directed, and particular prices should be considerably less influenced by deliberate governmental policies.

Conclusions to Chapters 11 and 12

The following remarks suggest themselves as a result of the foregoing foray into the relationship between systems and growth.

(a) Many other variables intrude upon the relationship between systems and growth and frequently render generalizations difficult. What often matters for growth is not so much the type of organization or ideology adopted (indeed, the latter can be a hindrance) but technical competence, rationality and a dedication to the growth objective. Given the latter qualities, diverse types of economic systems may yield relatively satisfactory growth performances.

(b) Nonetheless, both *a priori* reasoning and the available evidence suggest that as a group the communist societies tend to be relatively successful in promoting increases in total output because of their sacrifice of consumer welfare and their greater ability to influence the factors responsible for growth. Models approaching *laissez-faire* would seem to yield the lowest growth rates. Mixed economies, including those of the fascistic regimes, occupy a middle position with respect to their success in stimulating growth. Most of the world's nations have, of course, opted for the form of the mixed economy which yields a combination of economic growth and some measure of personal freedom.

(c) Governments participate widely in economic affairs in both the developing nations and in those that are more mature economically. Poverty dictates to the members of the more numerous first group that they adopt somewhat more authoritarian systems and that their governments intervene much more at the microeconomic level than is true of the richer countries.

(d) Finally, it should be useful to recall the earlier discussions, in Chapters 1 and 11, of the many functions that are performed by a political and economic system. This diversity of functions imposes an important constraint upon the social scientist. He can establish the means for ranking systems on the basis of a single criterion, but he cannot order them according to several criteria without entering into problems of weighting and value judgments. Thus the subject matter in the last two chapters has concerned the relation of growth to systems, and it has been possible to rank various systems on the basis of their growth performances alone. Even in this discussion, however, it seemed necessary to include some observations about opportunity costs, such as the possible effects of exceedingly rapid growth upon personal freedom. It is to be stressed that the rankings attached to various systems on the basis of their ability to grow do not imply similar gradations of political-economic systems taken in their entirety.

Review Questions

Chapter 1

1. To what does the term *economic system* refer and what are the basic questions which must be answered by any economic system?

2. Describe the distinguishing characteristics of each of the three major types of economic systems—capitalism, corporatism and socialism.

3. What are the success criteria which Professor Balassa has selected for the purpose of evaluating economic systems? Can they be used to develop a completely objective ranking of systems? Explain fully.

4. Describe carefully the concepts of static and dynamic efficiency.

5. Explain the difference between the actual growth rate and dynamic efficiency.

Chapter 2

1. Describe the economic characteristics of the Middle Ages in Western Europe.

2. Describe the important factors contributing to the industrial revolution.

3. What was the economic situation of the laboring class in England during the industrial revolution, and what were the major factors contributing to it? Explain carefully.

4. Describe the significant economic ideas and accomplishments of Robert Owen.

5. Compare and contrast the stages of industrial capitalism and financial capitalism.

6. Describe briefly some of the important departures from a strict *laissez-faire* policy which have occurred in the United States since 1914.

227

Chapter 3

1. What conclusion did John Stuart Mill draw concerning the long-run trend of economic development and through what reasoning did he reach it?

2. Describe briefly the important developments in Marx's life to the period when Engels and he began their collaboration.

3. Why did Marx and Engels write *The Communist Manifesto*, and what important thoughts were developed in it? Explain carefully.

4. Compare and contrast the thinking and activities of Marx and Lassalle.

5. Describe the nature and history of the First International and Marx's role in it.

Chapter 4

1. How did Ricardo eliminate rent and capital in the determination of relative exchange values, and how valid is the labor theory of value? Explain carefully.

2. What does Marx mean by the term *constant capital*, of what components is the flow of constant capital composed, and what does he consider to be the contribution of constant capital to the value of the goods which it helps to produce? Explain carefully.

3. Has Marx's concept of the contribution of constant capital caused any difficulties for the Communist regime in Russia in the making of investment decisions? Explain.

4. Using the letter notation adopted by Marx, show the total value of the output of a firm for a given period and also its total cost of production. Explain carefully Marx's concept of the difference between these two totals.

5. Compare and contrast Marx's concept of the *rate of surplus value* and his concept of the *rate of profit*.

6. Would aggregating Marx's concept of the gross value of the annual output of individual firms in the economy give the figure for GNP? If not, what adjustments would be needed to give a closer approximation of GNP? Explain.

7. Explain carefully and evaluate critically Marx's transformation analysis.

8. Explain carefully Marx's concept of the *reserve army of labor* and indicate the importance of this concept for his analysis of the capitalistic system.

9. Why did Marx reject the so-called *natural laws?* Explain.

10. Given the weaknesses in some of Marx's basic arguments, what accounts for the wide attention which his book, *Capital*, has attracted over a long span of time? Explain carefully.

Chapter 5

1. In accepting Say's Law and the concept of savings as a function of the rate of interest, what conclusions about the trend of an economy characterized by conditions of *laissez-faire* and pure competition did the neoclassical economists tend to reach? Explain carefully.

2. What conclusion about the behavior of a mature capitalistic economy did Keynes draw from his concept that savings are primarily a function of the level of income? Explain.

3. By what reasoning does Schumpeter reach his conclusion about the long-run prospects for capitalism? Explain carefully.

4. What does Galbraith mean by the "technostructure" and what role does he say that this group plays in a mature capitalistic economy like that of the United States? Explain.

5. Why does Galbraith consider that there has been a breaking down of the free market in mature capitalistic systems?

6. Are there any theses concerning the possible long-run future of capitalism other than those suggested by Marx, Schumpeter and Galbraith which may be plausible? Explain.

Chapter 6

1. Under what circumstances did communist societies develop in the Greek period? Explain and give examples.

2. How did Plato view the existing society of his time and what proposals for change did he make? Explain. How did Aristotle's views differ from Plato's? Explain.

3. Compare and contrast the communal society of the Spartans with that of the Essenes.

4. What were some of the important thoughts developed in More's *Utopia*, and what is the historical significance of this work? Explain carefully.

5. How did Rousseau view the existing legal structure, and what was his attitude toward private property? Explain carefully.

6. What ideas are common to some of the Utopian writers and to Marx? Explain.

Chapter 7

1. What is the basic distinction between utopian socialist thought and *scientific socialism*? Explain carefully.

2. Summarize the Hegelian dialectic and describe carefully the adaptation of this dialectic formulated by Marx.

3. How did Marx view the concept of the class struggle from the historical standpoint? Explain.

4. What shortcoming did Rosa Luxemburg see in Marx's analysis and what line of thought did she develop to overcome it? Explain carefully.

5. What led Bernstein to develop his doctrine, and basically what was this doctrine? Explain carefully.

6. Did Marx's writings provide useful operational guidelines for Lenin's new communist regime in Russia, and was this regime able to institute comprehensive planning quickly? Explain.

7. Describe briefly Pareto's view concerning the problem involved in determining an efficient allocation of resources under socialism.

Chapter 8

1. Describe carefully Mises' theory of value.

2. What is the significance of free market prices in Mises' analysis? Are they objective or subjective? Explain.

3. Explain carefully why Mises believes that socialist systems cannot attain economic efficiency.

4. What conclusion did Professor Robbins reach concerning the attainment of economic efficiency under socialism? Explain.

5. What would be the practical implications of the conclusions of Mises and Robbins if they were valid? Explain.

Chapter 9

1. In what sense did Mises' criticisms of socialist doctrine represent a challenge to socialist theoreticians? Explain carefully.

2. Describe Professor Taylor's solution to the economic efficiency problem under socialism and explain how it avoided the mathematical difficulties described by Hayek and Robbins.

3. Explain carefully the concept of prices which Lange considered to be relevant for a socialist system.

4. Describe the nature of the markets which characterize Lange's system of liberal socialism and explain how equilibrium would be approached under this system.

5. Evaluate carefully the advantages which Lange claims for a system of liberal socialism.

6. What would be the role of the interest rate in Lange's model of liberal socialism, and how has Russia's authoritarian socialist system handled the interest rate question? Explain carefully.

7. What is Sweezy's concept of the monopolistic and imperialistic stage of capitalism? Explain carefully.

8. What questions can be raised concerning both the determinateness of equilibrium and the determination of the social welfare function under socialism? Explain carefully.

Chapter 10

1. Describe carefully the distinctive characteristics of corporatism.

2. What was the objective of early nineteenth century corporatist thinkers? Were they able to achieve it? Explain carefully.

3. Describe carefully the philosophy of Social Catholicism as it developed in the latter half of the nineteenth century.

4. Develop a critical analysis of Italian fascism.

5. How did the Fascist regime in Italy view the policy of *laissez-faire* and the institution of private property? Explain.

6. Describe the nature of corporatist developments in the post-World War II period.

Chapter 11

1. How do past and present views differ concerning the attainment of greater economic and social justice? Explain.

2. A change in organization is often a necessary but not a sufficient condition for the attainment of satisfactory growth. Comment.

3. The relationship between a nation's growth rate and its mode of organization depends upon the wide variety of functions which its economic system may be called upon to perform. Comment.

4. The wide diversity of factors affecting economic growth greatly complicates any discussion of the relationship between growth and systems. Comment carefully.

5. What historical sequence of stages did Marx detect, and how valid does his sequence seem to be in the light of recent history? Comment. What revision may be needed in the sequence proposed by Marx to make it more realistic?

6. Systems are in part correlated with and in part dependent upon levels of per capita income. Comment carefully.

7. On *a priori* grounds one would expect the communist countries as a whole to perform relatively well in the area of economic growth, but at the expense of personal freedom and improved planes of living for consumers. Comment carefully.

8. What can be said of the growth rates in the East European communist nations other than Russia and Yugoslavia during the 1950's and the first half of the 1960's? Comment.

9. Do incremental output-capital ratios in the communist countries seem to have been rather low or rather high? Explain.

10. Can any clear-cut conclusions be drawn about the product-per-man-year performance of Germany, Italy and Japan during their fascist periods in relation to that of a selected group of non-fascist nations during the same period? Explain.

Chapter 12

1. Discuss the relation of government intervention to growth and freedom.

2. Why does the mixed economy tend to yield economic results that are superior to *laissez-faire?* Explain.

3. Do the appropriate functions of government tend to change as an economy advances? Explain.

4. An operating price system in an underdeveloped country may direct economic resources effectively in the immediate period yet help to retard the long-run growth of the economy. Discuss carefully.

5. As an economy moves into middle income status and beyond, in part through proper governmental contributions, the government should be prepared to terminate most of its interferences at the microeconomic level. Explain.

6. What are some of the important questions that would have to be answered in the affirmative if a country is to be considered as relatively advanced and ready for the operation of the price system?

7. Describe the nature and use of shadow or accounting prices in relation to economic development.

Selections for Further Reading

Aitken, Hugh G. J., ed., *The State and Economic Growth*. New York: Social Science Research Council, 1959.

The American Assembly, The President's Commission on National Goals, *Goals for Americans*. Englewood Cliffs, N. J.: Prentice-Hall, Inc., 1960.

Argarwala, A. N., and S. P. Singh, eds., *The Economics of Underdevelopment*. New York: Oxford University Press, Inc., 1958.

Balassa, Bela A., "Success Criteria for Economic Systems," *The Hungarian Experience in Economic Planning*. New Haven, Conn.: Yale University Press, 1959, pp. 5-24.

Barach, Arnold B., *U.S.A. and Its Economic Future*. New York: The Macmillan Company, 1964.

Baran, Paul, *The Political Economy of Growth*. New York: Monthly Review Press, 1957.

Barone, Enrico, "The Ministry of Production in the Collectivist State," reprinted in *Collectivist Economic Planning*, ed. Frederick A. von Hayek. London: George Routledge & Sons, Ltd., 1935.

Bauer, Pèter Tamàs, and Basil S. Yamey, *The Economics of Underdeveloped Countries*. Chicago: University of Chicago Press, 1957.

Bergson, Abram, *The Economics of Soviet Planning*. New Haven, Conn.: Yale University Press, 1964.

Berle, Adolf A., *Power Without Property*. New York: Harcourt, Brace & World, Inc., 1959.

——————, *The 20th Century Capitalist Revolution*. New York: Harcourt, Brace & World, Inc., 1954.

Berlin, I., *Karl Marx, His Life and Environment*. New York: Oxford University Press, Inc., 1963.

Bernstein, Eduard, *Evolutionary Socialism*. New York: Schocken Books, Inc., 1961.

Beveridge, William H., *Full Employment in a Free Society*, New York: W. W. Norton & Company, Inc., 1945.

Bird, Richard, and Oliver Oldman, eds., *Readings on Taxation in Developing Countries*. Baltimore, Md.: The Johns Hopkins Press, 1964.

Blough, Roger, *Free Men and the Corporation.* New York: McGraw-Hill Book Company, 1959.

Bober, M. M., *Karl Marx's Interpretation of History,* 2nd ed. Cambridge, Mass.: Harvard University Press, 1950.

————, "Marx and Economic Calculation," *American Economic Review,* 36, June 1946, 344-357.

Borgese, Giuseppe Antonio, *Goliath.* New York: The Viking Press, Inc., 1938.

Bornstein, Morris, "The Soviet Price System," *American Economic Review,* 52, March 1962, 64-103.

————, ed., *Comparative Economic Systems: Models and Cases.* Homewood, Ill.: Richard D. Irwin, Inc., 1965.

Borstein, Morris, and Daniel R. Fusfeld, eds., *The Soviet Economy: A Book of Readings,* rev. ed. Homewood, Ill.: Richard D. Irwin, Inc., 1966.

Boulding, Kenneth E., *The Organizational Revolution.* New York: Harper & Row, Publishers, 1953.

Bruton, Henry J., *Principles of Development Economics.* Englewood Cliffs, N. J.: Prentice-Hall, Inc., 1964.

Brzezinski, Zbigniew, and Samuel P. Huntington, "America and Russia: Converging Nations?" *Columbia University Forum,* Winter 1964, pp. 12-17.

Buchanan, James M., "Social Choice, Democracy, and Free Markets," *Journal of Political Economy,* LXII, April 1954, 114-23.

Buckingham, Walter S., Jr., *Theoretical Economic Systems: A Comparative Analysis.* New York: The Ronald Press Company, 1958.

Bunting, John R., *The Hidden Face of Free Enterprise: The Strange Economics of the American Businessman.* New York: McGraw-Hill Book Company, 1964.

Cairncross, Alexander Kirkland, *Factors in Economic Development.* London: G. Allen & Unwin, Ltd., 1962.

Canes, Richard, *American Industry: Structure, Conduct, Performance.* Englewood Cliffs, N. J.: Prentice-Hall, Inc., 1964.

Cheit, Earl F., ed., *The Business Establishment.* New York: John Wiley & Sons, Inc., 1964.

Cole, George Douglas Howard, *Fabian Socialism.* London: G. Allen & Unwin, Ltd., 1943.

————, *Socialist Economics.* London: Victor Gollancz, Ltd., 1950.

Committee for Economic Development, Research and Policy Committee, *How Low Income Countries Can Advance Their Own Growth.* New York: C.E.D., 1966.

Crosland, Charles Anthony Raven, *The Future of Socialism.* London: Jonathan Cape, 1956.

Demas, William G., *The Economics of Development in Small Countries: With Special Reference to the Caribbean.* Montreal: McGill University Press, 1965.

Dickinson, Henry Douglas, *Economics of Socialism*. New York: Oxford University Press, Inc., 1939.

―――――, "Price Formation in a Socialist Community," *Economic Journal*, Vol. XLIII, June 1933.

Djilas, Milovan, *The New Class: An Analysis of the Communist System*. New York: Frederick A. Praeger, Inc., 1957.

Dobb, Maurice Herbert, "Economic Theory and the Problem of a Socialist Economy," *Economic Journal*, Vol. XLIII, December 1933.

―――――, *On Economic Theory and Socialism*. London: George Routledge & Sons, Ltd., 1955.

―――――, *Political Economy and Capitalism*. London: George Routledge & Sons, Ltd., 1937.

―――――, *Studies in the Development of Capitalism*. London: George Routledge & Sons, Ltd., 1963.

Domar, Evsey, *Essays in the Theory of Economic Growth*. New York: Oxford University Press, Inc., 1957.

Downs, Anthony, "A Theory of Bureaucracy," *American Economic Review*, 55, May 1965, 439-46.

Drewnowski, Jan, "The Economic Theory of Socialism: A Suggestion for Reconsideration," *Journal of Political Economy*, LXIX, August 1961, 341-354.

Durbin, Evan Frank Mottram, "Economic Calculus in a Planned Economy," *Economic Journal*, Vol. XLVI, December 1936.

Eastman, Max, *Reflections on the Failure of Socialism*. New York: The Devin-Adair Co., 1955.

Eckstein, Alexander, "Individualism and the Role of the State in Economic Growth," *Economic Development and Cultural Change*, VI, January 1958, 81-87.

Enke, Stephen, *Economics for Development*. Englewood Cliffs, N. J.: Prentice-Hall, Inc., 1963.

Finer, Herman, *Mussolini's Italy*. New York: Holt, Rinehart & Winston, Inc., 1935.

Fisher, Allan G. B., "Alternative Techniques for Promoting Equality in a Capitalist Society," *American Economic Review*, XL, May 1950, 356-68.

Friedman, Milton, *Capitalism and Freedom*. Chicago: University of Chicago Press, 1962.

Galbraith, John Kenneth, *The Affluent Society*. Boston: Houghton Mifflin Company, 1958.

―――――, *American Capitalism: The Concept of Countervailing Power*. Boston: Houghton Mifflin Company, 1952.

―――――, *Economic Development in Perspective*. Cambridge, Mass.: Harvard University Press, 1962.

_____, *The New Industrial State.* Boston: Houghton Mifflin Company, 1967.

Goldman, Marshall I., ed., *Comparative Economic Systems, A Reader.* New York: Random House, Inc., 1964.

Golob, Eugene O., *The "Isms": A History and Evaluation.* New York: Harper & Row, Publishers, 1954.

Gordon, Margaret S., "U. S. Welfare Policies in Perspective," *Industrial Relations*, 2, No. 2, February 1963, 33-61.

Gray, Alexander, *The Socialist Tradition: Moses to Lenin.* London: Longmans, Green and Co., 1947.

Green, Robert W., ed., *Protestantism and Capitalism: The Weber Thesis and Its Critics.* Boston: D. C. Heath & Company, 1959.

Grossman, Gregory, "Notes for a Theory of the Command Economy," *Soviet Studies*, 15, October 1963, 119-23.

_____, ed., *Value and Plan.* Berkeley: University of California Press, 1960.

Hacker, Andrew, ed., *The Corporation Take-Over.* New York: Harper & Row, Publishers, 1964.

Hagen, Everett E., *The Economics of Development.* Homewood, Ill,: Richard D. Irwin, Inc., 1968.

Hall, R. L., *The Economic System in a Socialist State.* New York: St. Martin's Press, Inc., 1937.

Halm, George N., *Economic Systems: A Comparative Analysis*, 3rd ed. New York: Holt, Rinehart & Winston, Inc., 1968.

_____, "Further Considerations on the Possibility of Adequate Calculation in a Socialist Community," in *Collectivist Economic Planning*, ed. F. A. von Hayek. London: George Routledge & Sons, Ltd., 1935.

Hansen, Alvin H., *The American Economy.* New York: McGraw-Hill Book Company, 1957.

Harbison, Frederick, and Charles A. Myers, *Education, Manpower and Economic Growth; Strategies of Human Resource Development*, New York: McGraw-Hill Book Company, 1964.

Harrod, Roy F., *Towards a Dynamic Economics.* London: Macmillan & Company, 1948.

Von Hayek, Frederick A., *The Road to Serfdom.* Chicago: University of Chicago Press, 1944.

_____, "Socialist Calculation: The Competitive 'Solution'," *Economica*, New Series, Vol. 7 (1940).

_____, ed., *Capitalism and the Historians.* Chicago: University of Chicago Press, 1954.

Von Hayek, Frederick, *et al.*, *Collectivist Economic Planning: Critical Studies on the Possibilities of Socialism.* London: Routledge and Kegan Paul Ltd., 1935.

Heimann, Eduard, "Planning and the Market System," *Social Research*, Vol. I, November 1934.

Heller, Walter W., *New Dimensions of Political Economy.* Cambridge, Mass.: Harvard University Press, 1966.

Higgins, Benjamin, *Economic Development*, rev. ed. New York: W. W. Norton & Company, Inc., 1968.

Hirschman, Albert O., *Strategy of Economic Development.* New Haven, Conn.: Yale University Press, 1958.

Hoff, Trygve J. B., *Economic Calculation in the Socialist Economy.* London: William Hodge and Company, Ltd., 1949.

Holzman, Franklin D., ed., *Readings on the Soviet Economy.* Chicago: Rand McNally & Co., 1962.

Hook, Sidney, *From Hegel to Marx.* Ann Arbor, Mich.: University of Michigan Press, 1962.

————, *Marx and the Marxists: The Ambiguous Legacy*, Princeton, N. J.: D. Van Nostrand Co., Inc., 1955.

Hoover, Calvin B., *The Economy, Liberty, and the State*, New York: Twentieth Century Fund, 1959.

Hoselitz, Berthold F., ed., *Theories of Economic Growth.* New York: The Free Press, 1960.

Hunt, R. N. Carew, *The Theory and Practice of Communism.* Baltimore: Penquin Books, Inc., 1963.

Hunter, Holland, "Optimal Tautness in Developmental Planning," *Economic Development and Cultural Change*, 9, July 1961, 561-72.

Jay, Douglas, *Socialism in the New Society*, New York: Longmans, Green and Co., 1962.

Johnson, Harry G., "Planning and the Market in Economic Development," *Pakistan Economic Journal*, VIII, June 1958, 44-55.

Kapp, William K., *Social Costs of Business Enterprise.* New York: Asia Publishing House, 1963.

Keynes, John Maynard, *The General Theory of Employment, Interest and Money.* New York: Harcourt, Brace & World, Inc., 1936.

Knight, Frank H., "The Place of Marginal Economics in a Collectivist System," *American Economic Review*, supplement to Vol. XXVI, March 1936.

Kolko, Gabriel, *Wealth and Power in America: An Analysis of Social Class and Income Distribution.* New York: Frederick A. Praeger, Inc., 1962.

Kuznets, Simon, *Economic Growth and Structure.* New York: W. W. Norton & Company, Inc., 1965.

Landauer, Carl, *Contemporary Economic Systems, A Comparative Analysis*, Philadelphia and New York: J. B. Lippincott Co., 1964.

————, "Value Theory and Economic Planning," *Plan Age*, Vol. III, October 1937.

Landauer, Carl, *et al. European Socialism: A History of Ideas and Movements*, Vols. I and II. Berkeley: University of California Press, 1959.

Lange, Oskar, and Fred M. Taylor, in *On the Economic Theory of Socialism*, ed. B. E. Lippincott. Minneapolis: University of Minnesota Press, 1938.

Leeman, Wayne A., ed., *Capitalism, Market Socialism, and Central Planning: Readings in Comparative Economic Systems*. Boston: Houghton Mifflin Company, 1963.

Leibenstein, Harvey, *Economic Backwardness and Economic Growth*. New York: John Wiley & Sons, Inc., 1957.

Lerner, Abba P., "Marxism and Economics: Sweezy and Robinson," *Journal of Political Economy*, 53, March 1945, 81.

————, *The Economics of Control*. New York: The Macmillan Company, 1946.

————, "Economic Theory and Socialist Economy," *Review of Economic Studies*, Vol. II, October 1934.

————, "A Note on Socialist Economics," *Review of Economic Studies*, Vol. IV, October 1936.

————, "Statics and Dynamics in Socialist Economics," *Economic Journal*, Vol. XLVII, June 1937.

Levine, H., "The Centralized Planning of Supply in Soviet Industry," *Comparisons of the U. S. and Soviet Economies*, pp. 151-75. Washington, D.C.: Government Printing Office, 1959.

Lewis, W. Arthur, *The Theory of Economic Growth*. London: G. Allen & Unwin, Ltd., 1955.

Lichtheim, George, *Marxism, An Historical and Critical Study*. New York: Frederick A. Praeger, Inc., 1961.

Litterer, Joseph A., ed., *Organizations: Structure and Behavior*. New York: John Wiley & Sons, Inc., 1963.

Little, J. M. D., and J. M. Clifford, *International Aid*. Chicago: Aldine Publishing Company, 1966.

Loucks, William N., *Comparative Economic Systems*, 7th ed. New York: Harper & Row, Publishers, 1965.

McGuire, Joseph William, *Business and Society*. New York: McGraw-Hill Book Company, 1963.

Machlup, Fritz, *The Production and Distribution of Knowledge in the United States*. Princeton, N. J.: Princeton University Press, 1962.

Marris, Robin, *The Economic Theory of "Managerial" Capitalism*. New York: Harcourt, Brace & World, Inc., 1954.

Marx, Karl, *Capital*, Moore and Aneling translation of the 3rd German edition, Vols. I, II, and III. Moscow: Foreign Languages Publishing House, 1961.

Marx, Karl, and Friedrich Engels, *The Communist Manifesto*, with an introduction by A. J. P. Taylor. Baltimore, Md.: Penguin Books, Inc., 1967.

Mason, Edward S., ed., *The Corporation in Modern Society*. Cambridge, Mass.: Harvard University Press, 1959.

May, Edgar, *The Wasted Americans*. New York: Harper & Row, Publishers, 1964.

Meade, James E., *Planning and the Price Mechanism*. London: G. Allen & Unwin, Ltd., 1948.

Meek, Ronald L., *Studies in the Labor Theory of Value*. London: Lawrence and Wishart, 1956.

Meier, Gerald, ed., *Leading Issues in Development Economics*. New York: Oxford University Press, Inc., 1964.

Meyer, Alfred G., *Leninism*. Cambridge, Mass.: Harvard University Press, 1957.

Meyer, Gerhard, "A Contribution to the Theory of Socialist Planning," *Plan Age*, Vol. III, October 1937.

Von Mises, Ludwig, "Economic Calculation in the Socialist Commonwealth," reprinted in *Collectivist Economic Planning*, ed. Frederick A. von Hayek. London: George Routledge & Sons, Ltd., 1936.

_____, *Human Action*, rev. ed. New Haven, Conn.: Yale University Press, 1963.

_____, *Socialism: An Economic and Sociological Analysis*. New Haven, Conn.: Yale University Press, 1951.

Monsen, Joseph R., Jr., *Modern American Capitalism: Ideologies and Issues*. Boston: Houghton Mifflin Company, 1963.

Montias, John Michael, *Central Planning in Poland*. New Haven, Conn.: Yale University Press, 1962.

_____, "Planning with Material Balances in Soviet-type Economies," *American Economic Review*, 49, December 1959, 963-85.

_____, "Socialist Price Systems," *American Economic Review*, 53, December 1963, 1085-93.

More, Thomas, *Utopia*, Everyman's Library edition. London: J. M. Dent and Sons, Ltd., 1928.

Morris, Bruce R., *Economic Growth and Development*. New York: Pitman Publishing Corp., 1967.

Mossé, Robert, "The Theory of Planned Economy: A Study of Some Recent Works," *International Labor Review*, September 1937.

Myint, Hla, *The Economics of the Developing Countries*. New York: Frederick A. Praeger, Inc., 1965.

Myrdal, Gunnar, *Beyond the Welfare State: Economic Planning and Its International Implications*. New Haven, Conn.: Yale University Press, 1960.

_____, *Challenge to Affluence*. New York: Pantheon Books, Inc., 1963.

_____, *Rich Lands and Poor*. New York: Harper & Row, Publishers, 1957.

Nove, Alec, "The Liberman Proposals," *Survey*, No. 47, April 1963, pp. 112-118.

Nurkse, Ragnar, *Problems of Capital Formation in Underdeveloped Countries*. New York: Oxford University Press, Inc., 1955.

Oxenfeldt, Alfred, and Vsevold Holubnychy, *Economic Systems in Action*, 3rd ed. New York: Holt, Rinehart & Winston, Inc., 1965.

Pierson, Nikolaas Gerard, "The Problem of Value in the Socialist Society," reprinted in *Collectivist Economic Planning*, ed. Frederick A. von Hayek. London: George Routledge & Sons, Ltd., 1935.

Pigou, Arthur Cecil, *Socialism versus Capitalism*. London: Macmillan & Company, 1951.

Pitigliani, Fausto, *The Italian Corporative State*. New York: The Macmillan Company, 1934.

President's Committee on National Goals, *Goals for Americans: Programs for Action in the Sixties*. Englewood Cliffs, N. J.: Prentice-Hall, Inc., 1960.

Prest, Alan Richmond, *Public Finance in Underdeveloped Countries*. New York: Frederick A. Praeger, Inc., 1962.

Radner, Roy, *Notes on the Theory of Economic Planning*. Athens: Center of Economic Research, 1963.

Reagan, Michael D., *The Managed Economy*. London: Oxford University Press, 1963.

Reid, Timothy E. H., ed., *Economic Planning in a Democratic Society?* Toronto: University of Toronto Press, 1963.

Robbins, Lionel, *The Great Depression*. London: Macmillan & Company, 1934.

Robinson, Joan, *An Essay on Marxian Economics*. New York: St. Martin's Press, Inc., 1947.

Rostow, Eugene V., *Planning for Freedom*. New Haven, Conn.: Yale University Press, 1959.

Salvadori, Massimo, *The Economics of Freedom: American Capitalism Today*. New York: Doubleday & Company, Inc., 1959.

Salvemini, Gaetano, *Under the Axe of Fascism*. New York: The Viking Press, Inc., 1936.

Schultz, Theodore W., *Transforming Traditional Agriculture*. New Haven, Conn.: Yale University Press, 1964.

Schumpeter, Joseph A., *Capitalism, Socialism, and Democrary*, 2nd ed, New York: Harper & Row, Publishers, 1947.

————, *The Theory of Economic Development*. Cambridge, Mass.: Harvard University Press, 1949.

Schwartz, Harry, *An Introduction to the Soviet Economy*. Columbus, Ohio: Charles E. Merrill Publishing Co., 1968.

————, *Russia's Soviet Economy*, 2nd ed. Englewood Cliffs, N. J.: Prentice-Hall, Inc., 1954.

Sharpe, Myron E., ed., *The Liberman Discussion: A New Phase in Soviet Economic Thought*, Vol. 1 of *Planning, Profit, and Incentives in the USSR*. New York: International Arts and Sciences Press, 1966.

Shaw, George Bernard, *The Intelligent Woman's Guide to Socialism and Capitalism.* New York: Brentano's, 1928.

Sheahan, John, *Promotion and Control of Industry in Postwar France.* Cambridge, Mass.: Harvard University Press, 1963.

Simons, Henry C., *A Positive Program for Laissez-Faire: Economic Policy for a Free Society.* Chicago: University of Chicago Press, 1948.

Singer, Hans W., *International Development: Growth and Change.* New York: McGraw-Hill Book Company, 1964.

Smith, Henry, *The Economics of Socialism Reconsidered.* London: Oxford University Press, 1962.

Solo, Robert A., *Economic Organizations and Social Systems.* New York: The Bobbs-Merrill Co., Inc., 1967.

Spiller, Robert Ernest, ed., *Social Control in a Free Society.* Philadelphia: University of Pennsylvania Press, 1960.

Sweezy, Paul M., *Socialism.* New York: McGraw-Hill Book Company, 1949.

_____, *The Theory of Capitalist Development.* New York: Oxford University Press, 1942.

Tawney, Richard Henry, *The Acquisitive Society.* New York: Harcourt, Brace & World, Inc., 1920.

Taylor, Fred M., "The Guidance of Production in a Socialist State," *American Economic Review,* Vol., XIX, March 1929.

Thorp, Willard L., and Wesley C. Mitchell, *Business Annals.* New York: National Bureau of Economic Research, Inc., 1926.

Tinbergen, Jan, "Do Communist and Free Economies Show a Converging Pattern?" *Soviet Studies,* XII, No. 4, April 1961, 333-341.

Tinbergen, Jan, and H. C. Bos, *Mathematical Models of Economic Growth.* New York: McGraw-Hill Book Company, 1962.

Titmuss, Richard Morris, *Essays on the Welfare State.* London: G. Allen & Unwin, Ltd., 1963.

Tsuru, Shigeto, ed., *Has Capitalism Changed? An International Symposium on The Nature of Contemporary Capitalism.* Tokyo: Iwanami Shoten, 1961.

Turgeon, Lynn, *The Contrasting Economies: A Study of Modern Economic Systems.* Boston: Allyn & Bacon, Inc., 1963.

Wakar, Aleksy, and J. G. Zielinski, "Socialist Price Systems," *American Economic Review,* 53, March 1963, 109-27.

Wallich, Henry C., *The Cost of Freedom: Conservatives and Modern Capitalism.* New York: Harper & Row, Publishers, 1960.

Ward, Benjamin Needham, "The Firm in Illyria: Market Syndicalism," *American Economic Review,* LXVI, No. 4, September 1958, 373-386.

_____, *The Socialist Economy.* New York: Random House, Inc., 1967.

Ward, Richard J., ed., *The Challenge of Development*. Chicago: Aldine Publishing Company, 1967.

Webb, Sidney, and Beatrice Webb, *The Decay of Capitalist Civilization*. New York: Harcourt, Brace & World, Inc., 1923.

Weber, Max, *The Protestant Ethic and the Spirit of Capitalism*, translated by Talcott Parsons. New York: Charles Scribner's Sons, 1930.

————, *The Theory of Social and Economic Organization*, translated and edited by A. M. Henderson and Talcott Parsons. New York: Oxford University Press, 1947.

Welk, William G., *Fascist Economic Policy*, Cambridge, Mass.: Harvard University Press, 1938.

Wellisz, Stanislaw, *The Economies of the Soviet Bloc: A Study of Decision Making and Resource Allocation*. New York: McGraw-Hill Book Company, 1964.

Wilcox, Clair, *Public Policies Towards Business*. Homewood, Ill.: Richard D. Irwin, Inc., 1960.

Wiles, Peter, *Political Economy of Communism*. Cambridge, Mass.: Harvard University Press, 1962.

Wolfson, Murray, *A Reappraisal of Marxian Economics*. Baltimore, Md.: Penguin Books, Inc., 1968.

Wootton, Barbara, *Freedom under Planning*. Chapel Hill, N. C.: The University of North Carolina Press, 1945.

————, *Plan or No Plan*. London: Victor Gollancz, Ltd., 1934.

Wright, David McCord, *Capitalism*. New York: McGraw-Hill Book Company, 1951.

————, "The Prospects for Capitalism" in *A Survey of Contemporary Economics*, ed. Howard Sylvester Ellis. Philadelphia: The Blakiston Company, 1948.

Zimmerman, L. G., *Poor Lands, Rich Lands: The Widening Gap*. New York: Random House, Inc., 1965.

Index